AN Officer AND A JUNKIE

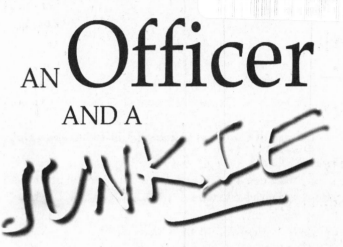

From West Point to the Point of No Return

MICHAEL WINDER

Health Communications, Inc.
Deerfield Beach, Florida
www.hcibooks.com

Library of Congress Cataloging-in-Publication Data

Winder, Michael.
  An officer and a junkie : from West Point to the point of no
return / Michael Winder.
    p. cm.
  ISBN-13: 978-0-7573-0639-6 (trade paper)
  ISBN-10: 0-7573-0639-X (trade paper)
  1. Winder, Michael, 1977–Drug use 2. Drug addicts–United
States–Biography. 3. United States. Army–Officers–Biography.
4. United States. Army–Officers–Drug use. I. Title.
HV5805.W57A3 2008
362.29092–dc22

          [B]

                                          2007048400

Publisher: Health Communications, Inc.
          3201 S.W. 15th Street
          Deerfield Beach, FL 33442-8190

Cover design by Larissa Hise Henoch
Inside book design and formatting by Dawn Von Strolley Grove

For my parents

Alan and Ruth.

Your son was (and still occasionally is) quite the jackass,

but you've always been cool.

Nothing but love.

CONTENTS

PREFACE

An *Officer and a Junkie: From West Point to the Point of No Return* is the story of my disastrous foray into drug and alcohol abuse. My tale unfolds chronologically as I tell my story month to month: first as a cadet at the United States Military Academy at West Point, then as an officer in the United States Army, and ultimately as a civilian.

My main intent is to paint a revealing picture of how ruthless and insidious the disease of addiction can be: it can strike anyone, anytime, anywhere, and such habits can be desperately hard to break.

Counterintuitively, part of the problem with addiction might be the seemingly logical push to deglamorize drug use. In a simpler, *Brady Bunch* world, "peer pressure" was the main cause of drug use in children. It might seem reasonable to think, then, that antidrug public service announcements should portray addicts as emotionally haggard and neglected misfits, lacking all responsibility, accountability, or motivation. The clear message has always been that drug and alcohol abusers are losers and failures. Although this message is difficult to argue, this addresses only the *consequences* of abuse. The *causes* cannot be simplified quite so easily, and this is obviously the next front of the war on drugs: the front end, not the back end.

My experience in drug use and addiction has shown me that addicts come from all socioeconomic and ethnic backgrounds, all ages, both genders, and all religions. Addiction does not appear to discriminate. Indeed, there is only one part of addiction that frequently seems to follow demographic lines: the drug of choice. Just as a poor background with poor prospects for future advancement can lead to substance abuse, the desire for continued success in a highly demanding environment can easily instigate and encourage addiction. In this way, and combined with an ingrained tradition of alcohol abuse, even prestigious institutions like West Point and the U.S. Army can be perfect breeding grounds for disaster.

I hold a high regard for truth in memoir and am well aware of its pertinence lately; accordingly, I have tried to keep this book focused on the facts. Trust me; it wasn't easy. Truth can be so very tedious. On the upside, I'm reasonably confident that I've written a book that's 99 percent kosher, with all events represented as candidly and accurately as possible.

That being said, I do not walk through life carrying a video camera or cassette recorder. Although I stand by all the events in this book and have not intentionally changed anything to support the progression of the story, I would like to remind the reader that *memoir* literally means "memory." Accordingly, all the events and dialogue herein are reflected to the best of my recollection and have been verified through external resources whenever feasible.

To maintain authenticity, I have used people's real names whenever possible. However, I have changed names for all those who might have done something that may be considered improper.

I initially began writing this book for cathartic reasons, to help with my recovery process. It was only after several months of writing that I realized I might actually have a unique and interesting story to tell. It also occurred to me that others might be able to learn from my mistakes—my story is first and foremost a cautionary tale. Finally, let's be clear on one thing: I shouldn't be alive to tell this story. If you come away from reading my book feeling inspired to try a drug, well, you are even stupider than I was. In that case, Godspeed.

ACKNOWLEDGMENTS

Special thanks to my brother, Jason, whose support of my writing has been nothing less than invaluable.

I am grateful to have such good friends as Vanessa and Josh: you're important.

Thanks to Dr. Daniel Mathalon and the rest of his fine staff at the West Haven, Connecticut, Veterans Administration Hospital: you're good people.

Finally, my appreciation also goes out to Gary Heidt and Stephany Evans of FinePrint literary management, who have given me two things everyone deserves: constructive criticism and a second chance.

Part One

JOINING
THE RANKS

1996–1999

1

R-Day
July 1, 1996

This was probably a bad idea, I think.

We pass through Thayer Gate. Everything is gray. All around us are large, drab, gray buildings. Military police usher us through the gates. They wear camouflage uniforms, with black field boots, white gloves, and 9 millimeter (mm) pistols holstered at their sides. Their rigid movements, deadpan eyes, and sharp, well-articulated voices are far, far too real.

I'm in shock. *What am I doing?* I wonder. This is only the first of a thousand times today that I will ask myself this question.

It's Reception Day ("R-Day") at West Point. R-Day is a new cadet's first day of Beast Barracks, simply known as "Beast," the affectionate moniker given to the six weeks of Basic Field Training undertaken by new cadets. For most cadets, military training and education begins on R-Day, when they enlist in the military, complete in-processing, take the Oath of Enlistment, review medical records, and begin practicing drill and ceremony movements that include learning to stand at attention, marching, saluting, and turning.

I had visited the Academy twice before, for my physical exams. I saw spectacular scenic views, the school's well-known distinctive buildings, cadets in uniform, and beautiful statues and monuments dedicated to important historical figures and alumni such as Generals Dwight Eisenhower, Douglas MacArthur, George Patton, and John Pershing.

On my previous visits I had not walked around the post or spoken with a single cadet about what the school was like, nor did I ever speak to any graduate. I had made a point of learning as little as possible, hoping that this might ease my trepidation and prevent me from changing my mind. I wanted to be a cadet, a part of the highly revered Long Gray Line, but I did not want to be dissuaded by the rigorous program. This was a challenge I deeply wanted to rise to, but I didn't have the confidence that I could to adhere to rigor and discipline, so I tried to avoid the knowledge of the specifics of training at all costs. Now everything looks so foreign to me. Everything looks so military. I think of Robert Heinlein's *Stranger in a Strange Land*. This is indeed a whole new world.

I am standing in the Holleder Center, on the floor of the Academy's basketball gymnasium, saying good-bye to my parents. I am determined to look calm, cool, and collected. I don't want to show how nervous I really am, especially in front of my dad—the six-foot-six, outspoken, tough-as-nails Jewish boy from the Bronx. My emotions are a weakness for me, an uncomfortable vulnerability.

"So, how are you feeling?" my father asks in his most relaxed voice.

"Good. You know. Fine." I glance at my feet.

"Nervous?" he asks.

"No, not really. Maybe a little. But that's probably to be expected," I say. *Is my anxiety that obvious? I hope not.*

"Of course it is." He gestures vaguely to the hundreds of other new cadets saying good-bye to their families. "Do you think any of these guys here aren't nervous about today? Of course they are! It's only natural. They're all going through the same thing. You're going to do fine."

Looking around, I wonder how many, like me, are seriously questioning their choice. *Did I make the right decision? What if it's too much for me? I don't want to fail. What am I getting myself into? The military? Me? Maybe I should just forget the whole thing? Is that possible? How would that look?* My brain is working overtime.

"Michael, you're going to do just fine. We are both extremely proud of you and have tremendous confidence that you can do it," my mother affirms.

"Thanks, Mom."

"Michael, I just want to reiterate what your mother said," my dad added. "We are really proud of you. You showed great determination and perseverance to get here, and it says a lot."

About a year ago, I had received a rejection letter from the U.S. Military Academy at West Point. Around my family I had been nonchalant about attending. Secretly, though, I yearned for the opportunity to do something that would set me apart from others, make me "special." I felt proud just telling people that I'd applied. I couldn't imagine how it would feel to say I was accepted, or better yet, that I had graduated.

My maternal grandfather, who lived in Germany, first made me realize the prestige of the Academy. Even though he lived in a small farm town on the other side of the world, he simply couldn't stop raving about West Point.

When I got my rejection letter, the verdict was in. I was average. Indeed, my parents were quite pleased at the notion of my attending the Academy, but it was I who secretly dreamed of being a member of this prestigious club. I was crushed. I walked into my room, lay down on my bed, and cried.

A few days later my father asked me if I'd given any thought to reapplying the following year.

"No. Absolutely not," I said. "I didn't really want to go anyway. I'm actually pretty happy about going to UConn."

Me, playing dress up with Grandpa, 1983.

DEPARTMENT OF THE ARMY
UNITED STATES MILITARY ACADEMY
WEST POINT, NEW YORK 10996

REPLY TO
ATTENTION OF

March 31, 1995

Admissions Office

Michael H. Winder
56 Partrick Road
Westport, Connecticut 06880-1921

Dear Michael:

I am writing to let you know the results of the Admissions Committee evaluation of your candidate file. Unfortunately, your physical aptitude record is not strong enough to qualify for admission to the USMA Class of 1999. It is the judgment of the Admissions Committee that you would not have a reasonable chance for success at the United States Military Academy if enrolled at this time.

This notification has no effect on other commissioning programs (ROTC or another Service Academy) for which you may have applied. We hope you will continue to pursue your goal of service to the nation in the Armed Forces, and, if you have not already done so, investigate ROTC options and the benefits available through Regular Army or Reserve Unit enlistment.

We regret that our reply cannot be more favorable, but you deserve to know your status so that you can make other plans for next year. Should you desire to compete for admission next year, please notify us to carry your file forward for consideration.

Sincerely,

Michael L. Jones
Colonel, U.S. Army
Associate Director of Admissions

Another few days went by, and my father asked me again.

"No. It's really not for me. Anyhow, there's no way Congressman [Christopher] Shays would give me a second nomination. And even if he did, there's no way they'd accept me. They made their decision."

Another few days went by, and my dad asked me again. I told him, "Well, my physical [examination] score was pretty low, so maybe if I improved it enough I'd have a shot."

The following day I announced, "I've got an intense workout plan set up. I'm going to start interval training, to get my speed up for the shuttle run, and strength training, so that this time I can do more than just two pull-ups." My father smiled.

I spent the summer training every day, confident that I could do much better. Shortly after starting classes at the University of Connecticut, I took West Point's physical entrance exam once again, this time scoring above average in all categories. My fine physical score, combined with two dean's list semesters at UConn and the fact that I had not been dissuaded by rejection, was enough to land me a congressional nomination for the second year in a row and, ultimately, admittance to the U.S. Military Academy at West Point.

My grandfather couldn't have been prouder.

Now, standing in the Holleder Center, I am aware that my dad is still talking and I haven't been listening. "You're going to do great. Just take it one day at a time. All right?"

"Yeah, thanks." The booming voice of the officer with the megaphone is suddenly instructing us to say our good-byes.

"I think they're calling your number," my father says.

"Yeah, I gotta go."

"How about a hug?" my mother asks. I dislike public shows of affection; however, it is impossible to say no to her. My mother, a very petite, reserved, kind, and soft-spoken woman from a small German farm town who moved to America in her early thirties, is the exact opposite of my father.

"I love you. You're going to do just fine," my mom whispers in my ear.

The United States Military Academy

The Admissions Committee of the United States Military Academy
takes great pleasure in announcing an

Offer of Admission
To

Michael H. Winder
Class of 2000

Michael L. Jones
Colonel, US Army
Director of Admissions

"Thanks."

"All right, Mike. This is all you," my dad says. "Take care. And give us a call as soon as you get a chance."

"Yes, please do give us a call," my mother chimes in.

"Will do. Bye."

With a halfhearted smile I grab my duffel bag and turn around, joining the countless other new cadets exiting the back of the building.

Passing through the doors, I cross into a new reality. I am no longer a civilian, I am a new cadet. Upper-class cadets, dressed in pristine white uniforms, usher us onto buses. There is not a hint of a smile or amusement on any of their faces. The upperclassmen look deadly serious as they shout orders at us.

For those relatively unacquainted with the military, as you might imagine, forceful corrections are a necessary part of our military's training process. Simply put: one must learn how to take orders before they can give them. The gravity of this training cannot be overstated, as it will almost inevitably play a role in one's combat decisions, thereby affecting the life and death of his or her troops.

"There will be no talking."

"Head and eyes forward."

"Form a single-file line and move with a purpose onto the bus."

Amid the flurry of directions, I scramble into line. As I find my seat on the bus, a cadet gives us the drill.

"New cadets, listen up. When I am talking, you will not be talking. When I am not talking, you will not be talking. You will not speak unless spoken to. If you have a question, you will raise your hand. You have four and only four responses that you may use when an upper-class cadet speaks to you: 'Yes, sir,' 'No, sir,' 'No excuse, sir,' and 'Sir, I do not understand.' Do you all understand?"

"Yes, sir."

"I said, do you all understand?"

"Yes, sir!"

"Good. When an upper-class cadet speaks to you, you will pop off [reply with a loud, firm voice]. Understood?"

"*Yes, sir!*"

"You will address all male upper-class cadets as *sir* and all female upper-class cadets as *ma'am*. Understood?"

"*Yes, sir!*"

"When this bus stops, you will all grab your gear and quickly exit in a single-file line, forming four equal ranks [rows] in front of the bus. Understood?"

"*Yes, sir!*"

"You will keep your head and eyes forward, you will *not* speak to your buddy, and you *will* move with a purpose. Is that understood?"

"*Yes, sir!*"

"Good. Today is going to be a long day, so remember to drink a lot of water and stay hydrated. Understood?"

"*Yes, sir!*"

Looking around, I notice that the smiles on the faces of my peers have rapidly faded. At least I'm not alone in my apprehension.

I'm from Westport, Connecticut—a small, affluent, predominantly white town, about forty-five minutes north of New York City. I grew up hating conformity, authority, discipline, stress, and physical fitness; the latter was especially grueling in light of my twisted spine—a thirty-one degree scoliotic curve. I came to West Point for the challenge; it was time to step out of my comfort zone and time to move to the top of the pack. I want to be a part of something exceptional. West Point cadets are the elite, our nation's finest—the best of the best.

When the bus stops, we quickly exit and form four ranks outside, as instructed. An upperclassman, a blurry white cyborg, indiscernible from the rest, steps in front of us and begins bellowing orders.

"All right, listen up, new cadets. From now on, when you are not in a fall-out area [a place that plebes can be 'at ease'], which includes the academic buildings, the gymnasium behind you, and your rooms, you will move with a purpose. Your hands will be clenched and arms locked out straight, swinging at your sides like so. You will keep your head and eyes forward and you will move out. When you pass the upperclassmen you will greet them with our regimental motto for Beast: To THE LIMIT. And when you are in formation, you will stand at the position of attention, unless instructed otherwise. Is that understood?"

"*Yes, sir!*"

"All right, now I want all of you to drop the bags you are carrying right where you are. You are leaving them here." He pauses while we comply.

"Good. And you're probably going to hear this about a thousand times today, but remember; it's going to be a long day, so drink plenty of water and stay hydrated. Now, starting with the rear rank, I want you all to move in a single-file line into the gymnasium behind you to begin your in-processing."

The process of stripping away our civilian identities begins. I shed my battered jeans and Pink Floyd T-shirt and don black army shorts and a white crewneck T-shirt. Soon after, I put on my army-issued dog tags for the first time. It feels good. I am going to be a soldier—an officer.

I spend the next few hours getting shots, reviewing medical records, and filling out paperwork. After that, I wait in countless lines, steadily filling up the large bag they have given me with numerous articles of army-issued clothing and accessories.

After this phase of in-processing is complete, our groups are attached to specific cadre (the upper-class cadets in charge of us), and I am taken to the cadet barbershop.

As soon as the clippers hit my head and the hair starts falling to the floor, it dawns on me that this is for real. This isn't a one-day affair. This is for keeps. The barbers don't care about preferences; there are more than a thousand new cadets whose hair must be cut today. It is fast and furious. There is an insane amount of hair on the floor. One second I am sitting down, and the next second the barber is pulling off my apron and ushering me out of the chair.

Regardless of the hairstyles we all have coming in, no male cadet leaves the barbershop chair without a "high and tight," and no female cadet leaves with hair touching her shoulders.

After the haircut, my group's cadre marches us back to the barracks. We enter Central Area, a large blacktop space in the heart of West Point, enclosed by extremely large (and extremely gray) buildings on all four sides and thus invisible from the outside. Visitors are not permitted in "the Area."

New cadets are frantically scuttling about while a torrent of voices reverberates throughout the vast courtyard. Upper-class cadets are shouting orders to their squad members. I see new cadets practicing marching, making facing movements (right-face, left-face, about-face) in place, and having their salutes adjusted. Others are "locked up" by upperclassmen, receiving forceful corrections at the position of attention. Still others are standing at parade rest, reading their *Knowledge Book*.

Parade rest is a variation of a standard position assumed by a soldier in which the feet are placed twelve inches apart, the hands are clasped behind the back, and the head is held motionless and facing forward. When we are at parade rest, we are often instructed to read the *Knowledge Book*, which is more than a hundred pages of West Point facts, mission statements, and excerpts from famous speeches. New cadets must memorize this book and recite it to their squad leaders during Beast. This position consists of a minor variation on the standard stance: one hand holds the book out in front while the other maintains its normal position on the small of the back.

Things are starting to get hazy. I dread our next task: reporting to the Cadet in the Red Sash. He is dressed in the same perfectly white uniform as the others, except that he also has a dark red sash tied around his waist. He looks ominous. We are given very specific instructions on exactly how we are to report to him. It is not terribly hard, but we are all a bundle of nerves, and this is our first time being put on the spot individually. If a new cadet makes a mistake, the Cadet in the Red Sash stops him or her, makes the necessary corrections, and sends the new cadet back to do it again. The new cadets who return look decidedly frazzled. Miraculously, I report to him properly on the first go-around. This is a pleasant and unexpected surprise. Maybe I'm going to be good at this!

The Cadet in the Red Sash tells me that I am in Charlie Company and to go report to my company's first sergeant. Reporting to my company's first sergeant does not go nearly as well. He immediately rips me apart. He tells me that he expects me to have proper military bearing at this point. There is no excuse. I had apparently been looking around and making facial expressions in front of him. He has no tolerance for disrespect, verbal or otherwise. He will not stand for it. He is going to run a tight ship. There is no room for "head cases" in his company. He has no patience for attitude. Do I have an attitude?

"No, sir!" I lie.

"We'll see, Winder. I'm not so sure. You haven't made the best first impression. I'm going to keep my eye on you."

My first sergeant tells me my company's motto, CHARLIE HUSTLE, which I am expected to use to greet all upper-class cadets in my company. He then dismisses me, sending me to report to my squad leader, Cadet Larkowich.

Cadet Larkowich is a bulldog. He is about five feet seven inches tall, but he is stocky and looks as if he is in excellent shape. He completely makes up for his relatively short stature, compared to my six-foot-three frame, by his intense demeanor. I can hardly look in his eyes. All the upperclassmen look serious, but Larkowich looks flat-out mean. I hope that his fierce haircut, which is more close-shaven than anyone else's I've seen, will not prove to be an accurate indicator of his personality. However, I can tell by the way he is looking at me that he is all business. Fortunately, a few other new cadets are standing alongside me.

"All right, new cadets, I am Cadet Larkowich. I will be your squad leader for the first half of your cadet basic training. I am going to be demanding, but I will be fair. Our squad motto is SQUARING AWAY THE REAR. When you see me, or when I dismiss you, you will sound off with this motto, and I will respond with SQUARING IT AWAY. Is that understood?"

"*Yes, sir!*"

"All right, I am now going to show you to your rooms, where you will wait for me or another upper-class cadet to get you for drill and ceremony practice. In the interim you will ground your gear and start getting moved in. There is a regulations manual in each room for how your gear should be properly set up. Is that understood?"

"*Yes, sir!*"

"You will not fall out until you are in your room. Understood?"

"*Yes, sir!*"

"Good. And make sure to drink plenty of water; today is going to be a long day. Understood?"

"*Yes, sir!*"

We walk into one of the adjacent buildings and climb several floors to our squad's barracks.

"Winder," Larkowich calls to me.

"Yes, sir."

"Your room number is 421. When I dismiss you, you will make a left down this hallway. What are you doing? I didn't say for you to look. When I am speaking to you, you will have your head and eyes forward the whole time. Is that understood?"

"Yes, sir."

"All right, your room number is 421. It's the last door at the end of the hall on the left. You're lucky; you have a prepster as a room-mate. He'll square you away. Understood?"

I was confused. I had some preppie in my room, and he was supposed to square me away? My mind zoned out as I wondered just how preppie this individual must be to have already earned him the nickname "prepster" from my squad leader.

"Winder! Where is your head right now? When I finish asking you a question, you will sound off with an answer. If nothing else, you will reply with 'Sir, I do not understand.'"

"Yes, sir."

"Winder, I didn't ask you a question. I wasn't looking for a response. I was telling you what you were supposed to do."

"Yes, sir. I understand, sir."

"Winder! Are you kidding me? First off, I just got finished telling you that you are not to reply if I do not ask you a question. In addition, what the heck is 'I understand, sir'? Is that one of your four responses?"

Silence.

"Jesus, Winder! Now you're starting to piss me off. I'm starting to think you're doing this on purpose. I just asked you a question and you stood there and just said nothing. Do you have an attitude, Winder? Are you going to be my project this detail?"

"No . . ."

"Don't answer that. I think you are. But we'll see. Now, thanks to your inability to grasp basic military etiquette, we're running behind schedule. Fall out and head to your room."

"Yes, sir." I turned and starting walking down the hall to the left.

"Winder!"

"Yes, sir?" I asked, as I casually turned around.

"All right, what position are you supposed to be in when speaking with an upper-class cadet?"

"The position of att . . . ," I began to say, still standing in the same manner.

"Don't answer that, just get there. Now do you know what you did wrong?"

"Yes, sir."

"And what was that, Winder?"

"I wasn't at the position of attention."

"And?"

Total silence.

"I told you that whenever I dismiss you, you are to sound off
with our squad motto. You heard the other two new cadets pop off
with it. Why didn't you?"

"No excuse, sir."

"Exactly."

Cadet Larkowich says that he doesn't have any more time to
waste here in the hallway with me; he'll talk to me more later. This
time I make sure to sound off with the squad motto. As I turn to
walk away, I notice out of the corner of my eye that he is already in
the stairwell heading back downstairs. With Larkowich gone, I have
the floor to myself. For a brief moment there is silence. Nothing
could sound more beautiful.

Wow! I think. *I'm really fucked. That guy already has serious issues
with me.*

I stroll down the hallway, again lost in thought over what sort of
preppie kid I have for a roommate. I am sure that Larkowich was
being sarcastic and meant it as a joke that this "prepster" would
square me away. As I approach the door I hear footsteps and realize that the hallway actually loops around to the right. I suddenly
see a white blur turn the corner, and I quickly turn away in a deliberate attempt to avoid this upper-class cadet. I pretend to be completely unaware that anyone else is on the floor with me. I have
only a few more steps to go to get to my room.

"Hey you, stop right there!"

Great. My plan has not worked at all.

I sigh, shake my head, and roll my eyes as I turn to face the
upper-class cadet. The short, hostile-looking cadet gets right in my
face. He is just inches away, yelling at me.

"Are you kidding me? It's the first day and you're just going to
stroll on by me without greeting me, acting as if you own the place?
And then you're going to just mosey around, rolling your eyes at
me?" Silence. He is livid, but his aggression seems comical to me,
given that I have fifty pounds on him. So I stay silent and just stare
this little "Napoleon-complex" down. He is far too close to my face

for comfort, and I want him to know that he has to back off. Napoleon is the first to break the silence.

"So that's it, huh? You're all attitude. Big, tough new cadet isn't afraid of anything." He has lowered his voice but is speaking in a more forceful, deliberate manner.

"No, sir," I say. I suddenly realize I am making a big mistake.

"Just look at you. You're a mess. All eight up. You know that? You're just all eight up."

I'm confused. "Eight up"? I think maybe this means that on a scale of one to ten, ten being the worst, I am an eight. Maybe that's it. An eight is bad, but at least I'm not a ten. (Later I will learn that he actually meant all "ate up," as in a complete mess.)

"This is just amazing. When an upper-class cadet is speaking with you, you will not display your emotions with facial mannerisms and gestures. Is that understood?"

"Yes, sir," I reply, my head instinctively nodding.

"My God!" He moves even closer to me. I can feel his breath on my face.

"Now you listen to me. When you reply with 'Yes, sir,' you will not nod your head, and when you reply with 'No, sir,' you will not shake your head. Your head and eyes will always be forward and you will not move your head or make any facial expressions whatsoever when you are speaking with an upper-class cadet. Is that understood?"

"Yes, sir," I say, my eyes wide open, glaring down at him. He is much too close for comfort and obviously just going out of his way to piss me off. Worst of all, he is pointing his finger right in my face. I hate that. He must sense my anger.

"Oh, so you want to hit me? You're a big, tough new cadet, aren't you? Well, why don't you do it? Do you want to hit me? Are you angry?"

"No, sir!"

"Yeah, you're going to be someone's big project. Who's your squad leader?"

"Cadet Larkowich, sir."

"Cadet Larkowich, oh, he'll square you away. And I'm going to make sure he knows about our little encounter. You are in dire need of a serious attitude adjustment. Is that understood?"

"Yes, sir."

"Now where are you going?"

"To that room over there, sir." I turn my head to the left and point at the door a few feet away.

"You just don't get it, do you? No, you're not a quick learner, are you? Did I not just get finished telling you that you will keep your head and eyes forward, with your arms at your side at the position of attention?"

"Yes, sir."

"Well?"

"No excuse, sir."

"I hope your parents stayed around, because you're not going to make it through the day. You're a mess. All ate up. Get out of here."

As he starts walking away I sound off with the regimental motto, quickly turning toward my room.

"New cadet, halt!" I hear him shout over my shoulder. I turn around, ensuring that I use proper facing movements and military bearing. He is shaking his head as he sneers at me.

"The regimental motto? You think maybe I'm in your company, since I'm in your company area? Duh? Hello? How about we start using our head a little?" he fires.

"Yes, sir."

"Oh, I don't have time for you right now. Just get to your room before you piss me off even more. I'll be seeing you soon, you can count on that," he says as he starts walking away.

I shout our company motto and then turn toward my room yet again. I am incredibly frustrated. This isn't what I expected. This is much, much worse. The way they really get in your face and make you know that they are your superiors and that they are giving you the orders is quite stressful and uncomfortable. I am starting to realize that I do not handle stress or taking orders very well. My hands are shaking from a combination of anger and anxiety. I take a deep breath to calm my nerves before entering. I walk into my room. I can't imagine a less inviting abode. There's a lot of empty space. There are three beds (two bunked together), three closets, three bureaus, and two desks with chairs. Everything is brown, gray, or off-white.

"The prepster" is sitting on a chair on the far side of the room, underneath the windows. As the door shuts behind me, he looks up and says hello. I see that he is intently shining his shoes. I guess that this is part of his being such a preppie.

"Hey, how's it going? My name's Mitch," he says with a thick Texan drawl, as he stands up to shake my hand. Mitch is about five feet ten inches tall, with broad shoulders and a reasonably thick frame. He looks as if he is in great shape, much better than I am, at least. I'm confident that he is quite the athlete.

"Mike," I reply. I am still trying to size this guy up. After all, in addition to being my roommate, he is the first new cadet I've spoken with since arriving.

"I take it that's your bed," I say, pointing to the one immaculately sheeted bed. Did he do that?

"Yeah, I don't think it matters which of the others you choose. So where're you from?" Mitch is seated again now, shining his shoes some more. He seems cool enough, but is he compulsive or something?

"Westport. It's about an hour from here in Connecticut. You?"

"Texas. Couldn't you tell?"

"Yeah, actually. Now that you mention it."

"So what do you think of our squad leader?"

"Larkowich? Seems like he's gonna be a prick," I say, as I sit down on one of the empty beds, taking off my shoes and socks. The army-issued footwear is killing me.

"Yeah, he's probably gonna be tough. Was that you I heard getting reamed in the hallway?"

"Yeah, some asshole stopped me for some bullshit. Hey, you mind if I ask you something?"

"What's that?"

"Larkowich called you 'the prepster' or something. Was wondering if you knew why he'd say that?"

Mitch looks up smiling. "No, man. He probably said '*a* prepster.' I went to the Academy's prep school. That's kind of funny, you thought I was like some preppie bastard or something? Funny shit."

"Yeah, well, I didn't really have a clue. I didn't even know there was a prep school. So you did that for a year. . . ." My sentence is abruptly interrupted by two thunderous knocks at our door. Mitch stands up to attention and whispers to me to do the same. I am once again completely clueless.

"Enter, sir/ma'am!" Mitch shouts. The door swings open and Cadet Larkowich enters, putting a doorstop down to hold the door open as he sternly enters the room.

"Sir, new cadet Smith, fourth squad, fourth platoon reports." What the hell was this shit that Mitch was saying?

"Smith, you can continue shining your shoes. Winder, it's been more than fifteen minutes and it doesn't look like you've done a damn thing. I gave you one simple task and you couldn't follow it!" Larkowich suddenly notices my bare feet. "Scratch that. Actually it does look like you've done one thing, you've gotten out of uniform! You are going to need to learn to pay attention to the orders you are given, otherwise this will be a very long detail with me. Understood?"

"Yes, sir."

"Now we're running behind. You understand, Winder? Right now you're keeping me from completing what I need to get done today. You've got exactly two minutes to get into uniform and meet me outside on the wall. Winder, what is that facial expression? What is with you and your facial expressions?"

"No excuse, sir."

"Do you have a question?"

"Yes, sir."

"Well, what is it, Winder?"

"Sir, did you mean the wall outside the building or the wall in the hallway?"

"Jesus, Winder! I mean the wall two feet outside this door. Understood?" He points his finger sharply to the door of our room.

"Yes, sir," I reply.

"All right. And I'll be back for you when we start parade practice," he says, pointing to Mitch.

"Yes, sir."

He kicks the doorstop, allowing the door to slowly close, as he exits our room.

"Squaring away the rear, sir," Mitch says.

"Squaring away the rear, sir," I chime in, having momentarily been saved from forgetfulness.

"Squaring it away," Larkowich says, as we hear his footsteps carry him back down the hallway.

"Man, he really likes you."

"Yeah, no shit."

"You'd probably better hurry up and get out there. You probably don't wanna piss him off any more than you already have," Mitch says, laughing mildly.

"Yeah, no shit." I quickly focus on getting into uniform and heading outside.

"Hey, aren't you coming?"

"It's a prepster thing. We've already done most of this shit."

"Lucky motherfucker. I'll catch ya later," I say, as I head out the door.

"All right, take it easy, man."

I rush outside to see Cadet Larkowich pacing away from me down the hallway. Having obviously heard me, he snaps around and looks at his watch. I jump against the wall next to the other new cadets standing there.

"All right, Winder, you are exactly fifteen seconds late. This is not acceptable. If you are late, we are all late, and that is simply not acceptable. You will learn to be on time. Is that understood?"

"Y-y-yes, sir," I stammer. All the forceful corrections on how I should and should not be doing things are starting to take their toll. I am becoming worn down. I don't want to be his project. I don't want to be the fuck-up. I don't want to be yelled at anymore. I want to be invisible. I've been here just a few hours so far, and already things are not going well.

The rest of the afternoon is grueling. We have only a few hours until the Oath Ceremony. Our parents are going to be looking on proudly from the stands as we march out onto the parade field for the first time and take the Oath of Enlistment. Accordingly, the overwhelming majority of our time is spent doing drill and ceremony practice in Central Area. The cadre moves at a fast, intense pace, determined to have us properly ready for the Oath Ceremony. It is nerve-wracking. It is miserable. It is a wake-up call to anyone who still doesn't know where he or she is.

The rest of the afternoon is "Right, face. Left, face. About, face. Present, arms. Forward, march. Parade, rest. Attention. Present, arms. About, face. Left, face. Right, face. About, face. Parade, rest . . ." mingled with the inevitable "Winder, try paying attention. Winder, what are you doing? Winder, stand up straight. Winder, hold your salute like this, not like this."

As the day progresses, things do not get easier—just the opposite. I thought the upper-class cadets had come out hard-charging and would slowly ease back, but as the day wears on they steadily demand more from us. By mid-afternoon there is no more leeway; we are expected to show proper military bearing and meet the appropriate standards. I feel caught in a whirlwind; after a while I am too dizzy to know if I am coming or going.

By the time the Oath Ceremony finally arrives, I think that most of the other new cadets are totally exhausted, just as I am.

The Oath Ceremony is for the parents. Less than twelve hours earlier, our parents dropped off their lackadaisical, undisciplined, unkempt teenagers, sporting their messy hair and long sideburns. Now here we are, with shaven heads in beautiful new uniforms, marching in formation to the beat of the parade drum.

After the Oath Ceremony, we march to the mess hall for our first meal together as a squad. This event is like a boxer beating his opponent when he's already down. Expecting to relax, finally, and eat a good meal, I am in for the shock of my life. There are so many rules and tasks to be performed at the table that I can't even begin to describe them all. Everything has to be announced, cut, poured, removed, opened, and served in strict accordance with Academy standards. We barely eat; Larkowich spends the entire meal engaged in a barrage of thunderous corrections. Listening to the cadets at the other tables around us, I can tell that we are all in the same boat. No one is eating more than a few bites of this meal.

To make matters worse, we are served spaghetti. This is obviously done quite deliberately, as Larkowich challenges us not to get our beautiful new white uniforms dirty. I have tomato sauce on my shirt after the first forkful. Apparently this is unacceptable. In fact, *most* of what I am doing is apparently unacceptable in Larkowich's eyes. I'm confident that the rest of my squad can already tell that I am going to draw a good part of his attention. This is a significant relief for everyone but me. No one, including me, wants to be singled out on the first day. Unfortunately, I have started off on the wrong foot.

It is just minutes before lights-out, and I am back in the hallway, locked up at the position of attention. Cadet Larkowich is standing in front of me, making more corrections. With his extremely grave expression and loud, intense delivery, he seems to be trying to kindle, through sheer force of will, some spark of military bearing inside me. It is not coming naturally to me. I was not trying to go out of my way to stir up trouble—far from it, actually. I had quickly grown quite tired of being yelled at. Now I simply wanted to be a ghost—unseen, unnoticed. It's just not in my cards, however. I stand out like a sore thumb, and for all the wrong reasons. I am a magnet for negative attention. My attitude is in dire need of adjustment; this I know. That doesn't make it any easier, though. I am still far too resistant to change. Larkowich says he has had enough for one day. *He and I both!*

Finally it's over. I fall on my bed and just crash. Flooded with self-doubt and apprehension, I feel as if I am drowning. I can't move. There is just total shock and more stress than I have ever experienced. I am completely drained, mentally and emotionally.

What have I gotten myself into? Do I want to do this for four more years? Can I do this for four years? Can I do this for even another month? Another day? Is everyone else in a state of such complete and utter disarray and confusion?

I can see that my roommate doesn't seem to be so affected. A recruited lacrosse player, he appears to be taking it in stride. I want to look tough, so I go out of my way to exude nonchalance. I pretend to be totally immune to Larkowich's harassment.

Our first physical training session is less than six hours away. *Can I do this? Can I? Can I finish Beast?* One day at a time, I tell myself. One exhausting day at a time. I slip into unconsciousness.

I will always remember R-Day. My parents later told me that my grandfather died that day. He was ninety-three years old. My mother said she thought that my grandfather was watching over me during Beast. I like to think that he was. Lord knows I needed all the help I could get.

At 3:00 AM, just a few hours after falling asleep, we are awoken for our first piss test. I am tired and absolutely miserable, but fortunately I have one thing to be happy about: I don't use drugs. Thank God there is at least one test that I'll be passing.

United States Military Academy
West Point, New York

Dear Mom + Dad,

I take it you stayed for the parade, and possibly may have seen me. Thus, the process of molding me into a "Westpointer" has begun. I am writing to you on the second day, and have nothing very exciting to tell you. So far it's been pretty boring, since all we've done is receive a lot of stuff and get yelled at—a lot. The officers here are trying to make it as miserable as possible. Everywhere I turn I am being yelled at for something, and then yelled at again for not responding right. However, despite their efforts this is not to say I'm having a bad time - it's actually mostly enjoyable, and I'm sure I'll get the hang of it. So far the physical aspect hasn't been a problem, I'll probably be writing you in another week,

Love, ~

2

Plebe

August 1996

A ttention all cadets, there are ten minutes until breakfast formation. The uniform is as for class. Ten minutes remaining."

Fuck! They're already calling Minutes. God damn! I hastily throw on my uniform and grab a razor.

Today marks the beginning of the academic year. Beast is finally over. My lack of attention and Larkowich's frustration with me were recurring themes throughout our time together. He was dead-on when he guessed that I'd be his major project during his detail. I was by no means singled out, though. There's a reason why 15 percent of my classmates have already quit. I never strayed from my R-Day attitude. The corrections I got, I deserved. I knew I could take them. My goal was not to complete meritoriously, but simply to complete.

The six most grueling weeks of my life are finished, and I have survived. It feels wonderful. Along with my classmates, I have been accepted into the Corps and am now officially a West Point cadet. The celebration didn't last long, however. After our acceptance there was Reorganization Week, which is considered by many to be the absolute worst time of the plebe year.

This transition week for all cadets, from summer leave and military details to academic year companies, is simply brutal—no one wants to be there, least of all the plebes. As rough as it was for me at the beginning of Beast, it is even more so at the beginning of the academic year. Just as I start to come to grips with my current reality, everything is flipped upside-down. Instead of nine new cadets for every upperclassman, there are now three upperclassmen for every plebe. The potential for me to be stopped and corrected has increased drastically, and so has my anxiety.

The one saving grace that makes the transition to the academic year bearable is that Mitch and I actually wind up in the same company. With thirty-two companies in the Corps, this is great luck.

Mitch is my idea of the perfect friend: honest, loyal, selfless, trustworthy, and thoughtful, with (as I will soon find out) a delightful penchant for self-destructive behavior and heavy drinking. He saved my ass countless times during Beast. He's also a recruited lacrosse player; I was right about him being quite the athlete.

I already know one other guy in our company in addition to Mitch—Mark, a fellow Jew whom I met at Shabbat services. He is a bit stiffer and more formal than Mitch, but he's a good guy nonetheless. His intellect and athleticism are also quite obvious.

I'm a bag of nerves. I feel like an emotional powder keg, walking on eggshells. At least I've lucked out again with my roommate: Pete, a tough Irishman from Vermont. A stocky five feet eight, he is extremely personable, wild, and absolutely the funniest person I've ever met. He is another obvious scholar-athlete. That seems to be a common theme around this place.

If I can hear Minutes being called, it usually means that I am running late. Pete left a couple of minutes earlier. Plebes are supposed to be out in formation, standing at the position of attention, ten minutes early. Hastily, I button my shirt and give myself a "dress-off." This involves pinching the back of my shirt with both hands and folding over as much material as possible so that my shirt looks as flat and tight against my body as possible.

At least it's not my platoon's duty to call Minutes this week, I think, as I quickly dart out of our room. Like most plebes, I don't look forward to standing in the hallway at the position of attention for what feels like an eternity, counting down the minutes until formation. Not only is it boring beyond belief, but we are extremely visible to the upperclassmen (and thus vulnerable to their unwanted attention)—much more so than when we are doing other morning duties (that is, cleaning latrines and delivering newspapers). These can easily be completed before the upperclassmen are even awake.

As I "ping" (the term used to describe a plebe's moving out) across Central Area, I can see that most of my peers, along with my team leader, Cadet Pietrantonio, are already in formation. Team leader is the first possible leadership position for cadets at West Point. As yearlings (the name for sophomores), cadets are given one or two plebes to watch over, mentor, and be responsible for in general.

Pietrantonio is a female cadet who refutes the stereotypes of women at military academies: she is in excellent shape and is quite attractive. I am quite relieved to have her as my mentor, because she seems to be laid back and just an all-around good person. Fortunately for both of us, she also has a great deal of patience, for the negative attention I draw certainly doesn't make her life any easier.

As I find my spot in formation and lock into the position of attention, I can see that Cadet Pietrantonio is shaking her head. She is not a morning person.

"You know, I shouldn't be out here earlier than you. All your classmates were out here on time. You should be, as well. It's the first day and everything. You weren't calling Minutes, were you?"

"No, ma'am."

"Yeah, just leave a few minutes earlier from now on. You have a chance to read the paper?"

"No, ma'am." One of our fourth-class (plebe) responsibilities is to read *The New York Times* in the morning. We have to know the weather, a few highlights from the front page, and the sports section. Similar to any other curriculum, the academy's military development program is fluid. Accordingly, reading the paper, along with many other academy particulars, have since been altered or completely done away with.

"All right, I'm not saying this to be a hard-ass, but reading the paper is part of your fourth-class duties, and I just don't want you to be ripped by other upperclassmen. So read the paper, okay?"

"Yes, ma'am."

"Did you shave this morning?"

"Yes, ma'am."

"Wow, you really didn't do a good job. You missed a lot of spots. You need to work on that."

"Yes, ma'am."

"Do you usually use an electric [shaver] or a razor?"

"I used an electric today, ma'am."

"Maybe you should try a razor from now on."

"Yes, ma'am."

"Let me hear the meals. You did look at those, didn't you?"

"Yes, ma'am. Ma'am, for breakfast we are having creamed chopped ham, with hash browns and biscuits. For lunch we are having broccoli and cheese delightfuls. And for dinner . . ."

"That's fine, that's fine," she says, signaling me with her hands to stop. She is smiling now; broccoli and cheese delightfuls are her favorite.

"So, are you excited about your first day of academic classes?"

"No, ma'am."

"Yeah, you're in for a treat. Plebe classes are wonderful," she says, smirking. "What gym class do you have?"

The Academy's gym classes are notorious. As plebes, male cadets take boxing and female cadets take self-defense; both also take swimming and gymnastics. The agenda for yearlings includes wrestling and combatives.

"Gymnastics, ma'am."

"Are you excited?" she asks, seemingly amused.

"Not really, ma'am. Should I be?" Around Pietrantonio I am somewhat lax with my four responses.

"No, definitely not. It's horrible. You'll really have to bust ass to get from the academic building to Arvin [Gymnasium] on time. All right?"

"Yes, ma'am."

"Winder, 'The Corps,'" shouts an upperclassman. Everyone is almost all in formation now. "The Corps" is one of the countless pieces of knowledge that plebes are required to memorize.

"Sir, 'The Corps, the Corps, the Corps, the Corps'! The Corps bareheaded salute it, / with eyes up thanking our God / that we of the Corps are treading / where they of the Corps have trod. / They are here in ghostly assemblage, / the men of the Corps long dead, / and our hearts are standing at attention / while we wait for their passing tread."

Silence.

"Winder, why'd you stop?"

"No excuse, sir."

"Do you need to start over?"

"Yes, sir. Sir, 'The Corps'! The Corps bareheaded salute it, / with eyes up thanking our God / that we of the Corps are treading / where they of the Corps have trod."

Silence.

"Winder, why'd you stop?"

"Not so sure, sir. Kind of just zoned out, sir."

"What the hell is that crap? Is that one of your four responses?" (The four-responses thing is a little tricky, because sometimes they really do want answers to their questions. I just always get it wrong as to when.)

"What's going on here?" my squad leader, Cadet MacIntosh, asks.

"Cadet Winder doesn't know 'The Corps.' And when I asked him why not, he said: 'Not so sure, sir. Kind of just zoned out, sir.'"

"Are you kidding me?" MacIntosh says. "Winder, that's just not going to happen in my squad. Understood?"

"Yes, sir."

"Wow, and your uniform looks absolutely terrible. You obviously didn't iron it. Did you even bother attempting a dress-off"?

"Yes, sir."

"Well, you need to do a much better job. This is totally . . . wait, did you even shave today?" he asks, as he moves in closer to inspect.

"Yes, sir."

"Well, you did an absolutely horrible job with that, too. You have little Winder-hairs popping out all over the place. No more Winder-hairs in the future, understand?"

"Yes, sir."

"So, what'd you read in the paper today?"

Silence. Becoming nervous, I swallow and make a facial expression that screams *I'm fucked!*

"Winder, now you're starting to piss me off. When I ask you a question, you will respond. And you will not make facial gestures. Is that understood?"

"Yes, sir."

"Well, not that I need to bother asking, but did you read any part of the paper this morning?"

"No, sir."

"Winder, this is not acceptable. You . . . ," he starts saying, now speaking very forcefully, with his teeth somewhat clenched and his eyes glaring at me. Fortunately, he is interrupted by our first sergeant.

"Company, fall in."

"Cadet Pietrantonio, you need to square your plebe away," MacIntosh commands. "Right now he's a complete mess. All right, Winder, we'll continue this at breakfast. You know we're at the same table now, right?" I am totally taken aback. No, I did not know this. I hadn't seen his name on the table list. This is not good.

As dreadful as table duties are during Beast, they are infinitely more horrible during the academic year. It's all about the numbers. As I mentioned earlier, during Beast there are nine plebes for every upperclassman at each table, whereas during the academic year it shifts to two or three of Us to seven or eight of Them. This is brutal.

"*Winder, ljfdl&kji#jtqjt!*"
"*Winder, poiohjj$#%gmq[tro!*"
"*Winder, owiettountett@!*"

It's all an incoherent jumble.

As soon as I get to the table, they start yelling at me, ripping me apart for doing just about everything improperly. I am an irrefutable magnet for harassment. And from here, things only get worse. My nerves are wearing thin, I am getting very rattled, and so I am steadily making more and more mistakes. In addition to performing our duties, the plebes are expected to entertain the upperclassmen with trivia and jokes. Today I have none. It's yet another thing I've forgotten. This does not go over well.

"*Winder, paoio&%dshggh!*"
"*Winder, aosgj$gjjr%$eh!*"
"*Winder, kltet*$%mmsdf!*"

Nothing is making any sense anymore.

Occasionally there is time to eat, but even then there are strict rules to follow: we are never supposed to have more than three chews of food in our mouths, and we always have to stare at the crest on our plates. This isn't enjoyable.

"Brigade Rise!"

This call, signaling the end of the meal, comes incredibly quickly. As soon as these words are sounded, I leap out of my chair, sound off to the upperclassmen with our company motto, and move out, pinging back toward my room. After an exhausting, incredibly nerve-wracking meal, I can't get back quickly enough.

For some reason, MacIntosh and the rest of the upperclassmen at my table have really gotten to me this morning. The prospect of dealing with this routine for the next nine months is completely overwhelming. I am so anxious that I start getting very dizzy, and I have to grasp the edge of the sink with both hands to keep from falling down. The nausea I have already been feeling from the creamed chopped ham doesn't make things any easier. It is all too much to handle.

Feeling extremely sick, I throw up in the sink. I attribute this to a combination of terrible food and anxiety, although I am unsure which plays the bigger role. It is at this inopportune moment that Pete walks into the room. I'm mortified. He will surely think I am an incredible loser.

"Ha, ha, ha, ha!"

Are you kidding me? I think. *Is he really that much of an asshole?* I wonder.

"You know, I even thought about you during breakfast," Pete says. "You can't eat pork, right? 'Cause it's not kosher and shit?"

"Yeah, exactly," I lie, relieved.

I knew he was a good dude. To my wonderful surprise Pete assumes that I have had an adverse reaction to the creamed ham because I am Jewish. He finds my situation hilarious. Bless his heart. I am glad that he doesn't see through my facade. I do my best to compose myself in front of my roommate, and I start cleaning the sink as he "squares away" his side of the room.

"Hey, I'll catch ya later. Hope ya feel better," Pete says, as he darts off toward classes.

"Yeah, thanks, man. Later," I shout after him.

Looking at myself in the mirror, I wonder if I am the only one who is still not adapting to this military regimen, or at least having such a hard time with it. Pete, Mitch, and the other guys I am friends with all find me quite amusing; I have become a source of entertainment for them. Upperclassmen and plebes alike are already trading Winder stories. I feign indifference, but really I am not happy about my current situation. Just as with Beast, life in my academic year company has started off on an extremely bad note. I have been in my new company for less than two weeks, yet I am reasonably sure that every single upperclassman already knows who I am—and not for good reasons. At least, that's how it feels: dozens have already had their chance to "lock me up." However, a small part of me thinks that perhaps it's mostly in my head. Perhaps many plebes, if not a majority, feel exactly like I do—like they are under constant attack. I disregard this notion (to my error) and continue to believe that this is personal. Glancing at my watch, I see that I am now running late for class. Hastily, I finish cleaning out the sink and brush my teeth. By the time I am done, though, I realize that I have dug myself into another ditch. I am already running far behind for the start of class, but I also still haven't finished cleaning my side of the room.

All four classes, especially plebes, have to keep their rooms open and immaculately cleaned and organized in accordance with the Academy's strict standards. The repercussions for my not having cleaned my room are at the discretion of my commander, and I really don't need to give my superiors any more reasons to yell at me. However, I calculate that being late for class will be even worse.

"Fuck," I say out loud to myself. I am screwed either way. "Ah, screw it. I'm outta here." I grab my stuff and leave.

The morning is brutal. Growing up, I never took well to academic classes. To say it is a challenge for me to pay attention is putting it mildly. This is so much worse, though. Our instructors are officers in the military; accordingly, they take military bearing and complying with West Point regulations very seriously. They have absolutely zero tolerance for talking, falling asleep, coming in late, or any other hint of disrespect. Any of these things can get a cadet "written up." Cadets dread getting written up, because it means that they are going to receive a certain number of hours of Area tours.

"The Area," as I mentioned earlier, is the common term for Central Area. Every Saturday morning, cadets with disciplinary violations line up in the Area in full dress under arms, to be inspected by the officers on duty. Then they march back and forth along the fifty-yard blocked-off piece of blacktop for the next five hours straight, with four ten-minute rests throughout. Area tours are especially undesirable for upperclassmen, who otherwise would typically be able to leave for the weekend. Until a cadet walks off all his hours, he has no pass privileges.

By far, the worst part of my morning is my final class right before lunch: gymnastics. I dread the opportunity to display my total lack of athleticism. The instructors waste no time jumping right in (no pun intended). I am already having serious problems with the basic tumbling they've shown us. My sense of balance, which is quite important in gymnastics, is extremely poor due to my severe scoliosis. Even though I had been recommended by prestigious doctors and had finally achieved fine physical scores, it's still somewhat uncommon for the military to provide a medical waiver for someone with a severe preexisting condition.

By lunchtime, most of my anxiety has transitioned into straight and thorough misery. There is never any letup. The pace is relentless and incredibly exhausting, but as I enter lunch formation, I can sense that things are actually about to get worse.

"Winder, I went through your room this morning for inspection. Know what I saw?" MacIntosh asks.

"No, sir," I say, even though I know this is a lie.

"Winder, why was your bed not properly made?"

"No excuse, sir."

"And your desk? Why was your desk a total mess?"

"No excuse, sir."

"And that wasn't all. Your windows were dirty, the floor looked like it hadn't been swept at all, the closets weren't organized correctly, and I could go on, but I won't. This is totally unacceptable, Winder. It's the first day, and already you're pulling this crap? You will start doing your duties properly. Both of you."

Wow, he is actually pointing to Pete now as well. He has suddenly noticed my roommate standing right next to me. I feel bad about getting Pete in trouble, but I have to admit that it does feel nice not to be the sole focus of his frustration.

"Winder, now you're getting me really mad. Didn't I tell you to shave before lunch?"

"Yes, sir."

"Well, why didn't you follow instructions?"

"No excuse, sir." The truth is far from acceptable: I forgot.

"I do not want to see your long, scraggly Winder-hairs in my formation anymore. Understood?"

"Yes, sir."

"And your dress-off still looks horrible. You know that?"

"Yes, sir." I'm not sure what to say.

"Well, if you know it, then fix it."

"Yes, sir."

"Winder, you are not starting off on a very good note. If you think you can just go through this whole semester doing your own thing, disregarding all orders and duties, you're in for a *big* surprise. Is that understood?"

"Yes, sir."

"Cadet Pietrantonio, can I speak with you for a moment?"

"Yeah," Pietrantonio responds, glaring me down with a look of total exasperation as she walks away. MacIntosh is obviously letting her know that she needs to take action and fix her jacked-up plebe. After that, I am on her bad side—but I know that this will last for only the rest of the afternoon. Fortunately for me, she is too easygoing to hold a grudge.

Lunch does not go much better than breakfast. The upperclassmen at my table, fueled by my squad leader's noticeable dissatisfaction, make it clear that they have a lot of problems with the way I am doing things. After lunch, life doesn't really pick up, either. My afternoon is long, exhausting, and thoroughly unenjoyable.

When I am finally done with classes, drill begins. Each afternoon, between academic classes and dinnertime, cadets switch off between drill and intramurals, and the varsity athletes have team practice. Drill is one of the most dreaded things a cadet does at West Point. It is two hours (or more, but also sometimes less) of continuous, mind-numbing parade practice in the most uncomfortable uniform imaginable.

After drill, I have to help deliver laundry. This final plebe duty is a rough one. It gives us ruthless exposure to the upperclassmen, but because it is such a large endeavor, all platoons pitch in and deliver—regardless of which platoon is listed on the current week's duty sheet.

This task is also unbelievably annoying. The laundry and dry cleaning of everyone in our company has to be brought into a room for sorting and distribution. The laundry must be organized to ensure that each upperclassman receives everything at once and that delivery is done properly, according to rank.

Delivering laundry puts a plebe on the spot more than anything else, including calling Minutes. When Minutes are being called, the upperclassmen are often in a hurry and don't want to take the time for "corrections," as they call it. However, during laundry, they have all the time in the world. Cadets from all three upper classes line the hallways, ready to stop plebes for anything wrong or just to rattle them; often it is the latter. When we find their rooms, we still have to knock on their doors and deliver the laundry to them properly. Clearly, this has no upside.

After delivering laundry, I have time for a quick lift. Lifting weights is crucial. Exercising is a vital stress reliever—enhanced by the fact that the gym is one of the few fall-out areas for fourth-class cadets, making it a safe haven where plebes can relax. In addition, weights provide me the means for leaving my lanky body behind.

Surrounded by stellar athletes, I desperately want to become bigger and level the playing field. Moreover, during the academic year it is a cadet's responsibility to stay in shape for the regularly administered fitness tests, composed of push-ups, sit-ups, and a two-mile run. Passing these fitness tests is mandatory for cadets; failure means expulsion from the Academy.

My lifting partner is Parker, another cadet in our company. Parker is a tough outdoorsman from South Carolina, originally recruited as a wide receiver for the U.S. Army's football team. In fact, he specifically excels at two things I have never been very good at: women and sports. To me he comes across as Mr. Everything: a very bright, athletically gifted football player and prom king who has no problem with the ladies. I instantly take a liking to him because he is intelligent, reliable, a great guy to drink with, and someone who obviously will never give up.

After lifting, there is "grab and go." Thank God for grab and go. There are no mandatory dinners except on Thursdays, so cadets go on their own time to the mess hall to eat. We are given the option of either eating in the mess hall or bringing the food back to our rooms in the carry-out cartons provided. Plebes almost always opt for the carry-out cartons. In the mess hall we are not permitted to speak and still have to perform duties, but with grab and go we can just bring the food back to one of our rooms and unwind.

Every night, five of us—Parker, Pete, Mitch, Mark, and I—get together in one of our rooms for a few hours of just totally relaxed bullshitting. Hanging out with my friends for dinner is by far the best part of my day and just about the only thing I look forward to at the Academy.

Unfortunately, our bullshitting eventually has to end. Lights-out is at 11:00 PM sharp, and there is generally a lot of homework that has to be done for each of our classes. Although none of us is extremely motivated toward schoolwork at this point, I am definitely the least academically inclined. I am adamantly opposed to doing any sort of work for any class unless I absolutely have to do it. Pete, at least, makes an attempt to study. I prioritize sleeping.

As I drift off to sleep on this first day, all the questions go running through my head again: *Is this really for me? Can I really do this for an entire year, let alone for four more years? Will tomorrow be this bad? Are others having as rough a time as I am? What will tomorrow bring?* Sometimes things have to get harder before they get easier. The next day is better, but just barely. Most of the first-day jitters are gone. However, as the academic year progresses, things actually get a bit tougher. The regimen itself does not get harder; it stays the same, and that is the problem. The intense daily grind and "corrections" from upperclassmen wear me down more and more. For a release, I drink quite heavily on the weekends with my friends. This is extremely risky, because neither plebes nor cadets who are under twenty-one are allowed to drink on post. Because I fall into both categories, if I am caught, it will mean serious punishment. I don't care, though. I need to drink. It makes my unhappiness bearable.

At times, I think about leaving. However, I'm relatively confident that most (if not all) other cadets are in the same boat. So I never leave, and eventually there is relief: Recognition. This significant rite of passage in a plebe's life comes shortly before spring break and is incontrovertibly the biggest and most eagerly anticipated hurdle that a cadet experiences in all four years at the Academy.

Recognition means no more sirs, ma'ams, pinging, or insane anxiety. We have first names again; an enormous weight is lifted off our shoulders. We've regained precious freedom and personal space. We are real people again. It gives me hope and makes me optimistic about staying at the Academy. I can do this thing.

3

Yearling
December 1997

As my plane starts its final descent at Amsterdam's Schiphol Airport, I am filled with an almost forgotten feeling: happiness. I think that everyone's heard stories about Amsterdam. I am not sure which is more famous—or infamous: the liberal drug policy or the legendary red-light district. I am excited, but not because I want to take part in either of these things. This vacation is the much-anticipated break I so desperately need. I am confident that the sheer distance from West Point will allow me to separate myself even further from the unhappiness and anxiety that have become my lot in life.

My yearling (sophomore) year is half over. I have made it through two summers and three semesters of incredibly demanding academic, physical, and military challenges. Visiting my older brother Jason is exactly the escape that I am looking for. It has been one and a half extremely harrowing years. I yearn for a different reality, even if it's only for a moment.

The constant corrections from the upperclassmen have been exhausting, but ultimately the two worst aspects of West Point life are the same two trouble areas that have always plagued my existence: women and athletics.

My trepidation about how I would fare in gymnastics was con-
cretely affirmed in the first several weeks. Despite receiving reme-
dial instruction from friends, I was ultimately one of just a handful
of poor plebes who failed the class last year. Fortunately, the only
consequence was for my grade point average.

After this disaster, I had to take swimming, which provided no
relief. I have never been comfortable in the water, but after nearly
drowning twice, my unease quickly changed to straight-up fear.
Both times I actually blacked out, forcing my instructor to jump in
and save me. Miraculously, I finished the class with a passing grade.
Thank goodness, all that remained was boxing, at which I actually
displayed some skill.

As far as the biannual fitness tests were concerned, I passed each
on the first go-around, but just barely. Both times I busted my ass
in preparation only to wind up crossing the finish line puking,
with just seconds to spare.

As for the woman situation, there simply isn't one.

There has been exactly one bright spot in academy life: my
friends, Pete, Mitch, Parker, and Mark. The five of us are inseparable. I am aware of the fact that West Point is known for fostering
such strong friendships, yet I am still caught off guard by how close
we have become. There's really no way to anticipate the bonds that
form between friends who rely on each other and look to each
other for support and laughter as they endure such a grueling experience together.*

After picking up my bags at the airport, I hail the nearest taxi
and give the driver the address of the hotel where I am supposed
to meet Jason and his friend Rob. If the driver thinks that I'm one
of those young, brash, uncouth Americans, completely oblivious
to his language, customs, and, moreover, the exchange rate, he's
right. I'm not too concerned with all that. *Charge me whatever you*

---

*Please do not assume from our close relationship that Mark, Pete, and Parker
ever joined me in any illicit activities. They did no such thing.

want, man. I'm here to do one thing and one thing only: drink.

As we pass through the city, my gaze is fixed out the window, sizing up this new place. I have not been to Europe often (or anywhere else outside the continental United States, for that matter); the last time was roughly ten years ago, on one of my mother's trips to visit our family in Germany. To be honest, I'm a bit surprised. Given Amsterdam's infamous reputation, I expected a very seedy atmosphere. However, the city really looks quite charming. With cobblestone streets, museums, fashionable boutiques, bridges spanning the numerous canals, and an eclectic assortment of tourists, it definitely piques my curiosity.

A drink would be fabulous, I think, as I hand the driver some cash. After the driver pulls away, I glance at my watch and see that I have an hour to kill before meeting my brother and Rob at our hotel. There's no reason to waste a good hour, especially on vacation in Amsterdam. Although I don't know my way around and I don't speak any Dutch, I'm confident I can find at least a handful of ways to be productive right now.

The room isn't ready yet, but the English-speaking hotel clerk is surprisingly responsive, and he allows me to leave my bags behind his desk in the interim. I'm not totally convinced that my bags are secure, but to be honest, I'm not too concerned. Right now all my thoughts are focused solely on securing a stool at the nearest watering hole.

Alcohol has played a prestigious part in my time at the Academy. I might not be the very best student, but I'm good at drinking. Actually, I should rephrase that: I am good at drinking a lot, often. I am still underage, and underclassmen don't get to leave post very often, but there are many ways around these minor obstacles. I crave alcohol. When I am drunk, I forget how depressed I am. Alcohol is the only means I have ever known to escape my feelings—until now.

En route to the nearest bar, I stumble across a head shop. I walk in and am immediately thrown into shock. The tie-dyed shirts, hemp jewelry, lava lamps, and psychedelic posters adorning the walls are what you would expect to find in any similar shop in the United States. However, there is one major difference here in Amsterdam: The sign in front of me reads FREE MAGIC TEA. PLEASE HELP YOURSELF. The rumors are true. I've come to the right place.

Stumbling across this little shop seems to be exactly what I need, although I'm not sure why. Specifically, I'm not sure when or how my strong convictions on drugs changed. I've portrayed myself to my West Point friends as someone who is well acquainted with drug use, who has done more than his fair share of narcotics, but this is a lie. I just wanted to look smooth, and I actually felt somewhat embarrassed by the fact that I had never done any drugs during high school and had smoked weed only once (at UConn) before entering West Point.

My one prior experience with drugs had not been an enjoyable one. I took one puff of that joint and started coughing uncontrollably, because I had never even smoked a cigarette in my life. There was absolutely no high, so there wasn't anything that made it worthwhile. (I wasn't aware then that it's standard not to get high the first time.) I decided that there was nothing there for me. I was confident that I would never use marijuana, or any other drug, for that matter, ever again. I am hardly the drug sophisticate I've pretended to be.

Times have obviously changed, and, apparently, so has my firm stance. Perusing the display case, staring at the hundreds of beautiful, multicolored mushrooms that fill all the various bins, I try to remain calm. I am equally nervous and excited, both emotions further igniting my heartbeat. The Dutch Rastafarian behind the counter can sense my inexperience and is trying to help me, pointing at the various mushroom names on the wall, but I'm not listening. I am captivated by the plethora of colorful, entrancing fungi.

"You know what sort of trip you're looking for?" the man asks me in fairly good English.

Silence. I have no idea.

"Well, usually I like lots of visuals and stuff," I reply, confident that this is a good answer. "So, is there like any real difference between these mushrooms?"

"Well, which ones have you done before?" the man asks with a wry smile. *Was I that obvious?*

"I'm not so sure," I stammer.

"Well, this one has strong hallucinogenic properties. Lots of visuals. If that's what you're looking for, it's a great trip," the man replies, as he points to the bin labeled HAWAIIAN (*COPELANDIA CYANESCENS*).

"Yeah, that'll be good," I decide, totally unsure.

"How much?" he asks.

"Um, what is normal? I mean, what's a good-size amount for just one person, just one time?"

"If you have not done it before, I would not get more than three, or possibly four, grams."

Looking at the prices on their wall, I see that this is their lowest ration. "Oh, okay. Well, I've done 'em before, just not in a while. I'll take seven grams." I have no idea why I care about this man knowing that I am totally ignorant about the world of drugs.

"No problem." The man starts to fill a small paper bag with the magical fungi.

"Cool—thanks, man." I pay, grab my 'shrooms, and leave the store. As I walk out, I am completely unaware of the fact that the specific flavor of mushroom I have chosen has the highest alkaloid content found in any hallucinogenic mushroom, producing two to three times the psychoactivity of its much more common (and much less potent) Mexican counterpart, *Psilocybe cubensis*. Had I even suspected that this was going to be on my trip's agenda, I would have done all the necessary due diligence beforehand; however, that was not the case, and all research would have to wait until I got back my computer at West Point.

As I walk back to my hotel, I keep the bag closed. As curious and excited as I am, my anxiety still reigns supreme. I am still undecided if I am actually going to consume the mushrooms, but I am glad that I at least have the option. Passing through the hotel's lobby doors, I immediately see Jason and Rob.

My brother Jason is seven years older than me, two inches taller, slightly more intelligent, and much more conservative. He's not overweight, but he's not muscular, either; he wears glasses and has thinning hair. Jason is working out of Brussels as an information technology consultant. For an American, this is especially impressive. Rob is his friend, a wiry, tattooed wild man from San Francisco, also in Europe on vacation.

After quickly dropping off our bags upstairs, the three of us stroll toward a quality Indonesian restaurant that my brother knows off the Leidseplein (a large square in the center of the city). I keep my magical bag tucked in my pants' right cargo pocket. Despite the conversation I am having with the guys, my thoughts are focused like a laser beam on this small concealed package. Overwhelmed with conflicting feelings, I go with my gut instinct, which tells me that I deserve this. (Some people pride themselves on having great natural instincts; I am definitely not one of these people.)

When I am confident that Jason and Rob are not looking, I quickly grab a mushroom from the bag and pop it in my mouth. The taste is god-awful. A minute later, I reach in and grab another and then just a couple more, to be safe; there are still some left for later.

I'm not even remotely pro-drugs at this point, far from it. But I am so unhappy and stressed out from Academy life that I am fully embracing the escape from reality. I feel especially safe with mushrooms because I know that these are not included in the drug tests. Although my firsthand knowledge in this area is not commensurate with the experiences I've led my friends to believe that I've had, I'm confident in the rather extensive research I've done on the subject.

Hallucinogenic mushrooms (active chemical: psilocybin) are found naturally in very warm, humid climates, such as Washington

State or Florida. Unless one picks them fresh, they are almost always eaten in dehydrated form. Throughout time, cultures ranging from the Aztecs and other Indian tribes to hippies, some of my cadet friends, and myself have all loved to munch on the magical fungi.

Mushrooms can be tons of fun: they provide a four-hour Alice-in-Wonderland journey that compares to nothing else. Some people can't handle the strong hallucinogenic properties associated with psilocybin, but one rarely knows this before trying the drug. The visuals can be overwhelming, but so can the altered thoughts and imaginary conversations that for some can feel uncontrollable.

Some people never have a bad trip, but everyone reacts differently to different chemicals, and certain drugs just suit some folks better. There are many people who cry, become depressed, or just plain lose their grip on reality from hallucinogens. Mushrooms aren't as bad as LSD for inducing craziness and severe instability, but in the end they're still *unpredictable*.

As I sit at the table with Jason and Rob, I am sure that everyone in the restaurant is staring at me. Everyone knows I am on drugs, and they are all talking about me. I am positive of this, and I wish I could understand what they're actually saying. Being surrounded by tables filled with people who aren't speaking English doesn't help to assuage the anxiety.

I can't stop sweating. I drink a pint of beer in an attempt to calm myself down, to no avail. The intensity of the trip is much more than I am prepared for. The "boom" I feel in the beginning stage of the mushroom dose is too much for me to handle. Either I've done too much or this drug just doesn't suit me at all. Either way, I'm not able to sit still any longer.

"Hey, I got to go," I suddenly announce, as I get up from my chair.

"All right, um, yeah, the bathroom's right over there. So anyway, Rob . . ."

"No, you don't understand, I've got to leave the restaurant."

"What? What are you talking about? We just ordered."

"Listen, I took some mushrooms and I really can't handle it right now, so I've got to go."

"So that was what was in that bag. I thought you were acting weird. Well, why don't you just drink some water, eat some food, and try to relax?"

"I just need to get some fresh air." Unable to stand there any longer, I walk out of the restaurant.

After throwing out the remainder of the mushrooms, I pace the sidewalk feverishly, repeatedly telling myself that I'll never do drugs again. This is it. Now I know for sure. Drugs are not for me.

Several days later, after spending most of my holiday in Brussels, where my brother lives, I am back in Amsterdam for one final night of festivities before I fly home. After my discouraging experience with the mushrooms, I have spent the rest of my week drinking extremely heavily. As far as I'm concerned, the trip was a fantastic success. I got drunk, often. However, I'm well aware that my brother has a slightly different take on things. He didn't make much of an effort to hide his desire to see me leave. Yes, this trip was many things for me, but a service to our relationship it was not.

Jason and I have never been very close; we are two very different people, but lately he has distanced himself from me even more. He is quite cultured and is noticeably pleased with how worldly he has become. He also doesn't hide his disapproval of his immature and uncultured younger brother. Furthermore, although he does not come out and say it, he sees himself as European now. During this trip Jason made numerous inflammatory, patronizing remarks about American tourists, and I was almost always the prime target. In simpatico with the upperclassmen at West Point, Jason seemed to find a lot of things about me to be unacceptable.

Although I had briefly seen Amsterdam's famous red-light district earlier in the week, as I wander alone through it now, it's a lot for me to take in. I never realized it was like *this*. Imagine a long street divided by a canal, lit with incredibly bright fluorescent red lights for as far as the eye can see in both directions. Imagine that both sides of the canal are lined with countless little shops whose storefronts are composed primarily of incredibly large windows. Imagine that standing behind these windows are some of the most gorgeous women you've ever seen, blowing kisses at you as they shake their bodies in their skimpy lingerie. As I said, it's a lot to take in.

As my drunken legs slowly carry me down the street, I can't help but stare at all the beautiful women, although I make sure to avoid any eye contact. Traversing this sea of sexual indiscretion, I feel embarrassed. I feel as if the invisible scarlet *V* I carry around with me has suddenly grown much larger, emblazoning itself on my forehead for all to see.

It's really funny how life works sometimes. I am going to turn twenty-one and have never dated a single girl. Of course, my friends know nothing of this. It kind of sucks going to a military school and having friends who are all extreme athletes when all you've got is a twisted back. So in addition to exaggerating my experience with drugs, I couldn't help but lie about my sexual experience to my asshole friends, who are all pretty much damn porn stars.

High school was where I first learned to embrace alcohol. I have always hated being sensitive and introverted, and I attempted to mask these qualities by being something of a clownish dolt in school and an oafish drunk at parties. I remember my high school graduation party, for example; it was classic. Within an hour and a half of arriving, I had consumed five bottles of Mad Dog 20/20. This sent me careening to the ground with alcohol poisoning, and from what I understand, I ruined the party because my parents had to be called to pick me up. Happy graduation! I was already on the right path.

Therefore, I've pretty much resigned myself to the fact that I am the sloppy drunk guy who repels girls into the arms of strangers. It is commonplace for me to watch my pretty friends slowly trickle out of a bar with beautiful women at their sides, while I sit alone on a stool, waiting for the lights to come on. The big problem (besides the fact that I drink way too much and act without any couth whatsoever around women) is that I have relatively high standards, and I won't sacrifice them just to hook up.

So with all that being said, let me just add that I'm not overly proud of the truth: I lost my virginity to a prostitute in Amsterdam at age twenty.

Sorry, Mom.

4

Cow

August 1998–May 1999

L ooking out my rearview window, I can see the cadets taking down my license plate number. If there was any uncertainty remaining, it's gone now. I'm fucked.

It's the first week of March, shortly before spring break. I'm looking to get a tan with a fellow cadet named Joe, in preparation for the holiday. I asked Parker if I could borrow his car; he is one of the only people I know who has a car, since Cows (the name for juniors) aren't allowed to have one until after spring break. Parker has slipped under the radar because he keeps his Trailblazer parked, against regulations, at a motel less than half a mile off post. Parker was cool about giving me his keys.

"*Fuck! Fuck! Fuck!* I'm screwed, man. I'm so fucking screwed!" I shout as my hands tightly grip the Trailblazer's steering wheel. I look to my right, but there's no response.

It all happened so quickly. The cadets came out of nowhere, jumping in front of the car as soon as we pulled out of the motel driveway. Then the questions came at me all at once, intertwined to the point of being almost indistinguishable, although one noticeably stood out from all the rest: "Whose car is this?" That was the deal breaker. I couldn't turn Parker in. So instead I did what thought was right: I lied. I said the car belonged to a Firstie (senior).

"Joe, what the fuck do I do?"

Joe shakes his head solemnly but says nothing. I've put him in a real bad spot.

At West Point, the Honor Code is simple: one cannot lie, cheat, steal, or tolerate those who do. In short, it is a cadet's duty to turn in his peers. Some cadets, like the fine young men who just stopped us, make it their mission to go one step further: to *seek out* and turn in cadets who are committing regulations violations. Personally, I find this mentality absurd.

I'm in shock. I keep repeating, "Fuck, Joe. What the fuck do I do? Seriously, Joe, what the fuck do I do?"

Joe finally breaks his silence with an unsettling and uncharacteristic look of gravity: "I dunno, man. I think they got your plate. Maybe we should turn back."

"*No!* Fuck that! We're going fucking tanning. If one thing's for sure, it's that the two of us are getting fucking tan this afternoon."

Joe is calm but serious. I know he knows that I'm fucked, and I also know he's aware that he's possibly screwed, too. For an easygoing California guy, Joe shows almost no sign of levity. His typical lighthearted demeanor is conspicuously absent. He has every right to be concerned: I'm in a lot of trouble, and if I don't do the right thing, so is he.

After a few minutes, I break the silence: "Hey, man. Don't worry. If I go down, I go down. None of this is going to be on you—trust me."

I'm reasonably confident that I can see his face—and the rest of his body, for that matter—subtly shift into a much more relaxed posture. "Yeah, I know," he says. "I'm just worried 'bout what's gonna happen to you. What'll you do?" he asks.

Even though we're not close friends, I'm certain that Joe's concern is genuine. I'm also confident that he knows I would never bring him down with me.

"I'm not sure, man," I reply. *That's putting it mildly!* "I'll worry about that later. Let's go get our tans on."

What should I have done differently? I wonder. It's still not clear to me.

My mind drifts to the movie *Scent of a Woman*, and Al Pacino's character: "I'm gonna shoot you, too. Your life's finished, anyway. Your friend George is going to sing like a canary, and so will you. And once you've sung, Charlie, my boy, you're gonna take your place on that 'Long Gray Line' of American manhood. And you will be through." His words feel especially relevant.

Is he right? I wonder. *Can standing by one's friends be dishonorable as far as the school's code is concerned, but still possibly be the right thing to do?*

A few hours later, our bodies finely tanned, Joe and I make the short (but seemingly interminable) trek back to the Academy. We don't talk much on the return trip, either. Joe's a good dude. I really appreciate someone who simply knows when to leave the damn elephant in the middle of the room alone.

Back on post, Joe and I part company. Although my mind is terribly confused right now, the first priority of business is irrefutably clear. I start walking toward Parker's room.

After telling him the story, I'm a bit surprised. I didn't expect him to be so angry.

"Fuck. God damn it, Winder! How could you be so stupid? Do you realize what you've done?"

"Yeah."

"Jesus, man. What the fuck! What were you thinking? You should've just freaking turned me in. Who cares if I get in trouble! Now *you're* screwed!"

You know, in a simpler world I might have turned Parker in. If I had chosen to approach life in black-and-white terms, I might have concluded that lying is wrong and that following orders is paramount. However, we do not live in that world, and the Nazis learned the hard way at Nuremberg that "I was just following orders" is not an acceptable defense. One simply cannot approach life as a lemming, or without a moral compass that accounts for the complex shades of gray that fill our lives. If I had used my brain, I might have turned him in, realizing either that it was wrong to lie or, if nothing else, that they would write down the license plate number as I was driving away, but I didn't.

I spare Parker my lesson in morality and just give him the Cliff Notes version: "Dude, I couldn't do it. It just felt wrong, you lending me your car and then me giving you up."

He's still shaking his head. "You should've just turned me in, Winder. Now what are you going to do?"

"I dunno, man."

"You know the Academy has access to law enforcement databases and such. They're gonna quickly trace the car back to me, anyway."

"Yeah, I know," I reply.

"Well, then, it's only a matter of time. As soon as they find you, you're fucked."

"I know that, too. I've thought about that."

"I mean, you're really fucked, Winder. You know that, right? If they find you first, they'll try you for honor, and then you'll be kicked out and forced to work as an enlisted soldier in the army for the next million years."

A cadet at West Point incurs his obligation to the army once he joins the Profession of Arms, which happens the moment he goes to his first class in his cow year.

"Yeah, I know all that."

"You should've just turned me in, Winder."

"Yeah, maybe so, but I didn't."

"So now what?"

"Now I do the only thing I can do."

"And that is?"

"Turn myself in, man. I got no choice."

So, to make a long story short, I turn myself in, and it isn't pretty. After my honor trial several weeks later, in which a jury of my cadet peers finds me guilty of committing an honor violation,

I am sent to see the superintendent, a lieutenant general. That's a three-star general in the U.S. Army, staring me down, ripping my shit. Talk about frightening experiences! He concludes that I need a full extra year at the Academy for ethics training before entering the U.S. Army's Corps of Officers, so he turns me back a year. I'm not happy.

The long and the short of my punishment is that I will remain a cow for one extra year. I will continue taking classes with my classmates, but I will not graduate with them, and when my cohort is gone I will begin taking electives. In addition, just to add insult to injury, my privileges as a cadet won't increase along with the rest of my classmates.

Now, if a cadet at West Point is found guilty of having committed an honor violation (as I was), yet he has done something redeemable to warrant his staying at the Academy (as I did by turning myself in), he is assigned an Honor Mentor. I draw Colonel Clemons. I have mixed feelings about that. On the one hand, I am understandably nervous, because he has a reputation for being one of the strictest, most demanding, hardest-ass officers on post. On the other hand, since Clemons is so highly respected, I have a good chance of graduating in December of next year after just one extra semester (in lieu of the extra full year I have been assigned)—that is, assuming he gives me a positive recommendation at my reevaluation the following fall.

It is hard for me to come to grips with the fact that I am not destined to graduate with the rest of my friends. I quickly conspire to take full advantage of the prime benefit that accompanies cow year: freedom.

Having made a commitment to the military, a cow's privileges are drastically increased. I am now allowed to leave campus almost every weekend, go to the Officer's Club, and participate in tailgates for football games. Basically, it all boils down to one thing for me: drinking. I have been given more privileges and freedom—to drink.

I am happier, but only because I am drunk more often. However, the positive mood change I feel quickly fades, replaced by renewed feelings of displeasure with my life. I'm not sure what specifically is making me unhappy, because there are too many issues on my table that I still haven't dealt with. However, I do know that alcohol and (when I am able to get hold of them) mushrooms and (if I am really lucky!) LSD are able to make all the bad stuff disappear for a while.

Despite my early protestations to the contrary, hallucinogens have become my thing. Disregarding my past unenjoyable experiences with drugs and the subsequent promises I had made to myself, I had tried LSD the previous semester. It was a matter of convenience. I was home for the weekend, became inebriated at a friend's party, and didn't give it a second thought when it was offered to me. An extremely pleasant trip with acid then pushed me to try mushrooms again, this time producing only favorable results. I love mushrooms; they will always be my drug of choice.

Now, with my honor-trial verdict in, I indulge even more in these self-destructive vices. Except for those precious psychedelic flashes of surreal escape, there is only the occasional fleeting moment of happiness to be found. In the midst of my misery, however, there is a sudden and unexpected oasis of relief: Dana.

Dana is my younger sister Vanessa's best friend from Brandeis University. Her exotic Middle Eastern features, slim body, and large, beautiful eyes make her a dead ringer for Jasmine in the movie *Aladdin*. She is quite attractive, but even more, she is bright, genuine, and sweet. We get along wonderfully right from the start, with our only noticeable incompatibility being our vast difference in size. The contrast of her extremely petite, five-foot frame next to my six-foot-three, 210-pound hulking body is somewhat amusing to both of us (and presumably onlookers as well!).

After seeing each other for a few months, the two of us fizzle out. Nevertheless, even though we don't click as far as dating is concerned, we become good friends and commit to keeping in touch. I feel relief not just from my West Point woes but also from the inescapable emptiness that has been lingering inside me for so many years now. I am twenty-two, and I have finally dated a girl. A real, live girl.

Maybe I am normal after all.

Part Two

BLURRING
THE LINES

2000

5

Kool

January 2000

My finger slowly makes its way down the piece of paper on the bulletin board one more time, but the result is still the same. I drop my bags and walk down the hall to the office of the commander of our company, Major Biagiotti. Coming back to West Point after Christmas break is never enjoyable for any cadet, but with all my current problems at the Academy, I really don't need this extra hassle.

You know, it's kind of funny how things work at West Point. There was no "Cadet Winder, you might be moved when you come back after Christmas." No forewarning, nothing. Nor do I hear, coming back after the holidays, "By the way, Cadet Winder, we shuffled you out of the company." There is simply a room list with one name absent: mine.

The tall, exceptionally broad-shouldered, bald, fortysomething major makes the walls quiver with his loud, Brooklyn brogue. His booming voice, combined with borderline comedic stubbornness and illogicality, make him a very imposing figure indeed. His enlisted background gives him a coarse manner of speech that immediately distinguishes him from the rest of his finely groomed officer peers serving at the Academy. His Special Forces patches reinforce his unique background and remind us of his tough-as-nails demeanor. Needless to say, he is an extremely intimidating individual.

Major Biagiotti has a few brief words for me: "Winder, you're out of F-3. Go see H-4; they should have you on their list. You're dismissed."

My commander has kicked me out of his company, just like that. I suppose he is entitled; after all, I *have* been turned back a year for an honor violation. He's probably tired of my antics. With me gone, there is one less problem for him to worry about. (The fact that nothing ever happened to Parker—that he was never charged with anything—assuaged a great deal of the grief I had about being turned back.)

In the big scheme of things, switching companies won't have much of an effect on me: same classes, same duties, and the same opportunity to see my friends. However, moving is still a major hassle, especially considering the apprehension I have about entering a company full of strangers. Changing companies like this is extremely uncommon, and everyone will immediately know that I did something wrong. I am ready for my role as the new pariah in town.

Leaving Major Biagiotti's office, I grab my bags and head outside to find my new company. The cold New York air is a frigid reminder of where I am and how I feel. My semester is not starting off on a very promising note.

When I find my new company, things don't get much better. Lots of sideways glances, false smiles, and hushed tones follow me wherever I go.

When I meet my new roommate, I have to laugh, because it's all too obvious. The new guy in the company, the outcast, has been paired with the poor guy no one wanted: "Kool."

"My name is Kolodzie, but you can just call me Kool!" he says, followed by some of the most unsettling laughter ever.

Is he for real? I wonder.

A lean, closely-shaven, five-foot-six, 140-pound individual is none too common around this school. After becoming aware of his obvious off-kilter demeanor, I immediately notice several other disconcerting things about my new acquaintance.

"So, Ranger goggles, huh?" I ask. He's wearing the field glasses used by the special unit known as the Rangers during their training in close-range fighting and raid tactics. "Yeah, always gotta be ready," he says, smiling, as he grabs a bayonet off the sink and starts making attack motions in front of the mirror, watching his own sharp-moving, shirtless torso in noticeable delight.

"So, what's your name?" he asks.

"Mike. I was turned back for honor and just got booted out of F-3 by my prick commander," I reply, hoping that this will be the end of any queries along these lines.

"Well, Mike, there are a few things you should know about me. Some people in the company are scared of me, or just don't like me, because I have my own little eccentricities," he says.

"Hey, no worries, man. Eccentricities I can handle. In fact, I almost welcome them." This is no lie.

"Well, first off, you should know that these goggles are part of my uniform in this room, because I regularly train in front of the mirror."

"No problem."

"But, more important, I've got my G.I. Joe army," he says. I follow his outstretched finger to his bookshelves, which contain few books and many action-hero figurines and plastic battle equipment.

I've no idea if any of this is allowed. Regardless, he is succeeding in catching me somewhat off guard.

"Cool, huh?" he says, genuinely excited to the point of scariness.

"Uh, sure, although I can't really say that I ever got into that shit—at least, not past like age eight or something."

"Ha! You kidding me? Joe is always cool!" he says, as he grabs some of the figures and moves them around.

"No doubt. Hey, your thing is your thing, Kool. No worries from me," I say, as I put some of my gear on my bed and prepare to start putting my stuff away.

"Hey, you haven't seen the best part."

"Oh yeah, what's that?" I ask, almost afraid to ask, yet still vaguely curious.

"Well, I haven't introduced you to the ranking officer of our room yet."

"What?"

I look over and see Kool saluting something on his bookcase. *What the hell is the crazy bastard doing?* I wonder.

"Hey, come over here, man. You gotta salute the General before you start moving in," he says, his salute still held high.

"All right, man. No problem." I'm willing to play along, because I'm definitely curious—and bizarre at least makes the day a bit more interesting, especially around here.

"So, what are we saluting?" I ask. I'm standing next to him now, saluting his bookshelf in kind.

"General Ducklas MacArthur. He commands my G.I. Joe army but basically watches over the entire room as well."

I am saluting a plastic duck that is wearing some sort of miniature army helmet, with a mini-M16 attached to one of his yellow wings.

"He already saluted back, so you can lower yours," he says, laughing.

I get the impression that Kool is hovering delicately in the gray region between strange amusements and carefree insanity. Suffice it to say that Kool is a raving lunatic (in a good, harmless way).

I quickly grow quite used to my new room (and new roommate) because I am confined to it all day except for meals, classes, and physical fitness. This is called room restriction, and it is a special added bonus to my punishment for the honor code violation. About two months ago, during halftime at the Army-Navy football game, I was caught drinking by Colonel Clemons. I am the only one, among all my friends, who felt any repercussions from that incident, because the officer who found us was not only my regiment commander but also the same man assigned to be my Honor Mentor. The severity of my current punishment—demotion to private rank from sergeant, fifty hours of Area tours, and three months of room restriction—is almost exclusively due to the fact that I had just received my honor decision from the superintendent.

Instead of doing homework, I spend most of my time reading for pleasure. Besides feeling too drained to use my mind, I have always been quite anti-schoolwork. My intellect is my main comfort, the sole advantage that I think I have over others. Nevertheless, I am quite happy getting by with just Bs while telling myself that if I had done the homework or studied, I would surely have done better than all the rest.

I don't think I could bear the thought of finding out that I am surrounded by individuals who are not just significantly better athletes but who are more intelligent as well.

The rest of my time is more or less devoted to Kool. At first I don't know if I should be amused, annoyed, or scared of the fact that I'd wake up in the middle of the night to find Kool wearing his Ranger goggles, either practicing knife moves in front of the mirror or saluting the plastic duck that commands his G.I. Joe army. In spite of all this, or probably due to it all, I really like him. He puts a welcome smile on my face.

6

Not So Kool

February 2000

I 'm not smiling.

Standing in my father's hospital room, I am taken aback by how overwhelmed by emotion I am. To see such a large, strong figure in my life suddenly appear so vulnerable and weak makes me quite uncomfortable. The rest of my family is gathered around him, offering all the typical words of encouragement and optimism, while I hover in the background, motionless, leaning against the hospital room wall. My mind traipses back to yesterday, recalling how I got here and consumed by an inability to remain in the present.

Yesterday I was just lying on my bed reading, trying to ignore Kool talking to his damn plastic army, when my phone rang. I can't think of a worse call I've ever gotten. My mother was on the other end of the line, telling me that they had found a large abscess on my father's brain and needed to perform urgent surgery the next day. I immediately saw my company commander, who gave me permission to take emergency leave.

Before leaving, needing some alone time, I took a shower. I'm all or nothing, especially when it comes to my emotions. I've always been annoyed by how sensitive I am, having learned at an early age the art of putting up walls in an attempt to ignore a situation so I wouldn't feel overwhelmed by the bad stuff. Standing in the shower, I suddenly found an opportunity to let it all go; I didn't stop crying for ten minutes. After the shower I was in a much better place, emotionally. I borrowed Parker's car and headed home to Westport.

I have yet to say anything directly to my father (or anyone else, for that matter) since entering his hospital room. I'm not listless or unaffected, but confused. I feel out of place, invaded by foreign feelings that are making me more uneasy by the moment. *Listless would be a blessing, right now,* I think. *And so would a drink.*

Less than six months ago, my father suffered a major heart attack. At that time, I was quite empathetic toward him as a man who suffered a trauma, but I also felt something empty in my heart, in that place where I wished I could relate to him on a more personal level.

This time, as I watch him lying in bed, his reason clouded by the abscess pressing on his brain, and struggling desperately to put coherent sentences together, I feel a void inside me momentarily become filled. Though I am aware of its transient nature, I feel a connection with him, in an uncharacteristically positive fashion. The surgery is supposedly safe, but there is always danger where the brain is concerned, and his condition afterward is not guaranteed.

Fucking asshole! Why'd he have to go and pull this shit?

To everyone else in the room, I do my monosyllabic best to remain silent and disconnected. The nurse finally comes in to tell us that visiting time is over. We all have to leave. *Thank God.*

I wait until I am the only one left in the room, so that I can have the chance to say a few quick words to him; this is the first and only time I've ever told him that I love him.

I have never been very close to my father. He is literally my exact opposite; we just don't understand each other. From where my father stands, I am always too sensitive, too quiet, and generally nonsensical, whereas I see him as a loud, arrogant, critical asshole. To be honest, of the four others in my family (my mother, older brother, older sister, and younger sister), my younger sister, Vanessa, is the only one I currently speak to regularly, and I speak occasionally with my mom.

The five of us remain in the hospital, our anxiety finally assuaged by news that his operation was a success. His surgery went as smoothly as anyone could have hoped. He is expected to make a full recovery, although for the moment his right side is paralyzed. We're told that this is a normal part of the recovery process, albeit quite frightening.

Nevertheless, as soon as I know the operation is successful, my heart shuts itself off again, and I reclaim my familiar emptiness. I feel overwhelmed by everything going on around me, and I am even sadder that I once again feel as if I don't truly care about what is going on with my father. I've blocked out his situation completely.

A few days later, back at West Point, I am back to being alone. As I sit in my room, I try to find comfort in the fact that nothing can get much worse. All I enjoy is lifting weights and reading, both of which I use to relax and relieve all my stress. I relish those moments when I am able to escape from things for a while. Thus, when I call my friend Mitch after dinner and he says that Jeff has some GBL (gamma butyrolactone), I don't hesitate to sneak off to Jeff's room to take a shot of the drug.

This is my first time doing GBL, the concentrated version of GHB (gamma hydroxy butyrate).* GHB is degreasing solvent or floor stripper mixed with drain cleaner. GBL works exactly like GHB; its effects include intoxication, increased energy, happiness, talkativeness, a desire to socialize, feelings of affection and playfulness, uninhibitedness, sensuality, enhanced sexual experience, and muscle relaxation. However, GHB has an additional compound that makes it odorless and tasteless, thereby making it an effective

---

*For the purposes of my story, the slight differences between GBL and GHB are irrelevant, so throughout the book I will refer to both compounds as GHB.

date-rape drug. I'd recently heard several stories in the national news about the law enforcement community's crackdown on the illicit drug because it is frequently used by unscrupulous club-goers to sedate and rape women.

Before I return to my barracks, my friends quickly brief me on this relatively new substance. They inform me that careful measurement is of paramount importance with GHB. One-half a milliliter too much could gracefully transition you into a five-hour coma. Ten milliliters too much could transition you into a grave. They also instruct me never to combine GHB with alcohol.

Since GHB (sometimes just called "G") has to be measured in small amounts, my friends find it practical to store it in an apparatus that allows for slow and careful dispensing. Bottles for eyedrops make perfect containers because they're so inconspicuous; one does not want someone else noticing one's drugs in the medicine cabinet.

GHB is an unnoticeable, clear liquid, but more important, it is not tested for by the army. As a result, G has become a mainstay of the dysfunctional Academy infrastructure.

This has created a serious and growing problem, with numerous individuals requiring hospitalization after overdosing. After three cadets suffer seizures, the Academy puts out a memorandum describing the dangers of GHB, citing these risks as reason for its definitive ban. I'm not deterred. To paraphrase Bogey, I can sense the beginning of a beautiful friendship.

7

Spring Break
March 2000

S he's perfect: tall, blonde, and curvy (but not overweight), with great big beautiful eyes, captivating girl-next-door looks, and most important, she's dancing with *me*!

I love to dance, but to be honest, I really just flail around like the tall wonky Jew I am—which is why I enjoy drugs (in this case, mushrooms) so much: they give me the confidence to just bounce all around the dance floor with a complete disregard for reality.

So here I am, careening around the club, bouncing along the clouds as I pour vodka down my throat, when I bump into this beauty. To my tremendous surprise, there is no look of disgust, but rather a pleasant smile, as she stays to dance with me. I am in uncharted territory.

I have no expectations anymore, especially here in Daytona Beach, besides getting liquored up. I imagine that for most of my friends, as with most other guys my age, spring break is, first and foremost, prime time for hooking up. My goal is even simpler: to get drunk—something I haven't been able to do in more than two months, yet I am confident that I am still quite good at it.

In light of my fifty hours of Area tours and more than twenty hours for other various infractions, it is quite likely that I am not going to be able to take a weekend pass anytime this semester. My one saving grace, therefore, is spring break. Except for plebes, everyone gets it, and it can't be taken away.

After what seems like an hour of swirling madness, I desperately need a rest. My body is completely drenched from the vodka and GHB-guzzling, psychedelic overdrive I've put it through. Now is the moment of truth. *Will she come have a drink with me?*

The club is extremely loud and crowded, so after a few unsuccessful attempts at soliciting a response, I decide to make things a bit simpler. I grab one of her hands and point with my other hand to her and then to one of the empty sofas in the distance. Another smile, coupled with a gentle nod. *Bless her heart!*

Thus far, my trip has gone as expected. The bottle of GHB and the ounce of mushrooms that I brought have been serving their purpose. I had been looking forward to a week that I was sure I wouldn't really remember, and in that regard I was succeeding swimmingly. However, now things were definitely taking an interesting, sudden turn.

After weaving through the masses, we reach our destination.

"Hey, I'm heading to the bar. You want something?"

"Yeah, thanks. A vodka-cranberry would be great."

Upon my return, as I hand her the drink, my eyes scan the Daytona Beach nightclub for the rest of my crew. *Damn, where are they when I need them?* I wonder. *I'd love for at least a couple of them to see me with this hottie.*

"Hey, so like I hope you're not offended by my asking again, but I couldn't get your name on the dance floor."

"Ha! I'm not telling. I've already told you three times, you know."

"I'm such a jackass," I say, as I stare downward, shaking my head. If I had any shot whatsoever, I figure it's over now.

Surprisingly, she puts her hand on my shoulder and starts shaking me a little bit.

"Hey, don't worry about it. It's Sarah. You're Mike, right?" she says, still smiling. *Why is she being so darn nice to me?*

"Yeah, it is. Now I really feel like a schmuck."

"No, seriously, don't worry. It *is* really loud in here, especially out on the dance floor. So, where're you from?"

What a cool, laid-back chick! I think.

"New York. I go to West Point."

"West Point? I'm sorry, I haven't heard of it." *Does she live in a bubble?*

"It's a military academy. The army. Trust me, it's not very cool. So don't worry. You're not missing much."

"Oh, okay, if you say so. Can't be that bad, though. I mean, they did let you out for spring break, right?"

"Yeah, I guess so."

Silence.

"So, how many of you army boys are there—down here, I mean?"

Thank God she is outgoing and taking the initiative in this conversation.

"Ten of us all together. We all drove down last weekend. So, how 'bout you? What's your story? Where're you from, and all that jazz?" I ask.

"Well, like I said, I'm Sarah. That was a bonus one for you—but trust me, it's not being mentioned again," she says, laughing.

"Thank God, you know I'd already forgotten again?" I say, joining in the laughter.

"Stop!" she says playfully, hitting me on the shoulder.

Really, though, I'm thinking: *Thank fucking God! Jesus, I need to remember that now. Sarah, Sarah, Sarah . . .*

"Anyway, I'm from Kentucky. I'm working part-time and taking classes at Eastern Kentucky University. It's all pretty basic stuff. Nothing nearly as *fabulous* as a military academy, though," she says, smiling.

I love her smile. It's so playful and genuine.

"Yeah, right. Trust me, 'fabulous' is not exactly the right word. So, who're you down here with?"

"Oh, I came down with a bunch of my girls, and couple of their boyfriends. There's like six of us altogether."

"That's cool."

This conversation seems like it's working—but how? There's no way I'm actually saying cool shit, is there? Is it possible that the mushrooms are making me sound somewhat cool?

"So, you mind me asking what you're on?" she says.

This is bad territory for a West Pointer. *Maybe she's like some undercover narc, and that's why she's being so nice to me,* I think.

"Huh? I don't . . ."

"Don't worry. Seriously. I'm not into the drug thing, but all my friends are, and they're all rolling tonight."

Wow, that I wouldn't have guessed. Such a sweet, innocent girl, I wouldn't have figured her to hang out with druggie types—like me, for instance.

"Oh, you're sure it's not a problem?"

"Yeah, definitely. So you rolling, also?"

"No, actually I ate some mushrooms."

"Ahh, gotcha. Yeah, I don't know much about them. My friends are all just really into X."

"Hey, I hope you don't mind me asking, seeing as how I just met you and all. But pretty much everyone in our group has wanted to try Ecstasy, and we figured Daytona would be the perfect opportunity. Since we've been down here, we've bought tons of pills from different sources, but they've all been bogus. So I guess you could say that our introduction into the world of X has mainly been a lesson in proper drug-purchasing techniques and general pill awareness."

Fuck! I'm rambling, and about drugs!

"So, what I'm trying to say is: do you think your friends could possibly hook us up?"

"Yeah, that's probably not a problem. I'll see what I can do. I know they didn't bring a lot down, but they definitely have a good connection for that stuff, so I'll ask them. But, hey. I thought army boys aren't allowed to do drugs?" she says seriously.

"Yeah, well . . ."

"Hey, I'm just messing with you," she quickly interjects, hitting me on the shoulder again, as she flashes that pleasant smile.

At this point Mitch, Dave, and some of my other friends notice me talking to Sarah (finally!), so I wave them over. I couldn't possibly be more pleased with the scenario. As shallow as it may be, everything is now perfect. Having a few of my friends validate not only her existence but also her good looks is absolutely crucial for my ego. While I go to get a couple more drinks, the guys keep her company.

As I return, I start to get nervous. There are a couple more friends of mine around her, and she's laughing hysterically. This is not a good thing.

Has she realized there are better options around here? I wonder, insecurely.

As soon as I get back, though, she quickly calms all my anxiety. After I hand Sarah her drink, she makes some room on the couch, grabs my free hand, and pulls me down next to her.

As we all continue talking, I am amazed at how comfortable Sarah is around my loud, wild, drunk-as-hell army friends. She is so down-to-earth and personable that it's almost scary. While they're all talking, Dave pulls me aside to ask me a quick question.

"Hey man, I just found this pill," he says, quickly flashing me something in his left hand.

"Where?" I ask.

"The back of the couch."

"And?"

"Well, should I take it?"

"I don't know, what is it?"

"I have no idea. It's yellow."

"Well, yellow's good."

"You think? Yellow's good?"

"I don't know, man."

"So, should I eat it?"

"I really don't know, Dave, but you're fucking nuts, man. You know that, right?"

"Yeah, I think I'll eat it. I mean, it *is* yellow," he says, laughing.

Before I have a chance to say anything more, Dave pops the little yellow pill in his mouth and swallows. Now I'm the one who can't stop laughing. I didn't think he was actually going to eat it.

"Hey, why are you laughing? I mean, it was yellow, and yellow's gotta be good, right?"

"Of course it does, bro. You're good to go."

I let Dave go do his thing so that I can continue hitting on Sarah. I keep expecting her to lose interest and leave, but she never does. In fact, the more we talk, the more attracted to me she seems to become. There is a genuine spark.

An hour or so later (time is hard to pin down on 'shrooms), Dave swings back over, with a noticeable kick in his step.

"Hey, man, I think it was like meth or some shit," he says, grinding his teeth. "Pretty cool shit!" he says.

"Yeah, I told you yellow was cool," I say.

"*Yeah! Definitely!* Yellow's always cool. Hey, I'll catch ya later, man," Dave says, quickly darting off, while I'm left laughing and shaking my head.

After dancing and talking with Sarah all night, I walk her back to her hotel, where her friends are all still rolling hard. They're a cool crowd, but not necessarily what I expected from meeting Sarah. Sarah's sweet innocence is a stark contrast to their edgy style.

When one of her friends offers me a hit of Ecstasy, I decide to try it, but once again, it's to no avail. I think I feel something, but from what I've been told about the drug and from watching Sarah's friends, I'm sure I'm not enjoying the full experience. I chalk it up to 'shrooms, GHB, and alcohol being combined with one really weak pill. Regardless, I stay up all night talking with Sarah. It's only when the sun comes up, and we realize that we're both totally exhausted, that we say our good-byes. Her friends, however, look undeterred, able and willing to go all day.

As I walk back to my hotel, the sun already beating down on my rapidly deteriorating body, I still feel a bounce in my step. All I have to do is remember that last kiss good-night and look at the piece of paper in my right hand. Things could not be better.

It's really funny how life works sometimes. I am about to turn twenty-three and have dated only one girl my whole life—and for just three months. This is why meeting Sarah my second-to-last night in Florida made my mushroom trip just that much more sur-real.

After sleeping half the day, I call Sarah and we make plans to meet again. *Would she still dig me the next day? Would she look as great?* We continue to get along marvelously, and without a doubt, she is beautiful, a total sweetheart from Kentucky. I could not possibly be more content.

Honestly, thank God she appeared when she did. A twenty-three-year-old guy on room restriction at a military school can only go so long without a girl in his life.

8

April's Fool

April 2000

A pril Fools'! It is the first nice Saturday of spring, my birthday is just three days away, and I am stuck in the Area. I am the fool.

As I walk around the Area, dressed in my parade uniform, my palm holding the butt of my rifle, which rests snugly against my right shoulder, I ask myself the question that often repeats itself in my mind: *How and why am I still here?*

As I reflect over the past four years, the answer is not totally clear. All I know for certain is that failure is unacceptable, and leaving would be failure. Beyond that, everything still seems so foreign, so surreal. It has taken almost my entire time at the Academy for it to all sink in, and I'm still not there yet.

As I march back and forth, alone with my thoughts, my mind meanders through the past four years, recalling the most vivid memories, good and bad.

I'll never forget R-Day. What a shock! I especially remember the first time I sat down in the cadet barbershop chair. More than anything else I did that day, including even the Oath Ceremony, my haircut was the defining moment for my entrance to the U.S. Military Academy at West Point.

Then I see Larkowich in front of me, that fierce bulldog, thoroughly ripping my shit. I remember how he once made me turn my chair around at the mess hall table and eat in the opposite direction because he couldn't stand looking at me. It was horrible. Now, for some reason, I find a peculiar comfort in this memory.

I recall watching Pete stare at me in disbelief the night before our first major inspection. I had just spilled black edge dressing (a strong black varnish used to coat the outside edges of the soles of soldiers' shoes) all over our floor, right after we finished countless hours of immaculate cleaning. I wouldn't change that for anything. Pete's great.

I remember marching in Bill Clinton's 1996 Presidential Inauguration Parade. Our company was chosen to go from the entire Corps, and I hated it. All the mind-numbing, incredibly exhausting hours of preparation practically drove me insane. *And for what? For a memory I'll never forget, that's what.*

I see countless upperclassmen, officers, and instructors yelling at me. Above all, I see my friends and myself laughing. Whether they're events in the gym, in one of our rooms, in a bar in New York, or tailgating on post, these are the memories I most often turn to. For me, they're the best thing this place has going for it.

It's interesting. Most cadets eventually learn to conform to the Academy's expectations, following orders and obeying the rules. If it's even possible, which it really shouldn't be, I had actually been getting *worse* at the whole military thing.

Thinking back to the how and why, my mind focuses on a particular conversation with my parents three days before I returned to West Point for the beginning of my cow year. I could not even begin to hide my unhappiness at going back. Although I was confident I'd be able to stick it out, I knew I was not even remotely close to entering the right profession. I dreaded entering that first class as a third-year student, thereby incurring my obligation to the army. I didn't want to join the Profession of Arms.

1996 PRESIDENTIAL INAUGURATION PARADE   ME!

As I talked with my parents, my state of mind could be summed up in two simple words: *anxious confusion.* I was torn between quitting and continuing with something that I knew was a horrible fit. My heart was in it, as far as never giving up was concerned, but that was about it. I had no desire to be there and no wish to do anything more than just get by.

My father took me aside and asked me to look at my mother, who looked as if she was going to cry at the thought that I might not go back. That wasn't fair. If ever I thought I might leave, I just had to think of my mom and how much she deserved to see her dream for me to graduate come to fruition.

My mom smiles while giving me a hug.

I remember the visitors looking at the spectacular scenic views, the well-known buildings, the cadets in uniform, and the beautiful statues and monuments, as well as watching us during our parades on Saturdays.

If only they knew the truth!

Cadets see a different side of the Academy. For myself and many others I know, it often feels much more like a prison. The parallels are striking: the rooms are small, our freedoms are obviously extremely restricted, and we are surrounded by the walls of extremely large, drab, gray buildings.

Except for a few minor differences, the quarters at West Point (much like the buildings themselves) are virtually all identical. Their meticulous layout and immaculate, unlived-in appearance only add to the cold, sterile feeling I get when I walk around campus. Moreover, the cadets' uniforms, which must be worn every waking minute whenever you step as much as a foot outside your room, are strictly regulated and enforced, serving as a constant inescapable reminder of where you are.

Overall, cadet life has been rough. I'm aware that in each entering class, approximately 20 percent of the extremely competitive, bright, physically capable individuals, all of whom went through the arduous process of receiving nominations and then appointments, and all of whom were confident that they had what it takes, will not make it to graduation. I find some comfort in the fact that, thus far, I'm not part of that group.

I keep thinking back to that first year. It was brutal. The Academy wasted no time assimilating me into this new culture, which first required an intense stripping away of my old behaviors and attitudes. The rest of the years weren't much easier.

As I see it, life at the Academy has been a relentless internal struggle, virtually entirely in my own mind. A great deal is demanded and expected from cadets, and I have constantly been forced to challenge myself through duties, projects, physical fitness, time constraints, and other stressors that can often feel overwhelming or even insurmountable. West Point has forced me to step out of my comfort zone at an early stage in my life. As I think about it some more, the hows and whys aren't really all that important. Even now, walking in the Area and not yet having received my diploma, there is one thing of which I am certain: the experience is invaluable. I am aware that I have received an unparalleled education, which reaches far beyond the classroom. Whatever challenges lie ahead, I feel much more confident in my ability to handle them.

Although I have been feeling miserable lately, and this day in the Area is no exception, as I march back and forth I find reason to be optimistic: the last weekend of April I am scheduled to be released from both room restriction and Area tours. I am very excited; not only am I going to be able to take off for the weekend, but Sarah is flying in from Kentucky.

Since spring break, the two of us have been talking almost every night. It is seriously comforting to have someone with whom I can let down my guard.

9

Ecstasy
May 2000

I am somewhat overwhelmed when I walk into Twilo. Twilo is an enormous dance club on the Lower West Side of Manhattan where individuals can bring in backpacks full of drugs without serious inspection, and ambulances are always waiting out back for the kids who miscalculate. (It has long since closed down, but back in those days it was really something.)

I instantly fall in love with the place. The main floor is simply one huge dance floor, the largest in the city. Upstairs, which isn't always open, there is a much smaller dance floor with sofas and the like. Beyond the interesting assortment of people we see, gorgeous women dressed in sparkling angel costumes are dancing on raised podiums, which lends a dreamy vibe to the place.

It's the second-to-last weekend in May. There is one week left of school, which is always set aside for finals and cannot be interrupted by urine tests. Thus, on a weekend when we all probably should be studying, six of us have decided to check out the New York City club scene. Our primary goal: to score Ecstasy.

As with my experience with mushrooms, I did ample research on the fashionable club drug. I know that "rolls" are a street name for the drug Ecstasy, which is the compound MDMA (methylenedioxymethamphetamine). Websites and friends I've spoken with have told me that MDMA shares the qualities of amphetamines (a family of stimulants) and mescaline (a hallucinogen). Although Ecstasy is often being labeled a hallucinogen, this classification is somewhat erroneous. The effects of MDMA differ noticeably from those of LSD and other psychedelics: Ecstasy lacks the perceptual distortions usually associated with these other substances. Anyway, it's supposed to be a fun ride.

After getting inside Twilo I take it upon myself to just start walking around asking everyone if they have any X; eventually I find someone who does. I know that the pills are supposed to be bitter, so before buying them I eat one, which tastes pretty damn nasty, so I figure it's legit. I'm right. Not only do the six of us spend the rest of the night rolling, but I get two dealers' numbers for future purchases. The evening is quite the success.

We are lucky, because we are at least taking legitimate MDMA. The sites I looked at on the Internet stress the fact that the majority of Ecstasy on the market nowadays is an unpredictable mixture of drugs not intended to be incorporated, such as DXM (dextromethorphan, the psychoactive chemical found in Robitussin cough syrup), caffeine, speed, ephedrine, or some other bullshit one's really not ready for. I can only imagine how it must suck to take a pill and have it wind up being something totally different than what you expected.

Nevertheless, these risks don't deter us. I find the effects of Ecstasy to be quite pleasant, characterized by strong euphoria and amazing sensations. Basically, it is unrestrained madness. I am able to get banged up and escape reality while remaining functional and able to talk to girls.

We all have an excellent experience and look forward to what will hopefully be a very soon next time. As a bonus, I meet two great guys from the Academy whom I hadn't met before: Eric and Chad.

The following weekend is painful and depressing as I watch my friends graduate. I have developed strong friendships—much stronger than I would have formed at any other college, I'm certain. Besides, at what other college do students take to the graduation podium in full dress under arms, wearing a saber at their left side, with the president of the United States as the keynote speaker?

Part of me still listens for where my name would be on the list, had I been graduating. When my name is passed over, even though I knew full well that it would be, a final ember of hope is extinguished. I feel as though I will never receive my diploma. It has been a long four years, especially the last two semesters, and my heart isn't so much in it anymore.

My friends are all leaving, I still have another year, and I am fraught with enormous anxiety about becoming an officer. I know it isn't really my niche. In addition, I'm not too optimistic about being allowed to stay, since I know I'm not well liked by my commanders. I will be walking on eggshells until graduation. I am so confused.

Receiving my diploma and being commissioned as an officer in the U.S. Army seems so far away. On the one hand it can't come soon enough, since I desperately want to leave West Point; at the same time it's totally undesirable, because it means getting serious about something I have no inclination to be part of.

Fortunately, Sarah flies in to Connecticut to visit me from Kentucky after the ceremony. I am happy to be back home; the only negative aspect is that I am forced to remember that my dad is still in the hospital. Nevertheless, I really enjoy my week with her before my summer details start.

At West Point, a cadet's military field training takes place during the summer. Before the plebe year there is Beast Barracks, or Basic Field Training, which serves to introduce and assimilate new cadets into West Point culture. After plebe year, the cadets attend Camp Buckner for Advanced Field Training, which focuses on much more hands-on training. The cadets are rotated through different blocks of instruction that provide them with the opportunity to see up close and personal what is involved with most branches of the army.

As upperclassmen, cadets may choose from an extensive variety of military advanced development programs. There are basically two slots open for each of the last two summers. I was a supply officer for Beast Barracks two years ago and was a shadow platoon leader last year for a scuba unit at Fort Eustis, Virginia. That provided me a lot of leeway for this, my bonus summer.

Still having to complete a training school, I lobbied for something easy due to my bad back, but also because I really didn't want to do anything requiring any serious discipline or a *soldierly* attitude. In lieu of the typical schools—such as Airborne, Air Assault, scuba, or High Altitude Low Opening (HALO) parachuting—I got my wish and was given the job of Bayonet Assault Course instructor. Most of the aforementioned schools require a good deal of effort, with the goal being to graduate and receive a badge; there is no badge in my future for helping to run the bayonet course.

My second detail, a leadership role, is also somewhat lacking in the military department: I am basically a camp counselor for a group of thirteen-year-old kids who are taking part in a three-week day camp that the Academy offers on its grounds. Neither the bayonet course nor the camp counselor gig is more than three weeks, which gives me just over four weeks of leave time; this isn't very common.

Sarah and I meet several of my Academy friends in the city, call one of my dealers for some pills, and then head over to Twilo to help them celebrate their graduation. With Sarah here, this night is even better than the last. She seems just as willing as I am to experiment with new chemicals. As the Ecstasy rushes through our systems, the two of us get real close, real fast, repeatedly telling each other how much we care for each other. A "great" thing about X is that two people can get lost in the moment, their emotions hyper-accelerated, causing them to say and do things that they would normally never do and almost certainly will later regret.

10

Porter

June 2000

F *ucking Porter, how the hell's he swinging this one?* I wonder.
Porter is one of two friends from high school with whom
I keep in touch (Josh is the other). My friendship with
Porter is kind of odd, because he is an extremely unreliable, obnox-
ious, selfish, cocky asshole. Yet in spite of this, we're tight. He's also
a ton of fun.

My thoughts about Porter's current enviable situation are being
somewhat overwhelmed by his incessant self-indulgent digres-
sions. Porter has convinced his parents that it's advantageous for
him to take a summer course at New York University (NYU), basically so they will pay for an apartment for him in the city. He has
one class, which I'm reasonably sure he doesn't go to very often
and almost definitely doesn't do any work for. (The amusing thing
is that although he passed the class, his credits didn't transfer over
to his regular school.)

"Yeah, so there's these three dope model honeys across the way.
Through this window, over there. Banging babes. I mean totally
banging. Well, at least two of them are. And I'm almost positive
those two have been sweatin' me. I look over through the window
sometimes, when I'm walking past in my undies, and catch 'em

checking me out. I kind of pose, to give 'em a little somethin'," Porter says, momentarily stopping to laugh. I know by now that his laughter is not by any means an indication that he's joking; it's simply a punctuation mark for his self-love.

I tune him out and then tune back in a few minutes later, only to get more of the same.

"Oh yeah! I mean, she was like some exotic model chick: half Persian, Brazilian, African, or like Puerto Rican or some shit. Fucking banging, bro."

Porter always speaks the same, regardless of the audience: parents, friends, teachers, coaches, or, in this case, Sarah. I like Porter because he is such a character, and I respect the fact that he never puts on a show—for although he might be a prick, at least he is a genuine prick.

"So we like pass each other on the street, and I'm totally checking her out like this," Porter says, as he pauses to give me his Zoolander (a Ben Stiller movie character) face.

Although I don't see it, Porter is supposedly quite good-looking (just ask him), and women are the only thing I've ever seen him take seriously. Actually, I shouldn't be so harsh. An athletic, trim five feet eleven with an olive complexion, Porter is good-looking. He's always quick to mention that other people tell him that he looks like Patrick Dempsey.

"And I know, I fucking *know* she's checking me out, too, bro. So, I . . ."

Porter's probably the funniest guy I've ever met, but only when he's just being himself, without actually trying to be funny. At the moment, however, any amusement is clearly being lost on Sarah. She's just not down with his misogynist sense of humor. Noticing her annoyance, I decide to change the subject back to reality.

"Porter," I say.

"So I cross over to the other side of the side sidewalk, and . . ."

"*Porter!*"

"Yeah, what's up?"

It's the last week of June. Having just finished my first detail, which was my camp stint, I have leave for the next ten days. I'm excited about my time off because Sarah has flown in again, and I have a chance to roll a few more times.

"Some X?" I say, smiling.

"No doubt! Yo, call that chick again!" Porter quickly replies.

"Yeah, maybe you should call her, Mike," Sarah urges. I smile, because this is one area that the two of them obviously agree on. Despite being a relative newcomer to the world of illicit drugs, Sarah unabashedly adores Ecstasy.

"Can't. I already beeped her twice."

Since my first visit to Twilo, I've maintained contact with a female dealer, Lizzie, whom I met there that night. She's expensive and sometimes hard to get through to, but in the end she's 100 percent reliable. She always comes through for me, and her pills are always totally rocking.

"Damn, man! What the fuck's her problem? Yo, wanna see a picture of this girl I've been bangin'?"

"Sure," I say, knowing full well that he'd show me anyway, and that there's no way to avoid the ever-increasing disgust that Sarah deftly doesn't show to Porter yet that I can see all too clearly in her eyes.

Why are you friends with this asshole? I imagine her wanting to ask me. It's a question I've heard often, from other friends and my family.

A few minutes later, my cell rings. The look of joy on my two comrades' faces is undeniable. To be honest, I feel like "the man." Porter's always been the cool party guy, but here I am getting the girl *and* the drugs.

Doin' it right, Winder, I think, smiling.

"Hello?" I say, trying to act nonchalant, despite my unequaled enthusiasm. Without her call, and more important, her Ecstasy, our evening would be an inevitable bust.

"Hey, Mike, that you?" Lizzie asks.

"Yeah, glad to hear from ya. Was starting to think I might not get a hold of you tonight," I say, honestly.

"No problem. Where you at?"

"Downtown. NYU dorm. Around Fifth and Eleventh."

"All right. I'm not that far. Give me a few minutes."

"Cool," I reply.

"Oh, and how many kids you see at the park today?" she asks. This is code for how many pills I want.

"Thirty."

"Wow, lotta kids today. See you in ten. Lata."

Yeah, it is definitely a lot—a lot of money, that is. I just want my time with Sarah to go perfectly. With Porter already snagging some of the pills for himself, I figure thirty is a safe number. The cost is high, but the benefits are huge, and I don't want to have to deal with any more purchases, especially from other dealers, whose stuff might not be legit.

"Bye," I say, after she's already hung up.

"So we good?" Porter asks, barely beating Sarah to the question.

"Yeah, she's meeting me outside in a few minutes. Told you she'd come through!"

"She giving you any discount or anything? I mean, you are buying thirty rolls," Porter says.

"No, I don't think so. Yeah, I know it sucks. Thirty bucks a pill is way high, but her shit's always top-notch, and right now she's the only good connection we've got."

"Maybe you can get her down to twenty, at least twenty-five. I mean, thirty is fucking kinda ridiculous," he replies.

"Would you rather we didn't have any, bro?"

I don't care about the money. Having parlayed my $20,000 West Point loan into $50,000 from day-trading securities, I have more than enough to focus on just the prime objective.

"No, but . . ."

"Listen, man, I'm not doing her any favors. She's told me before that she and her boss don't negotiate, and that their primary clientele is the uptown Wall Street guys."

"Yeah, I know. I just think we need a new source."

"Yeah, definitely. Shit, she said last week that she brought over a couple hundred pills to some investment banker who was having a weekend party in the Hamptons. Her boss didn't even offer one fucking free pill, and what's more, she said the rich fucks didn't care about the price at all and even tipped her a few hundred. We're small potatoes, man. He don't give a shit about bargaining with us. If we call, they know we need their shit. And that's it," I reply, as I head out the door.

Once I am back in Porter's room, with X in hand, everyone is energized. I am personally overwhelmed by feelings of elation. I've found that the only thing that compares with the actual euphoria of Ecstasy (and other comparably wonderful substances) is the acquisition and subsequent anticipation of the drug.

I immediately take out the pills, and Sarah and Porter inspect them with the careful awe and elation that I expect an anthropologist would feel in unearthing an ancient civilization. Actually, I believe that Sarah and Porter's wonder and joy far exceeds that of scientific discovery. It's a chemical thing.

"Yellow smiley faces," Porter says.

"Yeah, they look cute. I wonder how good they are," Sarah says.

"I heard about them. Supposed to be pretty good. Anyway, her shit usually is. You pay full price?" he asks.

"Yeah, of course. There was no freaking negotiating. She was out of there like a gunshot."

"Ah, whatever. Let's just look these up real quick online," he replies.

Since Sarah was already looking at Porter's favorite Ecstasy verification website, it took us just seconds to find the pill in its registry and verify that it was totally legit. Any irritation Porter had about the cost has completely vanished now, because it seems that these pills are not only pure MDMA but also extremely potent and very user-friendly. We are all very happy.

After a few hours of drinking, we head out to Exit. On our way out, we decide to play it safe and stash our pills in Sarah's bra. One can't be too careful, and this club's discretion might not match that of Twilo's. This uncommon act of prudence proves quite beneficial, because Exit's security team thoroughly searches us, but to no avail. The whole process of just getting in is so exhausting that I almost want to head somewhere else. However, despite having a wait of more than an hour, Exit is well worth the trip.

The club is unparalleled. It makes Twilo look like a little shoebox, and I can't imagine that there's another club like it anywhere else in the world. With four floors and ten to twenty rooms, including an outdoor area with a beautiful waterfall, Exit has something for everyone (on drugs). It's a drug user's paradise.

Sarah and I barely see Porter. He's off making out and getting numbers from an amazing array of different women. I can't imagine, though, that there's anything as exhilarating as rolling with a sexy woman who's into you. The sensual nature of the drug makes our simple touches and kisses practically orgasmic.

"I really care about you. I mean, I *really* like you," Sarah says.

"I know, I really like you, too," I say, as we start making out again.

Despite the fact that we've seen each other only a few times, the two of us have been getting really close, really fast.

Walking around the enormous chemical wonderland that is Exit and taking everything in consumes just about the entirety of our six hours. As the sun comes up, we slowly begin meandering out. Just a month ago I was wary of doing a couple pills in one night, but now I've no problem doing four or five.

"Yo, who was that guy I just saw you talking to?" Porter asks, as we leave the club.

"DJ Scab. At least that's what he called himself. I don't know if he's actually a DJ, though. Kinda doubt it, actually."

"So, what's his deal? Why were you getting his number?"

"You got that guy's number?" Sarah asks, somewhat alarmed.

"He's gonna hook me up," I proclaim.

"How?" Sarah asks, still confused.

"With rolls?" Porter says.

"Yeah. Supposedly he moves large quantity. Says he can get me a good deal."

"How much for how much?"

"I said I was looking for around three hundy, and he said he could do me around tenish on the first deal, and then we'd go from there."

"That's all right. Definitely a lot better than what we've been getting," Porter says.

"Yeah, but he seemed kind of shady, didn't he?" Sarah asks.

"Yeah, I guess, but it probably comes with the territory. And if this works out, I won't have to worry about getting pills or paying high price anymore. I'll always have my own stash. Plus, maybe I'll start selling a little on the side to the guys at school, and the shit'll basically pay for itself."

"True dat, bro. Sounds good to me, man. That's kinda like what I've been doing up at school, except I was the go-to coke dealer on campus," Porter says, "the real-estate broker of drugs," he says, laughing with glee.

"Well, it sounds like a good plan, I guess," Sarah says cautiously.

"Yeah, it's all good," I say, as I grab her hand, pull her close, and kiss her.

The three of us, still rolling hard, grab a cab and head back to Porter's place. During the time that Sarah is visiting, we spend most of our waking hours, at least our nights, hanging out with Porter in the city. Our Ecstasy-induced travels send our relationship soaring to tremendous heights in an extremely short period of time. Although I initially enjoyed the intensified intimacy levels, I now find them (and the accompanying propensity to share feelings that are incredibly exaggerated) totally undesirable and reason enough not to do the drug anymore around a woman with whom I am actually involved. Memo to self.

11

Scab

July 2000

S cab."

"Hey man, it's me," I say.

"Who dis?"

"Mike."

"A'right, cool. Yeah, I gotcha, Mike. Just checkin'. Can't never be too safe."

"Gotcha," I say, confident that I'm a fast learner in the drug arena.

"You at our spot?"

"Yeah, I'm still here. Where're you . . ."

"Be there soon." (Click.)

I've already been waiting thirty minutes. Oddly enough, an otherwise irksome wait under the hot Manhattan sun has actually eased any anxiety I have about being swindled. The way he acts is similar to Lizzie, as if he's doing me a favor.

There's no way I'm getting fucked, I think to myself.

Although my summer military assignments were admittedly not very arduous details, the constant military focus still completely drained me. Finally, however, I am done with the Bayonet Assault Course and all West Point obligations. With two and a half weeks leave until I have to sign back in to the Academy, I am looking forward to some quality unrestricted drug use.

I sleep at Porter's probably four days a week, doing Ecstasy every night. I am really enjoying the New York scene and grow more attracted to partying with drugs each time I do them. I love being able to go nuts and totally forget any displeasure I have with my life, while dancing in a state of fantastical happiness that I haven't ever come close to achieving with just alcohol.

With one week remaining until the start of school, I decide that I might as well take the prudent option and buy a large quantity of pills at one time, instead of continuing to purchase in small, and much more expensive, piecemeal quantities. The deal I'm getting from DJ Scab is 300 pills for $2,700; this isn't too great a bargain for the quantity, but it will have to do. So it is the middle of the day, and I am waiting for him on the corner of a highly populated block on Seventh Avenue. I am a little antsy, which is primarily due to fears of him being undercover or possibly under surveillance, since he gives the impression that he moves quite a bit of product.

After waiting another fifteen minutes I begin to get nervous, but now these feelings are all focused on whether he'll even show up; the more I wait, the more I know I have to have the rolls. I want a personal stash for the coming semester, and I calculate that if I decide to sell about half, that will more than pay for my half. Porter made roughly $10,000 selling drugs at his school this past year, so I don't see any reason why I can't make some nice "bank" myself.

When DJ Scab finally shows up, I am relieved, and for some odd reason I have no worries. Scab definitely doesn't try to make himself look less nefarious or intimidating. *Convict* is the only word I can think of to describe him, although a much more accurate description would be *dirty, shady-as-fuck-looking convict*. Strangely, none of this bothers me.

He looks like a serious drug dealer. I gotta be good.

"Yo, Mike?"

"Yeah, Scab?"

"True. You a cop?"

"Uh, no. You?" I answer, trying to act like I know what I'm doing.

"Nah. Yo, where's your car?"

"Huh?"

"Where's it at, man? Fuckin' po-po on everyone's ass these days. Can't be too safe when movin' weight."

"Well . . ."

"What? You didn't think we're doing this shit here, did you?

"Uh, no," I lie. "It's in a parking lot over there."

"A'right. Let's go."

The two of us, the good DJ and I, stroll over to my car. I feel cool. I feel confident. I feel *so* excited.

Three hundred fucking pills! I shout inside my head, wishing I could let the outside world hear me.

Two hours later I'm in a dive bar in the Village, using Porter and vodka to console me. As I have previously stated, I tend not to use my brain nearly enough, so when DJ Scab told me that we had to drive to Weehawken, New Jersey, to pick up the X, I was totally cool with it. I'm far too naive and trusting sometimes—which I credit to my mother, since her genuine spirit is legendary, to the point of bordering on the comically gullible at times.

On the drive into Jersey, he counts the money; the $2,700 is all there. Now, what happens when we get into Jersey is a little questionable. The basic gist, however, is irrefutable: I get robbed.

I feel so low and despondent. I can't tell if I'm depressed and agitated at my own stupidity, over the enormous loss of cash, or simply because I don't have any Ecstasy. Porter is the only person that I've decided I'm going to tell about the incident, probably because I know he'll believe what I say without question.

"We drive to his place, and like a dumb ass I go up to his apartment. When we get there, I go in first, and he shuts the door behind me. I'm sizing up two of his friends sitting on the couch when I hear him speak from behind me: 'A'ight, just throw the money on that table in front of you, turn around, and get the hell out.' I quickly turn around, and he's holding a gun. He says, 'I told you to throw down the money and walk out. Think about it, you can't do shit. What are you going to do, tell the cops? "Oh, officer, I just got robbed during a drug deal." Throw the shit down and get the fuck out of here.' So I throw down the money and leave."

As I finish telling Porter my tale, I am dumbfounded. I suddenly realize that I'm starting to believe this ridiculous tale. Porter is actually quite cool about everything, and he gets me sufficiently inebriated to the point of near-forgetfulness and bliss.

I am a moron—the most impulsive, thoughtless individual on the face of the planet. Yes, I even impress myself with my stupidity, I think to myself, bizarrely amused by this notion.

My mind reviews the day's actual events one last time, confident that no one else (including myself, eventually) will ever be the wiser.

Upon arriving in Weehawken, DJ directs me to a Wendy's. When I pull up to the curb, he's still holding the money, and he says he has to go in alone to get the shit from his friend and will be back in a few. For some reason, no alarms go off in my head. "Sure man, I'll be here."

And there I sit, listening to music, for probably a good thirty or forty minutes. Finally, I figure something might be questionable, so I walk in, only to find no DJ, just an empty Wendy's with a beautiful rear exit leading to a back alley.

So, as I mentioned earlier, Mom is going to have to take full blame for this one.

12

Too Nice

August 2000

As I cross the Appalachian Mountains, the only thing on my mind is my relationship with Sarah. She is a great girl, but I am unnerved by the fact that things have gotten so serious so quickly. The last time we were rolling I'd let slip an invitation for her to move up to Connecticut and live in my parents' spare bedroom. She immediately said yes. *What was I thinking?*

With school about to start, my visit to Kentucky is going to be an extremely short one, two to three days max. I miss Sarah and look forward to spending time together, but primarily I need some time alone with her, off drugs, to figure out what the hell is really going on with us.

As soon as I get there I am quickly reminded why I like her: she is beautiful, always in a good mood, and super nice—too nice. I regret that one of Sarah's best traits is also what I find to be one of her worst.

As I sit on her couch, watching her put away my clothes and cook dinner for us, both completely unsolicited, I realize that she is waiting on me hand and foot. As I think back, it occurs to me that she has always been like this, and I just haven't seen it because 99 percent of the time we are either doing drugs, recovering from drugs, or having sex. I'm sincerely down with having such a sweet girlfriend, but I can't stand being around someone who seems to put me above her.

She is simply way too nice!

Although I know that things aren't clicking for me, I can't say anything, because she keeps making it apparent, by her words and obsessive actions, exactly how much she likes me. Because this is only my second relationship, my experience with women is admittedly quite limited. Unbeknownst to her, I decide that the best thing for both of us is to keep things normal while I am visiting. Our time together is great, but when I drop her off at work on my last day there and watch her walk away, I know that it is the last time I am going to see her.

I feel absolutely terrible. However, the guilt that consumes me is a distant second to the thought of actually telling her how I feel face-to-face and dealing with her reaction. I know I can't lie to her, and I simply can't envision myself telling her that she is far too codependent, obedient, and servile.

Upon my arrival back at school, my semester starts off on a much better note than the last. My new roommate, Ryan, seems quite cool; there is no room restriction or Area tour; I don't have to switch to a new company where I don't know anyone; and my father is out of the hospital and doing much better. In addition, I have finished all my economics classes, so I can take whatever electives I want and, if I'm lucky, do even less work than usual.

Opening my trunk, I lay the aspirin bottle filled with Ecstasy tablets at the bottom of my lockbox. Undaunted by getting scammed, I bought 100 pills through Porter before coming back. I don't want to do anything too risky, but I figure that taking them on three-day weekends and occasionally on a Friday isn't too dangerous. It is comforting to know that I don't have to worry about acquiring drugs—at least for a while.

The phone rings, but I don't pick it up; I know who it is. I hear Sarah's voice on my answering machine and wonder how long it will be before she stops calling. All I have ever known to do when negative emotions are involved is to shut myself off and avoid them; I am a pro at that. I attempt to block her out of my mind— but this is rough, even for me. Overwhelmed by guilt and sadness, I *almost* pick up the phone. After she hangs up, I *almost* call her back. Instead, I do a shot of G, and moments later I go back to unpacking my trunk, and all the negativity is gone. There is nothing but ecstasy.

13

The ~~Holy~~ Grail

September 2000

Looking in the mirror, I really like what I see: a six-foot-three, 215-pound, golden-brown bodybuilder.

I was quite lanky when I first entered the Academy, but those days are over. Most of it was a mind-set change, which I attribute mainly to the intense, physically competitive culture in which I found myself immersed. Once the hardest part of the assimilation period was over, I began focusing on weight lifting. I decided that although my crooked back would never allow me to become truly athletic, I could at least *look* athletic.

I was unsure about doing steroids, but it was Greg, the former tight-end recruit and devoted bodybuilder, who finally convinced me that the downside is totally exaggerated and heavily outweighed by the positives. At six feet six inches tall and 275 pounds, with less than 10 percent body fat, Greg is just one fucking giant. Like me, Greg had not graduated on time due to disciplinary issues. We both have had our share of problems involving alcohol, the only real difference between us being his driving under the influence (DUI), which is one road that I'm adamant about not heading down.

I wanted to look more like Greg. I was reasonably big before, but now, after just one month of steroids, I am completely jacked. Giving up drinking for Ecstasy and GHB has only helped to make me even more ripped. I like the new me.

I found a guy living in Holland who was selling GHB over the Internet, shipping the stuff in fifty-dollar bottles labeled CONTACT CEMENT CLEANER AND REMOVER. The first time I ordered the stuff I was pretty wary. For one thing, I was having it delivered to the West Point mail room, and for another, I really didn't know what the hell I was about to be drinking. Fortunately, it was all good.

I'm convinced that doing GHB is better than drinking: it's a lot cheaper than alcohol (buzz for buzz), doesn't make me belligerent, and actually increases my metabolism. In fact, I don't see much of a downside to doing GHB at all—and since I have plenty of it, and it's cheap, it doesn't seem unreasonable to do it four or five days a week.

Along with having developed my newfound muscularity, I have also become a familiar face at the local tanning salon, thus rounding out my journey into the land of the superficial. I'm surprised (and perhaps somewhat irked) by how things that I have always been so critical of, which should mean nothing, are making me more confident than I have ever been and ever thought I could be. I'm changing before my very eyes, and again, I like the new me.

At some point in my personal reverie, I'm startled out of my deep trance by an unexpected visitor. I turn to see Malibu walk in, look to make sure that Ryan isn't around, and then shut my door.

Malibu is a lunatic, a good-looking linebacker for the army football team. He makes up for his relatively small stature (five feet eleven inches and 185 pounds) by his complete disregard for his own safety on the field.

Here is a brief story from high school that perfectly describes Malibu's mentality. One evening he's driving a few of his friends around when his car suddenly starts spinning out of control. They're heading directly into oncoming traffic, and Malibu assumes that, like in football, when two moving forces make contact, the one that's going the fastest and hits the hardest usually wins. So instead of slamming on the breaks and attempting to avoid a collision, Malibu actually hits the accelerator and flies head-on into the oncoming car. By some miracle no one was seriously injured.

If Malibu is a little bit annoying when he's sober, he is a walking disaster when he drinks; nothing is out of bounds for him. Malibu, like Greg, has also received repeated alcohol violations that resulted in his being turned back for another year at the Academy.

"Hey, man, cool if I come in?" he asks, perhaps somewhat after the fact.

"Yeah, of course," I say, quickly moving past him to get to the T-shirt I'd thrown on my bed.

"Damn, man, you're getting fucking big," he says, as he grabs my arms, momentarily stopping me from attempting to cover up my secret.

"Look at those fucking guns!" he adds, squeezing tightly.

"Thanks," I say, as I push off his hands and throw on my shirt, hopefully concealing the evidence.

"Seriously, bro, you're a fucking monster, man!" Malibu says. He's obviously not letting this one go. The kid never knows when to shut the hell up.

"Yeah, all I basically do these days is lift. Everything else here blows," I say. Malibu might be cool, but my business is my business.

"No doubt, man. No doubt. You're fucking ripped and huge as all shit, man!" he says for the three-hundredth time. I'm getting very tired of our conversation.

The whole time he's been talking, Malibu has been poking his head around the room, as if someone could possibly be hiding in my tiny, immaculately cleaned, ten-by-fifteen-foot cell.

"So what's up?" I say quickly. There is no need for me to deal with his weird bullshit any longer.

"Dude, Ryan's not here, is he?" he asks nervously. His anxiety seems out of place, compared to his typical laid-back California beach-bum persona.

"No, he's obviously not here. What's up?" I ask again. Now he's piqued my curiosity. In a fleeting moment I've switched his status from "loud-mouthed jackass who needs to be on the other side of my door" to "potential." The only question remaining is, what he's bringing to the table?

"Listen, man," he says, drawing closer, "I've got some serious shit to talk about with you."

"Well, shoot, bro. You've got no worries here," I say, trying my best to restrain myself. I've got a hunch that he's got something really jazzy.

"This is on the most extreme down low, bro. You gotta promise me, Winder, this shit stays between you and me," he says, looking around again, as though we were suddenly surrounded by officers who had been wearing their invisibility cloaks.

"Goes no further," I reply. "Whatever it is you want to tell me, I can absolutely guaranfuckingtee you it goes no further."

"Well, here's the deal, bro. I've got some information that I'm willing to trade, but I need to know something first," Malibu says.

"And that is?"

"Can you get me some sweet Alice-D?" he asks.

"Alice-D? What the fuck is—oh, right, LSD, now I gotcha," I say. (Apparently even a burgeoning drug kingpin like myself can learn some new drug lingo now and then.)

"So, can you do it or not?"

"Yeah, no problem," I reply, rather disingenuously. I have no clue if I can get the shit. Malibu had obviously combined some of my acid-tripping stories from sophomore year with my current notoriety among West Point's insidious underbelly and concluded that I could get anything, including LSD, anytime.

"You sure, bro? 'Cuz a lot of people say they can get that shit, and they always end up bailing on me," he presses.

"Yeah, I'm sure," I lie. I could care less about his LSD. Right now

I just want to hear what could possibly cause him to approach me, like this, out of nowhere.

"Sweet, man. I fucking *love* acid, bro. It's my absolute favorite! Love that shit, man. Fucking seriously lovely shit. Have I ever told you that I have Jim Morrison's soul, bro?" he asks, grinning from ear to ear like a Cheshire cat. He reminds me of a little boy—a psychotic, manic little boy who is celebrating Easter, Christmas, and his birthday all at once.

"No, you didn't, but why . . ."

"Yeah, man. He and I are the same fucking person. Damn, bro! Gonna go run through the fucking forest naked, screaming, 'Winder, *you're the fucking tits, man!'* Fucking sweet, man. Can't wait to eat a whole sheet of that shit, blow some lines off that model whore I've been banging, and have a twisted orgy with all her slutty little friends."

I'd actually heard the Jim Morrison thing several times before, and, as always, he truly seems to believe it. Nothing he says fazes me anymore.

"So, watcha got?" I press again, trying to bring him back down to earth and keep him from becoming the first individual to trip from just sheer anticipation.

"All right, here's the deal, bro." He pauses. "You sure you can get me that shit, bro?"

"Yeah, it's solid. Just get on with it, Ryan's gonna be back soon," I lie again.

"All right, man. You know how I kind of take this military shit seriously, right?" he asks.

I nod my head yes.

"Well, I don't want to get kicked out of here, and I wanted to make a good impression, so this past summer I asked for a high-profile job to get some points with all the upper-echelon jackasses. You following?"

"Yeah," I say, not certain how this is at all going to connect with me getting him LSD.

"Well, to make a long story short, they gave me a job working for the post's sergeant major. You got me, bro?" Malibu asks, with a strange grin beginning to show.

"Yeah, I gotcha. So what of it?"

"You wanna know what one of my duties was?"

"Listen, man, can you please just . . ."

"*Bam!* Right there! That's it!" Malibu shouts, as he slams a single piece of paper on my desk.

I turn the paper over. It appears to be a calendar, a schedule of some sort, with all the West Point company names on it.

"What is this shit?" I ask.

"Listen bro, that copy's for you. But remember, it goes no further," he says gravely.

"Yeah, but what the fuck is it?" I ask again.

"You still don't get it, bro? Catch this: So the sergeant major walks up to me one day and gives me a calendar and a bunch of little squares of paper and asks me to arrange all the squares randomly on the calendar. The interesting thing was that the pieces of paper had all the company names on them. *It was the fucking urinalysis schedule, bro!* He was asking me, *me*, to make the entire Corps piss-test schedule! Can you believe that shit, bro?"

"Holy shit! No, I fucking can't!" I exclaim, telling the truth for the first time. "Wait a minute," I add, suddenly suspicious. "How do you know this shit's legit? What if they changed it around after you turned it in?"

"Bro, after I turned in my list, I waited until the sergeant major was gone. Then I snuck back into his office, checked his e-mail, found the finalized copy of the calendar that he sent off to the company commanding officers—which, by the way, I'm pretty damn sure was exactly the same as what I'd given him—printed that shit out, and voilà," Malibu says triumphantly, pointing to the sheet in front of me.

"Yeah, but how do we know for sure?" I ask, my mind starting to comprehend the possibilities of what this might all mean.

"Look at the list, bro. If you don't believe me, just check who's been tested so far and match it up with the dates on that sheet. It's all totally fucking straight, man. You believe that shit?" Malibu asks.

I do and I don't.

Looking at the dates and companies on the list, I see that everything seems to match up perfectly. This indeed appears to be the piss-test schedule, but I simply can't believe it. My mind won't let me comprehend the full impact of what I'm seeing. Something inside me knows that everything is about to change, that this is a potentially pivotal moment in my life.

At that exact same moment, Ryan walks in. I'm glad. I put the paper in my desk, and Malibu quickly leaves, telling me he'll catch up with me later. A few minutes later, Ryan leaves for class, and I'm left alone with my new best friend. My fingers glide over the paper, confirming its reality, as my eyes gaze through the unfolded sheet, staring far beyond, into a realm of graciously welcomed, uncharted madness.

Suffice it to say that the piss-test schedule is the Holy Grail for a cadet who uses drugs at West Point. There would be no more worried nights and no more unnecessary abstinence; all restrictions have been lifted, and all gloves are now officially off.

14

Hawaiian Trip
October 2000

S itting in dense traffic on I-287 while Malibu hangs his head out the passenger-side window like a golden retriever, I stare at the clouds swirling above, dancing in their ever-changing animal forms. I totally came through for him, and we're both tripping hard. The thought occurs to me that dropping four hits of LSD before leaving the Academy might not have been such a great idea.

This is already the third time I've done acid since I acquired the two bottles at a Phil Lesh concert last weekend, each container filled with 100 hits of the psychedelic liquid. I absolutely love the drug; it is better than I remember.

Acid creates more unconstrained craziness than Ecstasy does, and the intense visuals that it provokes make it much more of a trip into the surreal than even mushrooms do. Unlike the effects of other drugs I've done, LSD's effects don't wear off completely when the trip is over; rather, the doors that are opened seem to stay somewhat ajar, virtually indefinitely.

So, with acid rapidly surging through our brains, we find ourselves standing still, trapped in my Nissan Altima on the Tappan Zee Bridge. Fortunately, things slowly pick up, and since we don't have that much farther to go, we're parking my car in Pleasantville at Pace University just as things start getting decisively too intense for me to continue to drive safely.

I met a woman I call Hawaiian Tropic Girl two weekends back, when some of my lieutenant friends came up for Columbus Day weekend. I had a fresh batch of two hundred rolls of Ecstasy waiting for them, having already gone through two hundred so far this semester. I'm now doing twenty a week on average, paying for them with the money I made in the stock market. Around the same time I got the piss-test list, I received my new platinum credit card. My combined spending limit is now near $40,000. This has paved the way for a much more lavish lifestyle. I've started staying in New York hotels every weekend, dining out whenever possible, and shopping for new, fancier clothes. I am completely oblivious to any impending financial disaster.

So there I was, rolling on the second floor of Exit, when I looked down to the main floor and noticed Greg dancing with a few girls, one of whom I thought easily hot enough to be a swimsuit model. Greg already has a girlfriend, so he might not have been putting forth that much effort, but when I strolled up to the group, flaunting my shirtless testosterone-engorged upper torso, it was sweet times indeed when I realized that Hawaiian Tropic Girl was unabashedly staring at me. After years of watching Greg and my other friends get the beautiful ladies, I was finally the one who got the number.

Note that I am not exaggerating when I call her Hawaiian Tropic Girl: she is five feet eleven inches, with long toned legs, ripped abs, extremely large breasts, and a golden brown tan. She is by far the hottest girl I've ever hooked up with, and I attribute it all to Ecstasy and steroids. I am a different man on drugs, the man I've always wanted to be: outgoing, happy, and confident. My attraction to this new world is growing by the minute.

So now, two weeks later, before stepping out of my car at Pace, Malibu and I each take a shot of G, which is swiftly becoming a staple of my daily routine. GHB doesn't take very long to kick in: it starts hitting us just as we're walking into Hawaiian Tropic Girl's apartment. Combined with the acid, it puts us on a different level.

We chug our bottles of wine as she and her friend get ready. We're in a wild, untamable state of idiocy. Now, the reason so many people stop being friends with Malibu is his propensity to become so easily unhinged. Granted, we are banged up on numerous substances, which probably combine to create a delightful mix of uncontrollable mayhem, but I am still caught a bit off guard when Malibu takes off his shirt and shoes, runs outside in his tight leathers, and starts a bonfire on the lawn outside the apartment complex.

The girls are getting a bit annoyed, so I do the only thing reasonable: I grab Hawaiian Tropic Girl's precious stuffed bunny, take off my own shirt and shoes, and run outside to join him, holding the defenseless rabbit over the fire, as Hawaiian Tropic Girl watches angrily from the upstairs window. No one besides us is laughing— but damn it, *we* are laughing!

Rest assured, I quickly come to my senses and apologize, although this is probably because I want to be let back inside and not have to deal with campus police. All is cool. We get our gear back on, and the four of us jump in my car. We are heading to the city (and guess who is driving!).

Damn, it sure as hell is one slippery freaking slope. Fucking amazing how quickly my convictions have overturned. Hmmm . . . oh well, c'est la vie! I think, as my hands tightly clench the steering wheel, eyes locked on the road ahead.

15

K-Hole

November 2000

S omething's wrong, I think, *something's definitely very wrong.*

It is the first week of November. I am standing at my mess hall table, waiting to be called to attention, when Eric and Chad, whose table I sit at, nervously walk up; something is obviously on their minds. Their grave expressions and jittery movements are a far cry from their typical confident, carefree attitudes. Indeed, they have extremely bad news.

Last night, the three of us, along with three other mutual friends, spent the good part of the evening snorting ketamine (a general anesthetic). Over the past couple of months, especially since I acquired the piss-test list, our group has gotten brazen with our drug use. GHB, ketamine, LSD, mushrooms, Ecstasy, and steroids are all stored in our rooms! Some of us sell the narcotics, some just use them, and others actually cook up ketamine in our quarters. We are too smart, above the law. It is this arrogance that has become our downfall.

Since trying LSD my sophomore year and realizing that I would more than likely experiment with other drugs, I have made myself two rules: no snorting and no injecting. At the start of the semester, I accepted the fact that I was now regularly doing some serious

106

drugs, but I was adamant about holding true to these boundaries that I had set for myself. It was roughly two months ago, at a club called The Sound Factory in Manhattan, when Chad got me to snort ketamine, thereby crossing one of the lines I had set for myself.

Although ketamine is used as a human anesthetic, it is primarily used as an animal tranquilizer. Its effects are described as dissociative because the mind separates itself from the body. This separation is often characterized by intense hallucinations and the feeling of entering an alternate reality that is commonly referred to as a K-hole.

What was ketamine really like? Well, although its effects were not nearly as enjoyable as those of other drugs—it did not make me very outgoing, happy, or confident—I did enjoy simply trying something new. Ultimately, I reveled in the fact that it was up the nose.

A wall was down and a whole new world was open to me. Snorting creates quite a unique feeling. The mucous membranes in the nose offer such a speedy metabolizing effect for any drug that snorting is almost always much more intense than taking something orally.

Within days of that night, I was snorting Ecstasy. I embraced the intense rush, craving the feeling one gets as the powdery madness shoots straight to one's brain. I could tell that my love affair with the nose was quickly going to grow exponentially.

"Yo, Winder. We're seriously fucked. I'd just take off right now, if I was you. Bad news to be around us, right now," Eric says.

"Why, what happened?" I ask, very alarmed. Despite my concern for the two of them, I admittedly can't help but wonder if by "we" Eric meant himself and Chad, or if I was included as well.

"Listen, bro. My roommate found a jar of K on his bed this morning and turned me in. Been interrogated by fucking everyone and their mother up the chain of command already, and more's to come this afternoon. We're fucked, but so far, you're all right. So I'd get the fuck away from us if I was you," Eric says, having regained that authoritative confidence I always attribute to him.

"All right, later, guys. Good luck! And keep me posted," I say, as I quickly depart, following his prudent guidance.

"Yeah, will do," Eric replies.

"Later, man," Chad says solemnly, seemingly taking it far worse than Eric.

That night, I get the rest of the story through a mutual friend.

Eric was ordered to provide a list of all the people in the room. Being in a different regiment, I was the one individual whom his roommate did not know. When Eric's command asked him who the tall kid in his room was, he was excellent and told them I wasn't involved, thereby avoiding having to tell them my name. If not for Eric, I would be suffering the same fate as the rest of them.

The five of them are all given piss tests, and although ketamine does not show up on West Point's normal drug test, their urine is sent to a special lab that screens for everything, and all but one of them comes up hot. Unfortunately for Eric, he is additionally screwed with a felony for possession, since his commanders have also searched his room and found Ecstasy and steroids stashed in his lockbox. Ultimately, all four individuals who came up hot on the urinalysis are told that they will be court-martialed out of West Point. I should be going with them.

Of course, I learn nothing from what happens to my friends. I continue my weekly routine, which now consists of two to three days of Ecstasy, two to three days of LSD, and seven days of GHB. I'm buying a hundred pills of X approximately every two weeks, for using and keeping the general populace content. My LSD consumption also slowly increases. Eventually, I begin saving Ecstasy for the weekends and do acid on weekdays, by myself in the barracks, often taking six or seven hits at a time.

As I mentioned before, acid seems to open doors for me—doors into artistic appreciation and expression. I have always enjoyed poetry, but only from the sidelines. I finally feel as if I have something in me that I need to start capturing with words. The more I write, the more acid I consume, and vice versa, because my poetry makes me feel so good and I don't feel creative on my own.

By the way, it is during one of these November LSD-GHB trips, toward the end of the month, when a few insanely incoherent phone calls terminate my friendship with Hawaiian Tropic Girl. It's poetic justice, I suppose: drugs got me in the door, so it seems only proper that they get me kicked the fuck out. I'm not sure why my close encounter with getting dismissed from the Academy has had no appreciable impact on me; all I know is that I am staying my course, believing that I know what I am doing.

At the end of the month I get the final word about my reevaluation, and I am ecstatic (no pun intended). In light of all the positive recommendations the superintendent has received, the most prominent being from Colonel Clemons, my graduation date has been moved up from next May to this December. This is crucial. At the pace I'm currently going, I have little confidence that I can hold it together at West Point for anything more than another month. For a moment I feel truly happy, because finally it all seems attainable. I have been so uncertain about making it through another semester, and I honestly just want it all to be over. I know that receiving a diploma will be something of which both my parents and I will be proud.

16

Graduation

December 2000

A s I turn off my alarm clock, my eyes scan the room, slowly putting into focus the same drab, gray surroundings I've called home for the past four and a half years. There is one difference, though: today the gray, the immaculate orderliness, and the cold space look absolutely beautiful.

It is already around noon, so I grab a quick lunch and then head back to my room to start getting ready. When my phone rings, I'm not surprised to hear my mom's voice; I think she is more excited than I am. I try to play it down because I don't want anyone to know how proud I truly feel about receiving my diploma. I am incredibly frustrated that it means so much to me to graduate from a place that has caused me so much anxiety and unhappiness. There is one saving grace that has made it all bearable: my friends.

Looking in the mirror, I couldn't be happier by what I see. With my close haircut, dark tan, large build, and spotless uniform, I've never looked better. My reflection is a stark contrast to that skinny, anxious Jewish boy who first put on a uniform so many years before. I look like someone who deserves to graduate from the United States Military Academy at West Point.

Sitting in the auditorium with a group of fifteen other

December grads, I block out the superintendent's voice. Instead I'm reflecting on the days since I first arrived for Beast Barracks. I already know that today will more than make up for all the road marches, shoe shining, room cleaning, uniform pressing, formations, Area tours, early morning physical training, field training, arduous academics, and relentless hazing (or "corrections," to be politically correct).

It *almost* all makes sense to me now. I understand why I stayed. I hate conformity, authority, discipline, stress, and physical fitness, yet it was for all these reasons that I knew I had to enter the Academy, and it was because I refused to fail that I never left. Nevertheless, how I made it this far is still something of a mystery to me.

After the ceremony, as my family congratulates me, it becomes abundantly clear from their shocked expressions that they, like me, had expected that I'd do something stupid (e.g., ketamine in the barracks) to prevent this day from ever arriving. Regardless of all the doubts, I am here, and bar none, December 22, 2000, is the best day of my life. There is nothing else that comes to mind of which I am so genuinely proud.

Eating dinner that night with my family, I am still riding high, but my mind starts asking more questions, such as *Do I really deserve it?*

As is typical of me, I have shut out what recently happened to Eric and Chad. While they were being court-martialed, I continued to keep a large amount of drugs in the barracks, using them regularly. The drugs were easy to hide, and I felt safer than Eric and Chad. Visine bottles disguised the acid and GHB, and aspirin bottles were the perfect storage container for Ecstasy. Although I felt comfortable that everything had a proper place, when the inspections came, I still felt a bit unnerved. By now, though, I felt almost untouchable. I wouldn't make mistakes like those made by Eric and Chad, and all the people who knew what I was doing had just as much to lose as I did. In addition, I'd gotten away with an uncountable number of regulations violations, and on the academic side I'd done just enough to avoid serious punishment.

In the words of the Academy, the mission of West Point is "to educate, train, and inspire the Corps of Cadets so that each graduate is a commissioned leader of character committed to the values of Duty, Honor, Country; professional growth throughout a career as an officer in the United States Army; and a lifetime of selfless service to the nation."

Since opening its gates on March 16, 1802, West Point has achieved this objective by developing cadets in four critical areas: intellectual, physical, military, and moral-ethical—a four-year process dubbed the West Point Experience. West Point graduates, whose ranks include the likes of Generals Ulysses Grant, Dwight Eisenhower, and George Patton, are awarded a bachelor's of science degree and a commission as a second lieutenant in the U.S. Army. Graduates serve a minimum of five years on active duty.

Using my intellect to justify things, I decide that making it, in and of itself, is proof that I truly deserve it; all that matters, I tell myself, is that I have received my diploma and commission as a second lieutenant in the U.S. Army. I have met all my goals. I challenged myself physically, as I never could before, met their rigorous challenges, and joined the elite as a graduate of West Point. The notion of active duty scares the shit out of me; nevertheless, I disregard all the angst I have about serving my five-year commitment and concentrate only on the near future: two and a half months of post-graduation leave.

After having dinner with my family, my sister Vanessa and I drive into Manhattan for some prime celebration. Vanessa is a slim five feet nine, with long black hair. She's extremely outgoing and friendly, easy to get along with, and somewhat insecure. She is two years younger than me, and she is my best and most reliable friend. I have three hotel rooms around the corner from Exit rented for two nights, as well as half a room upstairs at the club reserved for roughly fifteen of us. Before we head to the club, most of my group dips into my bag of fun that, thanks to recent purchases, now contains 4 ounces of mushrooms, 150 hits of Ecstasy, 1 ounce of weed, two bottles of GHB, and one-quarter bottle of acid. Extra-special occasions merit extra-special risks.

Despite all this and an additional $1,800 worth of champagne, I buy a couple of jars of ketamine in the club as well; I just can't help myself. Within minutes, I am being searched by the club's undercover security. Fortunately for me, all they find are the two jars of K, since one of my boys is holding my rolls upstairs. I tell the security guys that I have just graduated from West Point, but this does me no service, for it actually seems to piss most of them off; ultimately, however, they discard the jars and let me go with a warning. I go back upstairs and drop another couple of rolls. This is my day, a day to celebrate.

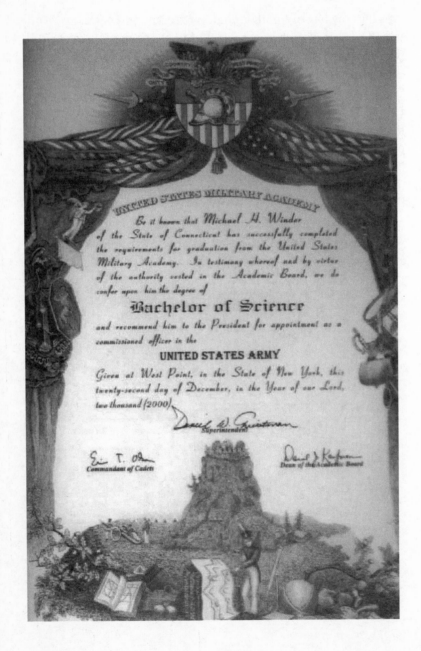

Part Three

AN OFFICER BUT NOT A GENTLEMAN

2001

17

Music and Animals

January 2001

D amn, *that sun is bright. Hey, where the fuck am I? I say to myself, half awake.*

"*Hey,* where the fuck am I?" I yell across the room.

"Are you fucking kidding me, bro?" Porter responds.

"Wha?" I reply, unable to complete even a simple one-word response.

"Are you fucking kidding me with this shit, bro?" Porter reiterates, laughing.

"Huh? What the fuck you talking about, man?" I respond, genuinely dumbfounded.

"Fuck! I don't fucking know!" Porter says, as he falls off his bed in a fit of hysterics.

Less than two minutes after waking up, Porter and I are already rolling on the floor laughing; we're stoned as shit. My new four-foot bong is already earning its keep.

In the five weeks that have passed since graduation, I have reached something of a definitive equilibrium: I go out seven days a week and do drugs seven days a week, and that's excluding GHB. (Because I do GHB so often, I really don't think of it as a drug anymore.) I am trying to make the most of my time off, and I really feel great about everything—it is definitely going to be a good year!

This has been the schedule for my first month off: wake up, run (every other day), shower, eat, read, write, lift weights, read, eat, and then prepare for drug and alcohol madness. Shortly after graduating, I bought Barnes & Noble's two twelve-book sets of classics. My hope is that I'll carry this venture into Officers Basic Course (OBC), as a substitute for my current (overindulgent) evening lifestyle. The books in these sets ought to be on everyone's bookshelf, in my opinion. They include such famous works as *The Brothers Karamazov, Moby Dick, The Adventures of Huckleberry Finn, Crime and Punishment, Oliver Twist, Phantom of the Opera, Jane Eyre, Pride and Prejudice,* and *Wuthering Heights.* On the few days a week when I'm not lifting or running, I just sort of move straight into the drug-and-alcohol phase of my day right after waking up. Today is one of those days.

It is Saturday, the day before the Super Bowl, and there we are, rolling on the floor of Porter's bedroom in his parents' house in Connecticut. I have been living in his house on an almost full-time basis now, and the two of us are inseparable—drinking, drugging, everything and nothing.

His parents seem to be gone yet again. As best as I can recall, they are looking to buy a home in Vermont, or perhaps they have already bought a home in Vermont; I'm not quite sure. The only important thing is that they aren't here. Our day is looking quite bright at this point.

Porter closes the shades; we don't need any sunlight right now. There is definitely no need to go outside today—at least while it is daylight.

We move downstairs, get more banged up, watch a little television, invite some people over, and start drinking. Eventually the sun goes down, and we go out. Then, after a few chemically hazy hours of inebriation, we come back.

We bring a bunch of people back from the bars to help us celebrate into the wee hours of forgetfulness. The very first thing we do when we get inside is set up shop—for cocaine.

Coke is a relatively new and unexpected addition to my repertoire. One of my friends from West Point called me a few weeks ago and told me that about ten of my college buddies were going to be in Atlanta for Super Bowl weekend; he wanted "mad white," and I told him I'd deliver. I had Porter pick up an ounce for me from his guy in the city. I was supposed to have left Wednesday morning and be there yesterday. I am avoiding all their calls. There is nothing enticing about a long drive down to Atlanta by myself. I feel bad that I haven't at least called them and let them know that I'm not coming, but I have a bigger problem. It seems that I have an ounce of cocaine and no one to give it to, so I get curious. I get stupid. I crush up a few lines, and I get real high.

It is around 3:00 AM when a couple of good-looking girls I don't know walk into Porter's place. Things take a sudden, almost magical shift. Drugs had been virtually consuming the entirety of my mind's attention, but now my eyes are focused on the new "eye candy."

Even though I haven't met them before, I recognize both girls from the bar. Amanda is the girl whose number Porter had gotten, and Lynn is her friend who has tagged along. Porter asked us to make sure to keep them occupied when they came over because he would be entertaining other ladies. I hadn't expected much, since Porter wasn't interested, and girls are all Porter's ever interested in. It turns out that Porter is just really annoyed by Amanda, a girl whose breasts are far, far larger than her intellect.

On seeing Lynn, I am more than willing to spark some conversation. She is five feet eight inches tall and blond, with fair skin, big blue eyes, a beautiful visage, a great "rack," and a reasonably good body.

Pretty damn cute! I think. I quickly introduce myself. "Hey, I remember you from the bar. I'm Mike," I say.

"Yeah, I remember you. Lynn," she replies.

"Wanna hang up your jack . . ."

"Hey, whose key chain is that?" she asks.

"Oh, that's mine," I say.

"That's yours? The one with the monkey? Wow! I absolutely *love* monkeys!"

Really cute, I think.

Some of the other guys must have been thinking the same exact thing, because a bunch of them quickly join in our conversation and pounce on these hot, young, unaccompanied ladies just moments after they've walked through the door. I'm not in the mood for a sword fight, so I decide to tend to more pertinent matters.

Ah, whatever. Back to business!

My focus is unobstructed; I go upstairs to do a couple more lines. It's really ridiculous how, with a little focus and determination, one can go through 28 grams of coke very quickly, even if one is a newbie. I enjoyed coke right from the start, and can't believe that I'd ever been wary of trying it. Different drugs just suit different people better, and coke is my kind of drug. It puts me in a great mood and makes me extremely outgoing and confident; this is just what I've been looking for. Despite my limited exposure to cocaine in particular, I'm experienced enough to know that the first line is the only one of purity and true significance; the rest is just maintenance, chasing the white angel, hoping you'll get higher, higher, and even higher still.

I fully embrace cocaine's "edge." It's rapidly becoming my favorite high. The best way I can describe the surreal feeling of confidence one gets from this drug is "rock-star-in-a-rock" (just add nose). On the flip side, I don't care much for coke's uncomfortable side effects: it can make me quite irritable, anxious, or just very aware that it has been almost twenty minutes since I've last done a line.

Standing in the bathroom, I stare at the image I have so carefully created in such a short time. Within days of graduating, I moved swiftly to embrace the new me, which is now almost fully realized just one month later. Staring back at me in the mirror is a good-looking young man with bleached blond hair, Elvis chops, a long black goatee, an earring, sky-blue contact lenses, leather pants, three-inch-heel boots, a tight shirt flaunting his steroid-engorged body, and a large black bag—his "mad satchel"—slung over his right shoulder. This bag has become something of a calling card, a presence felt keenly by those who know its capable contents: coke, Ecstasy, GHB, mushrooms, acid, marijuana, opium, and sometimes even alcohol. I enjoy being the traveling broker of purely unwholesome fun, watching people's eyes light up as they explore the options of the satchel. There's something for everyone.

I rummage through the sack. There are so many options, but only one will be the perfect complement to my coke high. I know that the little voice in the back of my head that sometimes spouts fear, anxiety, or disgust can easily be silenced by the perfect inappropriate combination of GHB and alcohol. I haven't done any GHB since this morning, so I decide that it's the perfect time to revisit that scantily clad devil.

With all caution and inhibition thrown to the wind, thanks to good old G, I walk out of the bathroom. I make sure to conceal my measuring syringe and G bottle; these sorts of paraphernalia tend to cross the line into infringing on nondrug users' space at parties. I especially make sure never to pull these measuring devices out in front of a woman—unless, of course, Porter or I have known her for at least a week or two. (These are the sorts of insights that we, the pragmatically dysfunctional, have gained from practical "hands-on" experience.)

I now have the tools I need to spark proper conversation. I head downstairs and sit down right next to Lynn, completely oblivious to any of the other guys in the room. I am a juggernaut. I am unstoppable. I'm the man.

"Hey, so how's it going?" I ask.

"Good. Ryan was just telling me about his band. Where'd you disappear to?"

"Oh, nowhere. Just bouncin' around. So, what's your story?" I ask.

"My story?" she repeats, giggling.

"Where're you from? Where do you go to school? You know, all that jazz," I reply.

"Well, I go to Vanderbilt, but I'm taking the semester off to take classes at Fairfield University. I'm living with my parents in Wilton," she says.

"Cool."

"And you, what's *your* story?" she asks, in a sassy tone.

"Guess," I say, confident that the overwhelming precautions I've taken to hide my "true identity" from myself will similarly thwart any outsiders' speculation.

"No clue."

"I'm in the military—an officer, actually. I just graduated from West Point," I say, happy to receive the look of astonishment that I had been hoping for.

"Really. Wow. Yeah, I definitely never would have guessed. Wait—are you just fucking with me?"

"No, totally legit. Ask Ryan," I say.

"Yeah, he's telling the truth," Ryan says halfheartedly, already realizing that he's being outmaneuvered.

"Wow. I can't believe that. Was that really your monkey—the one on the key chain?"

"Yeah, my sister gave it to me."

"Oh. So, do you like really like monkeys, or is it her thing?" she asks.

"Well, we're both cool with animals and go to zoos all the time, but I'm definitely down with monkeys," I say, stretching the truth just a bit.

"Wow! That's crazy! I love monkeys, especially apes. I can sit for hours outside the primate cages at the Bronx Zoo and just watch them."

"Honestly. No joke. I'm exactly the same way," I say, now completely lying.

"Yeah," she says excitedly, "they're like people. Big, hairy, gentle people."

"Yeah, totally."

"So, I'm just curious. Who's your favorite performer?"

"That's easy. Jim Morrison. He fucking kicked ass," I reply.

"Oh, my God! You've got to be kidding me! Are you serious?"

"Yeah, why?" I ask, somewhat disingenuously, realizing that she must have similar tastes.

"I adore him. I'm even reading this book, *Wild Child*, that's this awesome unauthorized biography about him that his mistress wrote. You read it?"

"No. Sounds cool. I'd love to read it when you're done," I say, truthfully.

"Definitely. I almost don't wanna ask, but what's your favorite music group of all time?"

"Ha! That's also an easy one. Pink Floyd. Without a doubt, nothing compares."

"*Oh . . . my . . . God!*" Lynn says, as she raises her hands to her face and stares at her friend Amanda. Although I don't see the coincidences as even remotely outrageous, given that at least half of all college-age kids like these bands, Lynn obviously finds the coincidences quite mind-blowing.

"Wow! You two are, like, meant to be together. It's fate!" Amanda declares.

Thanks, Amanda, I think. *You can't buy that sort of marketing.*

Lynn just stares at me for a moment while I simply return the stare. She probably thinks that I'm reflecting on our destiny; however, I'm actually contemplating the best way to leave to go upstairs and do some more cocaine.

Fuck, I want the coke. I need the coke. But things are going so well! I might not get this chance again, especially with all these dudes ready to jump her bones. Maybe I can bring her with me. Yeah, that's it, Mike. Good thinking!

"Hey, not to be shady or anything, but I have to go upstairs for a second. Wanna tag along?"

"Sure," she says.

I don't scare her, I think, *which is a good thing.* Or is it? I have to wonder why I don't scare her.

A few moments later Lynn is watching me do a couple lines of cocaine. And even though she doesn't touch the stuff, she doesn't appear to care that I do, and she actually grins from ear to ear when she looks inside my bag.

"So, what are you? Some sort of crazy dealer or something?" she asks.

"No, nothing like that. Just the bearer of goodwill," I say.

"Wow! There's a lot of goodwill in here. You've even got mushrooms. Jeez!" she says, laughing, as she rummages around.

"You want some?" I ask, as I snort my second line.

"No. I'm good. But, I'm definitely down for mushrooms sometime."

"Cool. Definitely," I reply.

This girl is hot, and she seems so down-to-earth, but why isn't she scared of me? Fuck, maybe I'm the one who should be scared! I think to myself.

After we hang out for several more hours, Lynn gives me her number and makes her exit; the sun is now shining brightly outside. We're both beaming as well. Meeting Lynn is quite an unexpected result of what had been just another typically destructive outing. Most delightful, indeed.

From where I sit, Lynn's hot, cool, and bright. She is also reasonably well read and interesting and has a good sense of humor—at least, she finds *me* amusing. In addition, Lynn was also something of a wild child in her youth and seems to be drawn to similar qualities. As far as Lynn's concerned, I'm some sort of crazy Jim Morrison spirit that destiny brought to her (or actually Porter's) front door.

After closing the shades to block out the sun, I walk back into the bathroom. I am quickly becoming a serious physical and mental waste. Drugs had illuminated everything around me all night with such intensity that nothing could stop my unwavering smile.

Now, standing in front of the mirror, I watch as the smile slowly corrects itself. I can see that look on my face: the drugs are starting to wear off. I realize once again that the high won't last and that soon I'll have to bear the horrible effects of my body's chemicals in free fall, leaving me exactly where I started, if not lower. I am on the verge of crashing badly.

All of my worries and problems are still there, only now they seem just that much worse under the dark shroud of day that all drug users know, fear, and pray they can sleep through. My eyes pray for darkness. I really need some sleep.

"Fuck!" I yell.

As I lie on my bed, I quickly realize that there is absolutely no way I will be able to sleep. My schedule is too messed up. In light of the myriad of amphetamines in my system, there is only one thing I can think of doing, besides Valium (which I don't have), and that is a hefty shot of G. This is something I wouldn't recommend to anyone—except, of course, to my own idiotic self.

I pour an amount about three times that of a conventional dose in my glass, mix it with some orange juice, and bottoms up. Basically I am sending myself into a nice, easy, velvet sleep. I make sure to get to bed in a most expeditious fashion—at least, I try.

You sometimes have just minutes before you feel the impending minicoma of a shot of G, and then there are the times when it takes only seconds before you find yourself waking up five hours later, lying on the floor of your friend's house staring at the ceiling with a splitting headache. This is where I am now. Since my mind and body don't seem to be working, I realize quickly that nothing productive is going to happen until tonight. Since no one else is home and the G is still in my hand, the only thought that runs through my brain is, *Why not just take another G banger and ride a nice, smooth G wave through the day?*

Fortunately, however, I come to my senses right before drinking, and I put the G down. In my completely lethargic and listless state, I notice two beautiful lines of coke left over from the night, or rather the morning, before. They are lined up majestically, like perfection, with a rolled dollar bill still conveniently lying adjacent.

I decide that I've had enough sleep for one day, or night, or whatever. Right now is not the time to be thinking anymore; it is time to start being productive. It is time to snort. And then: clarity!

18

Hear No Evil

February 2001

I wish I didn't have to work," Lynn says.

Lynn has to bartend at some restaurant in Fairfield.

"Yeah, that definitely sucks. No worries, though. I'll see ya tomorrow," I reply, feigning frustration.

"Yeah, but I want to hang with you today. Maybe we can get together after work."

"Trust me, I do, too. And maybe I'll stop in," I say, knowing full well I have no desire or intention to do so.

"That would be fabulous! And then maybe tonight?"

"Yeah, and regardless, I'll see ya tomorrow," I say, doggedly avoiding her suggestion.

"Yeah, that sounds great. Can't wait. But do stop in," she says. It's obvious that she doesn't want to come across as too needy or annoying.

"Lynn, honestly, if I can, I will. I just got some shit I got to take care of that has to be done this afternoon," I say, quite honestly.

"Hey, and your friend Vicki's coming over tomorrow, right?" she asks.

"Yeah, we'll probably just do dinner, and then we'll all hang afterwards. Cool?"

"Yeah, definitely. Bye!"

"All right, take care," I reply, and I hang up the phone.

I fucking love Lynn. Not really—but I love having a girlfriend, and a hot, cool one at that, I say to myself.

A couple of hours later, I'm taking care of business.

I feel reasonably confident in what I am doing. The preparation is relatively easy; the purer forms of heroin require only water to dissolve. In addition, I have recently acquired a digital scale (which I will soon hastily throw out) for measuring the 20 milligram (mg) dose I need; from what I've read, this is a decent beginner's dosage.

I am still a virgin to the needle, in terms of injecting illicit drugs, and I want that to change. I find lately that not only am I breaking all the boundaries I had previously set for myself, I am also realizing great enjoyment from doing so. Nothing new is a letdown; my cravings aren't for any single drug but rather for trying new substances, new combinations, and new levels of intoxication.

A few weeks ago I'd gone into Manhattan to pick up a few sheets of acid, which has now realized its place in my life as my absolute, without a doubt, favorite drug. However, when my dealer pulled out a small vial of what he called "China white" (a relatively pure form of heroin), I couldn't resist; the desire to try something foreign, to feel a high I had yet to feel, was simply too great to control.

Porter's parents had recently returned. While I initially saw this as just a major downer, I quickly realized it could be incredibly opportune, allowing me a chance to delve into my small vial in the privacy of my bedroom back at my parents' house. Porter is clearly cool with drugs but, similar to most recreational drug users I've met, heroin ventures one huge step past his comfort zone. As I waited for a day when I'd be alone at my parents' home, I spent a great deal of time doing research on the Internet. I was actually quite nervous, given the harsh stigma associated with heroin, and I was generally uncertain about how I was going to take it: snort, smoke, eat, or inject. After deciding quickly on injection (my last frontier), the next question was which method to use: skin popping (under the skin), mainlining (into the veins), or muscle popping (into the muscles). I have concluded that muscle popping is the prudent choice, because my body cringes at the prospect of trying to get one of my sister's relatively short diabetes needles into one of my veins, and, moreover, it seems simplest just to jam the needle into my shoulder.

With the big day at hand, and using my Internet sites as references, I cook the heroin properly, although I forget to use the recommended cotton filter. Despite this oversight, the injection mostly goes off without a hitch. However, I have very mixed feelings about the experience. Much as I anticipated, it is extremely euphoric and pain numbing; however, I surprisingly get a bit energized as well.

Despite all these pleasant feelings, however, I prefer something less likely to make me so damn nauseous; I have a very weak stomach, and heroin just tears the hell out of it. I've thrown up from just about everything, even tobacco, so it isn't a surprise when I find myself "praying to the porcelain god," repeatedly, about an hour after my injection. Taking advantage of the period when most of my decisions are made (that is, in the heat of the moment), I wash the rest of the white powder down the kitchen sink. I will not be trying heroin again.

The following day Vicki arrives. She's very thin, very good-looking, and very smart. The only time I've ever truly been in the scenario where I'm hanging out with a hot, cool chick, it never crosses my mind to try to hook up with her. (To be honest, though, the list of hot, cool chicks I've hung out with probably wouldn't take too long to read!) Vicki went to West Point with me. She seriously refutes the stereotype of what a female cadet looks like, because she would turn heads at any university in the country. I have always known Vicki, but when all my guy friends graduated in May 2000, I started hanging out with her a lot more. Since she isn't graduating until 2002, and I have all this time off, we've been partying together. She comes down and stays with me for weekends such as this one.

It will be my last hurrah in the area before starting work. When

Vicki gets to my house, I consider telling her about my recent foray into heroin use, but despite the almost overwhelming urge to share the experience, I resist.

"So, who's this Lynn girl? How'd you meet?" she asks coyly.

"She's from the town over. Met her at Porter's about a month ago," I reply, as vaguely as possible.

"So, how are things going?" she asks persistently, grinning from ear to ear.

I pause for reflection. In the four weeks that Lynn and I have been seeing each other, we have gotten along marvelously, hanging out virtually nonstop. I am in such a delighted state, sometimes I even feel genuinely happy. I know that she finds me exciting, out of the ordinary, with potential, and hopefully malleable. I have indeed changed, but it has been for the worse. "She's cool. Mad cool. Thing's are going great," I say.

"So, she's fine with all the crazy shit you do?" Vicki asks.

"Yeah, definitely. At least, I think so. I mean, she knows that I have two sheets of acid that I walk around with at all times in my wallet. She knows that I do fifteen hits a week and speak to her family when I'm all tripped out and banged up."

"Really?"

"No doubt. She tells me she is amazed at my ability to maintain such composure and articulation while under the intoxicating effects of any and all narcotics."

"Are you kidding me?"

"Nope. And as far as Lynn's parents are concerned, I think they are impressed. I'm a West Point graduate. I'm an economics major. I run every other morning and lift almost every day. I've read a little bit of everything. I write poetry, draw, drink like a fish, and snort coke in the bathroom of *their* house."

"You're such an ass!" Vicki says, giggling.

"Hey, if I come across as cocky, remember: Nothing can touch me," I reply, joining in her laughter. "To be honest, I don't totally know what Lynn's deal is. I think maybe I'm some sort of experiment for her. All I know is that for whatever reason, she finds me interesting. And to be honest, I find her interest, in itself, quite interesting," I say.

As far as my parents are concerned, this is what I tell them about my lifestyle: "Yeah, there are definitely some drugs at that club, but we stay away from all that. Frankly, I don't understand people in that scene; why do they need to do drugs to have a good time? It's really quite pathetic."

Remember, Michael, although the delivery has to be good, it's not that hard to sell; hear no evil, see no evil, I always tell myself.

Just once, for a solitary moment, do my parents open themselves up to the real possibility that I might be using drugs. It happens today. Vicki and I have to eat dinner with my family before we head out. This will prove disastrous.

Before dinner, I bust out my old friend, Georgia Home Boy (that is, GHB). I've done this countless times, so there is no reason for concern. Unfortunately, I do too much. Anyone who's done slightly too much GHB knows exactly what I mean. Billy Idol knows what I'm talking about; when he passed out in front of a club and went into a peaceful coma, he felt the thunder of what he called "a really nasty drug." GHB doesn't play around, but I do.

At the table I can feel the craziness of G coming on, and I start doing my Winder thing, making Vicki, my sisters, and even my parents laugh at my antics. After a short while, however, I am quickly crossing serious lines. I have lost my hold, thrown my silverware away, and started to eat with just my hands.

I am acting like a drunken Neanderthal, being driven on by the unyielding laughter of Vicki and my sisters, but my parents are saying something now, aren't they? Wait, are they yelling at me? Shit, how long have they been yelling? My mom stands up, putting her hand on my shoulder. "Mike, I want to talk to you in the other room for a moment."

We have to go all the way to the back bedroom for this conversation; there is no way she will talk to me of such things with anyone in earshot. Even in the bedroom, with the door shut, it's still a whisper. (Isn't it always just whispers behind closed doors?)

She asks me what I am taking. "You aren't on any drugs, are you?" The word *drugs* is barely audible; it almost can't escape her mouth. I somehow manage to put on my game face, reclaim my grip, and tell her the following: "Sorry, Mom, I took a bunch of these Hydroxycut things before dinner. You know, those weight-loss pills? They have all this ephedrine in them, and they make me act real weird sometimes. I guess I took too many." She seems relieved. Things are fine. Disaster avoided. Hear no evil. . . .

The next week I pack up all my stuff and start the 2,200-mile drive to El Paso, Texas, where I am scheduled to begin OBC at Fort Bliss in less than two weeks. It is time to transition back into military life and my officer's uniform. It is time for things to change. Unfortunately, the party is over.

19

Bliss

March 2001

G od, if you're listening, please help me out just this once. If
you do, I promise I'll never do drugs again. Never. I promise. I know I've been a shitty person up until now, but I
need your help just this once. Just this once," I say aloud, tears running down my cheeks, as I maintain what I believe (despite my
Jewish upbringing) to be the "standard" prayer position: knees on
floor, hands clasped, and elbows resting on my bed.

My cell phone rings. I can see Lynn's name pop up on the display. I'm thankful for the break, and that despite my move to Texas
and Lynn's return to Nashville, the two of us are still maintaining
our relationship. I wipe the tears from my cheek and answer the
phone.

"Hello?" I say, assuming my typical Winder "chillax" tone.

Be cool, Mike, be cool, I tell myself.

"So, how are things?" she asks.

"All good. No problems here," I reply.

"Any word yet on that piss test?"

*No, God damn it! Nothing! Not a goddam thing! It has been three
weeks of nail-biting hell! I fucked up! I royally fucked up! How fucking
stupid can I be, not even to know when OBC starts!*

I arrived in El Paso on the Friday before OBC began, believing that it started on the following Wednesday when it actually started on Sunday. It's a complete disaster: Acid, Ecstasy, and G early Friday morning, and then a piss test Sunday morning! What a great fucking way to start my transition to a "normal" military life!

"No, not so much. The rumors are still floating around that someone came up positive. To be honest, I've kind of come to grips with whatever goes down," I say, lying through my teeth. I wish I could be honest with her about what I was going through, but it's just too painful.

"Well, that's good. I'm glad you're doing all right," she says.

No, God damn it! No, I'm freaking not! I am scared shitless. One way or another, I just need to know. Not knowing is the worst part of all.

"Yeah, well, I may not like being in the army, but the last thing I want is a dishonorable discharge," I reply, providing a rare glimpse of honesty.

"Yeah, I can imagine. So, how are things otherwise? How's everything else going?" she asks, gracefully changing the subject and putting me at ease.

"Well, okay, I guess. I mean, thank God that Mitch is stationed here."

"How are things with him, you know, as far as the test goes and stuff? Any word yet?"

"Well, since he failed his last fitness test, he's got just one more chance to pass before he is discharged from the army. He's pretty unhappy with himself right now."

And I'm unhappy as well, but with what, I do not know. I have been feeling empty for so long, I've forgotten when and why it all started, or if I've ever really known at all.

"So, you guys get to hang out at all, what with your schedule and everything?"

"Well, every day I wake up around 5:00 AM for PT [physical training], eat, have class instruction, then some military instruction, followed by a lecture, lunch, then more lectures, some more military instruction, final class time, and then, around 6:00 PM, if I'm lucky, it's all over and time to head to Mitch's place."

"You're such a drama queen. You make it sound so awful."

"No, well, it isn't that any of it is hard; it is simply worthless—to me, at least. You know, to be honest, Lynn, although I never really liked the military, I always thought that things might change once I was out of West Point. I really thought and hoped that life as an officer in the regular army would be more enjoyable. It isn't."

"Mike, a lot of that is just your anxiety talking. You know, you're doing a great thing here. You really ought to be proud of yourself," Lynn says, marvelously calming me once again.

"Well, yeah, you know, I don't want to give the impression that I don't respect the uniform." In fact, I have strongly come to admire our armed forces, which is the exact reason I don't believe I should be an officer. "I am seriously miserable," I add, with unabashed sincerity.

Lynn lets my comment slide. "You guys hanging out tonight?"

"Yeah, actually I should already be over there."

"Any big plans?"

"Funny girl. You know the two of us don't like to go out—*ever!*"

Right on cue, my cell phone starts lighting up; Mitch is calling.

"Hey, Lynn, I gotta go. I'll call ya tomorrow."

"All right, Mike, take care of yourself. I'll talk to ya tomorrow."

"Yeah, bye."

"Bye, Mi . . .," Lynn says, as I switch over to Mitch.

"What's up, bro?" I ask.

"It's almost seven, man, where you at?"

"En route, as we speak. Was just talking to Lynn."

"All right, cool, man. See ya in a few."

"Definitely."

After hanging up the phone, I throw down a quick shot of G and then jump in my car. I show up at Mitch's around half past seven, prepared for the typical routine: shots of G followed by vodka. Every single night I pass out on Mitch's couch.

When it comes to defiling ourselves together, Mitch and I are a perfect fit. We are distressingly comfortable with hanging out alone together, drinking ourselves into oblivion every single night. We're both disgusted by the prospect of having to interact with the "normal folk," all flaunting their worthless grins, prancing about in their emptiness, interlaced, interlocked, interdependent. . . .

Tonight is different, though, because lately it's gotten to the point where we can't reach the passing-out point, at least not in a safe and effective manner. We decide to switch our protocol: shot of G, glass of vodka, shot of G, glass of vodka, and so on, until we fall asleep. Together the two of us drink an entire handle (1.75 liter bottle) of vodka. We are becoming well acquainted with the fringe benefits a drunkard reaps from chronic GHB use.

The following morning I wake up around 5:00 AM and drive twenty minutes from Mitch's apartment to the physical training field, prepared for yet another day of the same.

Man, I feel like hell.

As PT begins, the angry, cold sweats begin pouring down my face. My dizzy brain is a fuzzy mess, barely able to remain grounded. This might be my regular routine, but it's quickly getting stale, and although GHB has made my body virtually impervious to the effects of alcohol, I don't believe that my internal organs were ever informed of this new regime. I am doing all this on about four hours of sleep, which are far from quality hours, considering the egregious amounts of liquor and GHB I am pouring into my body just to fall asleep. My body might be ignorant, but it is far from impervious.

I briefly wonder if anyone else notices that something is wrong with me, but then I stop caring. I'm simply too dizzy and fully overwhelmed by nausea. As soon as physical training is over, I drive to the local Popeyes Chicken for a morning breakfast sandwich.

Needless to say, this is a bad idea. I should've known that I wouldn't be able to keep food down very well, much less greasy fast food. Huddled next to the toilet, the vomit still running down my cheeks, I now feel worse than hell. I feel desperate. I need an answer. I need a supplemental boost. I need Brian.

20

ᏠᏌᎥᏟᏋ

April 2001

B rian knows all about steroids. At West Point, he lifted
weights and was juiced on a daily basis; he was absolutely
jacked up. Nowadays he is just drinking and sleeping, and
from his appearance, one would never guess him to be the same
person. At five feet eleven and 215 pounds with a dark olive complexion, Brian looks healthier and much more toned than he actually is—and that isn't saying much. He looks like the large guy who
used to lift all the time but who let his muscles get soft from the
shitload of beer he drinks.

Now that I am suddenly interested in steroids, too, it's "go
time"—to Mexico, the land of prescription drugs without a prescription. Juarez is a leisurely jaunt (just ten minutes) from Fort
Bliss, immediately across the border. Have you seen the movie
Traffic? It is no exaggeration; it is always "snowing" in Juarez. The
pure white angel, her wings a soft embrace, blankets everything
around the lazy army town.

My first impression of Mexico is exactly what I expected.
Walking over the bridge into Juarez, I find unpaved dirty streets
lined with dilapidated run-down buildings, littered sidewalks, and
pushy merchants at every turn. This is all just across the border, in

"the tourist district," mind you. I can only imagine what lies farther in from the border. My mind pictures something akin to the movie *From Dusk Till Dawn*, presumably without all the vampires. I'm so tempted to explore deeper, but Brian keeps me kosher. (Note to myself: It's a bad thing if Brian's judgment is the only thing that's keeping me kosher.)

Brian reminds me that we're here on business. We're not here to get coke, get high, or get stupid. Also, we've been repeatedly warned not to venture too far over the border. It's simply not safe for Americans, especially American soldiers. I wish my mind didn't work backward. Someone can tell me, "Don't go into Juarez, but if you do, don't go to any of the seedy inner-city bars, and definitely don't do any cocaine," but what I actually hear is "Head across the border, find the most deviant and sordid strip club, and blow lines till the wee hours of the morning." This is just how my brain works. Brian points down the road, refocusing my eyes on our first pharmaceutical candidate.

As we walk down the street, I feel confident with Brian. In most other cases (that is, on the other side of the border), Brian would be a liability. He is simply too dangerously unpredictable. However, I presently feel a surprising amount of comfort alongside him, for the honest reason that he blends in (he's part Latino) and speaks Spanish. His unkempt, curly black hair and long sideburns only add to the effect. From my perspective, the locals see only one real gringo among us. My closely shaven hair is a stark contrast to his own, and I presume that it serves as something akin to a flashing billboard to all the locals that I am a U.S. Army soldier. We walk from pharmacy to pharmacy, pushing farther away from the tourist district, as Brian scours the various stores for his complete shopping list. This is all Brian's show; I'm just along for the ride.

I'm anxious—not just to find what we need but also to find a place to do some G. (You didn't think I'd leave home without it, did you?) The eyedrops bottle I'm carrying is burning a hole in my pocket. It's been almost forty-five minutes since my last dose, and

I can feel myself starting to get quite antsy. Brian finally finds every-thing he's looking for. At this point, I can give two shits about the price, or anything else for that matter. I just want to go throw back some GHB.

With vials and syringes in tow, Brian and I head farther down the street toward a bar he sees. It's my idea, or rather the G's idea—it's demanding attention, and fast. Ultimately, this ends up being the per-fect scenario. A bit off the beaten tourist path, Brian and I walk into a dive bar that's really no different from any you'd find just over the border, or even back in Manhattan, for that matter. (Actually, it is probably a bit dirtier, but otherwise the same.) It's midday, so there are only a few other patrons, and Brian and I are obviously the only Americans. First things first: we grab some beers and head into the bathroom together. We dump a few capfuls of GHB into our cervezas and swirl it all around really well before we chug them back. GHB is never something to be devoured slowly over time, nor is it something that should ever be consumed with alcohol (another memo to self!). As we walk back to our table, everything suddenly becomes perfect. All anxiety is gone. The two of us are all high-fives and smiles. Mission accomplished—at least, partly.

"Sweet. Little bit a G-sus sure hits the spot! Whatcha wanna drink, Mike?" Brian is one of the few people, including my girl-friend, who actually calls me by my first name.

"Whatever ya got."

"You down for some shots?"

"Obviously."

"Oh, right, I forgot who I was talking to."

Brian orders a couple more beers and several rounds of tequila. He grabs the bottles and saunters back to our table, grinning from ear to ear, as the bartender loads a tray with shot glasses and starts drowning them with tequila.

"So, when's your girl coming?" Brian asks.

"Two weeks. That's enough time to get me somewhat jacked up, right?"

"Yeah, definitely."

I haven't lifted weights once since arriving in El Paso, and my body has been deteriorating fast. I wouldn't care about my rapid decline if it weren't for Lynn's visit in a couple of weekends. I don't feel like showing off the slob I really am. With just a little physical training, I know that steroids will give me incredible, overwhelming results. I naturally have a very high metabolism, and with steroids it should be ridiculous. I'll have what I need to make it through the day. I'll have the energy to wake up early, do physical training, go to class, and then drink all I want, while actually increasing muscular definition. It's the perfect plan!

"Sweet. This shit's clutch. Thanks for helping me out, bro," I say. I avoid talking about Lynn, intentionally downplaying my excitement to see her. The fact is, though, I really miss her. I desperately need her and the reality she brings with her. For those brief periods that I'm even just speaking with her on the phone, I feel amazingly alive.

"Mike, forget about it. I've been wanting to come for a while now, anyhow."

"Cool. So, you mind if I ask how your shit's going? You heard anything yet?"

About six months back, another officer (who also happened to be a West Point alumnus) had been busted for doing drugs, and in the process he implicated Brian. Brian was ordered not to shave his head so that his commander could administer a hair test the following day. Hair tests can be a pretty scary proposition to an addict, since traces of virtually all chemicals can still be found in one's hair several months after their use. All the bleach, drain cleaners, and other scalp-burning chemicals Brian poured on his head that night did nothing to deter his positive result for cocaine.

Coming up "hot" on a drug test in the army is definitely a poor turn of events for an officer; one gets a dishonorable discharge, and possibly jail time as well.

So like me, Brian's time in El Paso is spent waiting. His

court-martial and dishonorable discharge are guaranteed, but his freedom is not. Although he doesn't express it, he's obviously quite nervous about the possibility of jail time. Brian just wants everything to be over, and he anxiously awaits trial. The way he's been partying these days, I'm not sure he will live to see it.

"Nah, I haven't heard anything. But to be honest, Mike, I really don't give a shit anymore."

"Yeah. I got you. Probably just want that shit to be over."

"Yeah—whatever," Brian says, as he stares through his beer, his index finger drawing a slow circle around the outside of the bottle. "I really just don't give a shit anymore. *Salud!*" Brian grabs his tequila glass and raises it toward me, urging me to do the same, as we down another shot of tequila.

Brian often tells me that he doesn't give a shit, and the sad thing is that I believe him. Brian used to be the sort of guy who would just laugh at what others said about him; he was his own man, the consummate rebel. Now he is still laughing, but his laugh grows louder and shallower with each breath; he is consumed and basically just pathetic. He has no more self-esteem or self-worth. I see it all in his eyes: he has accepted what others say about him and given in to the fact that he is nothing. I feel bad for him; he is bright, harmless (to everyone but himself), insecure, and severely depressed. I wonder for a moment why his commander doesn't get him into some sort of counseling, or maybe even drug rehab—but I suppose that things just don't work that way.

"You read that book I gave you yet?" Brian asks, changing the subject.

"No, not yet."

"Read it, man. Dostoevsky's good shit. Trust me on this one, Mike."

What makes the biggest impression on me is that despite everything, Brian still finds time to read, every day. He does a magnificent job of keeping hidden all inklings of how well read he is. It would never cross your mind that his book collection contains the works of Ernest Hemingway, Kurt Vonnegut, and John Steinbeck.

"Yeah, I will. Just haven't had the time, really."

"Don't bullshit me, you fucking G-hound," Brian says, as he starts laughing. I can't help but join in, because he called me out on point.

"You must be glad as shit to have that whole piss-test thing behind you," Brian says.

"Yeah, most definitely. That's the understatement of the year. Dude, I thought I was royally fucked. When they said someone came up hot on that test, I was positive it was game over."

"Yeah, and it turns out it's that old dude with the wife and kids. Who would've thought?"

"Yeah—crazy shit," I say, taking my turn to stare through my bottle, lost in a momentary trance. *It should've been me*, I think, *not some old guy with a wife and kids.*

For the past month I'd been constantly on edge. The day I learned that I was in the clear, a tremendous weight was lifted from me, and I felt compelled to turn to God once more. I said that I was indebted and that I would make the most of this wake-up call and begin a new chapter in my life. I would hold true to my promise and further strengthen my newfound spirituality. (I sometimes wonder if God ever feels used or even really listens to the false promises of addicts and losers.)

Brian brings me out of my daydream. "Mike, you know, you got pretty damn lucky with that G shit, too, bro. That shit was fucking you all up! You could've been wrecked," Brian says, grinning.

"Yeah, I know. Aron really saved my ass. You know, this G shit is no fucking joke."

Over the past couple weeks I had quickly learned that cutting back one's G intake, after taking it virtually every day for six months, can have seriously debilitating ramifications. My shipment from Holland wasn't expected for at least another week. In total desperation, I had called Aron, another friend from West Point, who is stationed at Fort Hood, Texas.

"You telling me, brother!" Brian affirms.

"Dude, I was seriously fucking tweaking. I mean, I didn't realize how much that shit would fuck me up by just cutting down how much I was taking."

"How long you been using it?"

"I don't know, a year. But it's been pretty much an everyday affair for the past six months."

Brian starts laughing. "Yup, that'll do it!" he exclaims. "*Salud,*" he says again, as we do another shot.

"Yeah, shit was pretty banged up. All the shaking, the anxiety, the sweating . . ."

"And tell me you weren't fucking hearing weird shit, too, bro."

"Yeah, all fucking night long I was hearing voices and shit. Didn't sleep a fucking wink."

"Yeah, bro. Been there, done that. Definitely not a pleasant experience. Surprised you didn't see shit, too. I had like little fucking insects crawling on me and shit one time."

"Yeah, only thing that helped was alcohol."

"Enormous fucking amounts of alcohol. *Salud!*" Brian exclaims, triumphantly, although his excitement at these revelations is almost unnerving.

"Yeah, Aron definitely came through clutch. Dude's fucking money. Right away he didn't even hesitate to hook me up with some of his stash. He even special overnighted that shit to me. Can you believe that?"

"My G brother. *Salud!*" Brian says predictably, as we drain yet another shot.

There is no more conversation. Brian seems just as lost in thought as I am. I'm not sure what's on Brian's mind, but I can't think about anything except what I hadn't told him about my phone call with Aron. Something quite serious had happened to Dave, one of our good friends from the Academy.

Dave is an absolutely excellent dude. He's your classically innocent, loyal, fun-loving, wild puppy dog. He is always in good spirits: smiling, running around doing crazy things, ready to make you laugh, and more than willing to help out a buddy.

Dave's roommate at Aviation School returned home to their apartment one night recently to find Dave lying in a pool of blood. Dave had a knife stuck in his throat and was bleeding to death. Due to the roommate's quick actions and an emergency tracheotomy, Dave's life was saved. The worst part: it turned out that Dave had stabbed *himself* in the throat. There is no one, absolutely no one, I had less expected to do such a thing.

I called Dave immediately to find out how he was doing and to offer my support. I didn't know what to expect, but Dave sounded like good old Dave. I could envision him smiling on the other end of the phone, and he made me laugh so hard that no part of me believed that it could possibly be true—but it was. Dave told me his version of the story: he had gone out to a bar, met some people he didn't know, they slipped him something in his drink, he went back to his place, he started panicking, and then he stabbed himself.

After hanging up the phone, I was frozen with fear, unable to move, barely able to breathe. I didn't buy his story. Dave is a G addict, like me. I couldn't help but wonder if G was partly to blame. It was a scary thought, because if it happened to Dave, then it could easily happen to me! Eventually an ironic wave of calm washed over me, however, as I remembered that I would be receiving more GHB by the end of the week. I put Dave out of my mind.

Several shots of tequila later, I figure it's time to finish this thing, so we can head back home. I feel the bartender's eyes on us as we walk back to the bathroom together again. Part of me wonders what he's thinking, but I don't really care.

Dirty floors, disgusting walls, and filthy, putrid-smelling toilets surround me as my bare white ass is suddenly being jammed with a needle filled with an unknown liquid, acquired less than an hour earlier from a sketchy Mexican man who spoke no English.

Brian fills a few bottles with the rest of whatever juice he has picked out (I don't bother to ask the names), he throws them in his shoes along with a couple bottles of clenbuterol, and we head back to the United States. As we walk through U.S. Customs carrying our assorted contraband, I imagine that my blood, rapidly filling with testosterone, must be racing with fury throughout my body, my heart, and my brain. With Brian taking all the risks, yet walking as though he's strolling down the beach, I feel hard-pressed to justify my anxiety. Nevertheless, between the German shepherds and the stern-looking officers with weapons holstered at their sides, I'm scared shitless. I'm confident my luck has finally run out. By some miracle, we walk through unhindered. Brian and I are all smiles; the two of us are fine now.

At the end of the month Lynn finally arrives. The steroids have worked their magic, and I look and feel great—even though I'm still drinking just as much as always and doing just as much GHB. I am totally exhilarated; for the brief time she is in El Paso, I feel wonderfully human. Lynn is confident that I have things under control, and so am I.

21

Gambling
May 2001

Looking in the mirror, I really don't like what I see: a six-foot-three, 215-pound, sickly facade.

"What's wrong with you?" I ask myself aloud.

My health has been rapidly declining. For a short while, now, the steroids have been the added edge I've needed. They've given me the energy for morning physical training, and they've gotten me through the rest of the day. Slowly, though, my body has grown accustomed to the increased testosterone levels.

After only a few weeks of juicing, while still continuing my regime of heavy alcohol, acid, and GHB abuse, I'm slowly starting to realize that steroids might not be the miracle drug I had initially thought. On the outside, I know I still look (somewhat) athletic. On the inside, however, my body tells a significantly different story. The steroids are not able to stop the stomach pains, the bowel problems, the headaches and dizziness, and the constant nausea.

"What happens when Lynn finds out what a loser you are; that you can't hack it? That you can't even handle the army's freakin' physical regimen anymore?" I exclaim in frustration.

I have become a regular at morning sick call. Initially, I had exaggerated my symptoms somewhat, to warrant more serious attention. Since then, I have honestly surpassed any imagined levels of poor health. I had only two options: give up drinking and G and try to make it through PT, or get a profile, which excuses me from all physical training. The latter was obviously the only pragmatic decision.

I look at the copy I've made of the profile I was given by the army doctors. I can't help but smile.

Good work, I think.

I start to walk away, trying to focus on something else, the day ahead, but my mind turns back to the piece of paper. I am acutely aware that although it's getting easier and easier to lie to others, it's getting harder and harder to lie to myself. I conscientiously work to push back any negative thoughts that slip through my mind's back door.

Am I doing the right thing? Fuck it! It's a fine line that I am more than willing to walk. And of course I deserve this!

Staring at the piece of invaluable paper, I am determined to keep it. I have come to the conclusion that maintaining a profile is not only my best option, it's my *only* option.

All I have to do is stay the course on my current destructive lifestyle, and with my already poor health, my continued presence at sick call should prove enough to maintain my profile. Ha! And my total disregard for my personal well-being will do the trick! I reflect, although my momentary joviality quickly takes another turn back toward the negative.

On those rare occasions when I am alone and sober, the intelligent, self-preservationist side of me sometimes shows its face. It occurs to me suddenly that I can use this time off from doing physical training to give my body the necessary time to recuperate. I know that I should try to stop drinking and doing G and that I really can't continue my drug and alcohol use indefinitely without negative repercussions; I know all this.

During such brief moments of sadness, which I typically hide even from myself, I know that these thoughts are no match for my insatiable craving.

Any time true tears almost form, perhaps accompanied by a heavy heart and sickness in my stomach, I rapidly pour myself some GHB and head over to Mitch's place. Today is one of those days, except that I have a pit stop to make.

A hypocrite is a person who puts on a false appearance of virtue. That's not me. I mean, I almost never drive drunk, and I condemn those who do. GHB doesn't count, does it? Fuck! Fuck! Fuck! Of course it does, you jackass. Fuck! Fuck acid, coke, and all that other shit; GHB is without a doubt the most dangerous drug I've ever driven on. How many times have I been wide awake, having the time of my life one moment, and without notice, one minute later, been in an uncontrollable stupor? Falling into the fierce decline and comalike state that no one, except fellow GHB users, can really appreciate. Wicked shit. No doubt, G's some crazy, fucked-up shit!

Quickly, though, the anxiety, uncertainty, and self-doubt give way to excitement. Today is Friday, the last weekend in May, but more significant is that Lynn is visiting again. I am dying for even the briefest glimpse of sanity, and I know that Lynn is my only link to the real world.

Scanning the throngs of people at the airport, my heart pumping rapidly in expectation, I am consumed with unbridled enthusiasm when my eyes finally find their target.

"You look great. Honestly, Lynn. It's great to see you," I say, as I pull her close to kiss her.

"You, too, Winder-butt!" Lynn says, as she kicks me playfully.

After we drop our stuff off at our motel room, Lynn and I stop at the liquor store and then head over to Mitch's place. The liquor store is conveniently located on the same street that Mitch and Brian live on; needless to say, the owners of this establishment have come to revere us somewhat.

Before we get to Mitch's, I tell Lynn the story of how Catalina and Andreea have come to live with Mitch. During her previous visit Lynn had met Catalina, but not Andreea. Catalina is nice enough, but Andreea is simply an irritable, unruly, extremely demanding and overbearing Romanian woman who, unlike Catalina, has not once in her three years living in the United States considered the notion that it might be of some practical worth to learn a bit of English.

Catalina, although Romanian, is not your stereotypical Eastern European drinker; in fact, she barely ever drinks, and she spends most of her time trying to convince Mitch to do the same. Catalina likes me, but only as much as any woman could ever like the evil enabling cohort of the man she's dating. Lynn and Catalina aren't down with GHB, understandably fearful of its negative consequences.

This creates a bit of a hassle for me, especially since Mitch is also somewhat weary of GHB in light of his latest episode. Mitch often passes out, blacks out, or—if his most recent use is indicative— falls asleep on his linoleum kitchen floor while he is cooking. It was lucky that I came into his apartment when I did, finding him passed out, the fire alarm blaring, and the stove a fiery, smoke-filled haze. By some stroke of luck, no one was hurt.

I quickly get down to business. I do a shot of G, and when Catalina isn't looking, I secretly pass Mitch some, kicking off our evening in proper fashion.

Lynn makes the mistake of leaving her purse on the table when she goes to the bathroom. Or, I should say, she makes the mistake of taking one of her prescribed Adderall tablets in front of me and then leaves the bottle unattended in her purse.

Her fault. That's something any girl dating "someone like me" should know not to do!

About thirty seconds after taking a few Adderall pills, I go across the hall, to Brian's room, and snort lines of Adderall; things are quickly getting interesting. I am unabashedly proud at how quickly I can crush the pills and carve numerous, majestically laden rows with the swift strokes of my trusty razor blade. By now, any drug, taken in any manner, can turn an otherwise bland evening into a potential carnival ride. Adderall, like Ritalin, is a drug used to treat attention deficit disorder. Adderall, however, is much harsher on the nose. Snorting Adderall burns like hell, and although snorting is a little more intense than taking the pills orally, in my opinion the quicker rush is not at all worth it.

I swallow another pill, go back over to Mitch's place, and drink for a while; I am content to hang around with Mitch and the guys, but after a while the ladies get a little restless. With Brian, a couple of his crazy friends, Mitch, and myself, there are more than enough characters around us to make Lynn laugh, but only for so long.

"C'mon, Mike. I mean, the last time I came to visit, well, it was great to see you and all; you know that. But, to be honest, we did absolutely nothing except hang out here, in Mitch's apartment, almost the entire time," Lynn complains.

"Well, um, this complex is pretty darn cool, so we could like party by one of the pools, lounge in one of the hot tubs, barbecue, or just get drunk and lie on a hammock and stare at the stars," I suggest.

I feel quite satisfied by this offer.

"Uh, you're not serious? Are you? Seriously, Mike, let's go *out* this time."

"Honestly, Lynn, there's really nothing to do. I'm not making this shit up."

"Listen, Mike. I don't care how shitty you say the rest of El Paso is. This time I'm serious about wanting to go out and actually do something," Lynn replies.

"Me, too," Catalina concurs.

I'm not excited at all by this prospect. I've grown extremely uncomfortable with leaving the apartment complex. I don't like speaking with normal people about normal things, especially when I am banged up.

Mitch and I think hard of a viable option—someplace the girls might like, and someplace we'd actually want to leave the apartment for. There is only one viable option, so a few minutes later we are in Mitch's car, heading for the casino.

"Thanks, Mike," Lynn whispers, as Mitch's Mustang speeds toward our destination.

Yeah, this is all for you, babe. I hate gambling!

As if I don't love gambling; I love casinos. My indulgent, compulsive personality lives for an insatiable need of more of anything—anything, that is, that provides some sort of high. I'm going to go out on a limb and say that it's quite likely that most drug addicts enjoy gambling.

"No problem, Lynn. I just want you to have a good time," I reply, with partial honesty. I do expect that this evening will be entertaining for Catalina and Lynn, for neither one has ever been to a casino before.

Once we get there, Mitch and I each go our own way, whereas Catalina and Lynn stick together; the two girls have a wonderful time just playing for the fun of it at the low-bet blackjack tables. I head to the higher-stakes blackjack tables; Mitch, on the other hand, loves craps, so he stays at the craps table most of the night (except for an occasional roulette spin).

I follow my usual casino routine: I drink, and I win money. I drink more, and more, and I lose money. I drink more, and more, and I lose much more. Lucky for me, just before leaving I throw a shitload of cash down on one hand and win most of my money back.

On the way home I find an Adderall tablet that I had lost earlier, and even though it is already 2:00 AM, I pop it. When we get back to Mitch's apartment I go to the bathroom, where I have hidden a spare bottle of GHB; I grab it real fast, and without properly measuring it, I drink a shot. After that, the night gets very spotty. Despite the Adderall in my system, I am aware that I have taken way too much GHB, especially considering my alcohol consumption. I am rapidly going down.

I remember leaving the apartment; it is raining very hard outside. I run off into the apartment complex, find the swimming pool, climb over the security fence, strip naked, and jump in the Jacuzzi. I don't know if I do anything else, really, but I do know that about an hour after leaving Mitch's apartment a security guard wakes me up in the hot tub.

I've passed out from taking too much GHB and fallen asleep naked in a Jacuzzi; good work, I tell myself.

Lucky for me, this particular security guard is the same guy who does cocaine with Brian. I know him, and his main concern is that someone might see me. I don't tell Lynn or Mitch that I've passed out in the Jacuzzi, or that the security guard found me; they are pissed enough that I disappeared in my state and then came back an hour later, totally drenched.

Fuck, I don't need this shit, I think.

The next week I am lying on the hammock, tripping fiercely, staring at the stars, when Lynn calls my cell phone. Lynn has gone out with some friends and is obviously drunk. She is pretty funny when she is banged up.

Everything is funny and amusing, though, when I am tripping, I think.

Somehow I mention that I want to get a dog someday—a pug, to be exact. Lynn says she loves pugs and begs me to let her get one. I tell her I'll pay for it; she can go pick it out the next day and just take care of it until I am settled in Georgia (where I will be stationed next).

She asks me repeatedly, and I tell her to go get it. Thus, it is done. The next day, Lynn purchases a $1,000 pug puppy, which she names Weenie after the pug in the Eloise children's book series. Weenie soon finds his most fitting description from Porter: "Crazy little fuck. He's so ugly, he's cute!"

22

Customs

June 2001

G *et a hold of yourself, Michael. You don't want Lynn to see you like this, do you?* I ask myself.

I am in pretty dismal condition. My health has declined to such a state that I am getting seriously depressed about it. I have incessant headaches, dizziness, stomach pains, and nausea, not to mention chronic diarrhea, and I am throwing up two to three times a day.

It is now late June. I have been at Fort Bliss for four months and have probably been sick more than 95 percent of the time. Now when I go to sick call I don't have to act; I am legitimately very sick. In addition to feeling shitty, I am starting to look the part.

Don't worry about it, man. You look good—a hell of a lot better than a few weeks ago, at least. Thank God you did what you did when you did it, I think.

A few weeks ago I was staring in the same mirror, feeling similar desperation, lost in similar ruminations. Remembering the bottle of clenbuterol tablets that Brian smuggled over from Mexico, I came up with a plan.

Conducting proper due diligence online, I learn that clenbuterol is a very unsafe pill that works as an extreme weight and fat reduction catalyst by artificially increasing the body's metabolism to dangerous levels. Although it's technically not a steroid, it's usually lumped together with steroids because of its similar abuse by athletes. All the websites make it abundantly clear that clenbuterol is also quite addictive and really just pretty rough all around on a person's inner workings.

Needless to say, I don't care, and I begin popping ten to twelve pills daily—a dose much higher than recommended, because I want to finish all 200 tablets by the time Lynn arrives.

Lynn is making a final visit to El Paso today. I don't know how soon I'll see her again after this visit, so I'm pretty worried about having her last impression of me in El Paso be one of disgust. By taking the clenbuterol and sticking to a diet of chicken, tuna, G, steroids, and vodka, I've dropped ten pounds of fat, slimming down to 210 pounds by the time I pick Lynn up at the airport. Although I am still athletic looking, I am much, much smaller than when Lynn first met me, and not remotely as ripped.

After we drop Lynn's bags off at a motel near Mitch's apartment, the two of us head over to Mitch's place to get something going. I've promised Lynn that we are actually going to do something interesting this time, and I know I have to deliver. Lynn has been asking about Mexico, and since Catalina has expressed similar interests, Mitch and I figure we'll take the girls to the Juarez city marketplace.

There are two words to describe why I am reluctant to take the trip to Mexico: explosive diarrhea. My bowels have been causing a riot in my body. All morning, every morning, I find myself, without any warning, running for my life to the nearest bathroom. There has not been even thirty kind minutes in a row yet. I see that Lynn really wants to check out Mexico, however, and since she quickly dismisses my idea of her going without me, I start eating Imodium AD like candy, chugging Pepto-Bismol as no one ever should, and generally consuming anything else I can find in Mitch's medicine cabinet. I figure, why not take everything? I want to make sure all my bases are covered.

Shortly after entering Mexico, we all decide we are kind of hungry, so we find a somewhat authentic, non-touristy, little Mexican street café. What I do next is pretty clever. Figuring that the best defense is a strong offense, I decide that I will not show any fear to my stomach or bowels, so I order a hot enchilada dish, which is served with beans, guacamole, and various other typical items.

I have been fine, as far as the bathroom is concerned, from the time we've left Mitch's apartment. That was about an hour ago, and since I've way surpassed even my top thirty-minute marker, I am pretty confident that there isn't much of a problem anymore. In addition, and probably of greatest importance, I don't want to look anything but cool and nonchalant around Lynn.

After we finish eating we start walking through the marketplace, and that is when I'm reminded of how much of a jackass I really am. The sharp, piercing gas pains in my stomach and the unyielding pressure of fluids trying to escape from my ass make it quite clear to me that I am in desperate need of a bathroom. Without saying anything to anyone, I start running toward one of the marketplace exits. I ask everyone where a bathroom is, and someone finally points me to the far side of the opposite street.

I can feel my body starting to shake a little, on the verge of giving in to a disgusting dark force. I sprint into the bathroom, and run right past the lady at the desk, who yells at me to stop. I turn around, and she says it costs fifty cents to use the bathroom. I toss her a dollar, but she says she has no change. (Right—no change.)

When I see the bathroom, it takes about three seconds for me to go into complete and utter shock. It's like the bathroom Ewan McGregor had to use in the movie *Trainspotting*—only worse. I see eight toilets: four on each side of the bathroom; there are no stalls, no seats, no toilet paper, no sinks, and shit and piss and God knows what else all over 85 percent of everything. Even the fucking ceiling has shit all over it!

I immediately turn around, run to the lady at the desk, and ask for some toilet paper; I know I'll never make it to another bathroom. The lady says there is a two-square limit per person, and each square costs twenty-five cents. As I grab two squares, I remind the lady that I just gave her an extra fifty cents a minute ago, but she doesn't understand what I am saying. (Right—no understand.) I toss her another dollar for the two squares, change obviously still out of the question, and run inside.

I have to say that it is quite disconcerting to find yourself hovering over a toilet, tremors rippling through your quaking body, shit spraying everywhere. My hands, with nothing to hold on to, firmly grasp my knees, which relentlessly buckle under the incessant explosions (or implosions), as the sweat streams down my face, cascading down the entirety of my smelly, disgusting body, while I use every last ounce of will to keep my ass cheeks from ever touching the toilet. The large Mexican man across the way stares at me as he basically does the same thing, although his cheeks rest comfortably on the rim.

It seems that bathroom doors (and bathroom stalls) are just one of those "modern conveniences" that I take for granted and that apparently haven't made it all around the world quite yet.

Several hours later, as we reenter the United States, the four of us first have to pass through Customs. As we stand in line, I notice that the border agents ask just two small questions: "ID, please?" and "U.S. citizen?"

It seems pretty ridiculous to me, because they are just taking everyone's word for it. The numerous German shepherds on duty further reinforce the obvious: the issue of illegal aliens is a distant second to the principal issue of drug smuggling. However, Mitch's attempts to influence Catalina's response are for naught; she gets flustered and says she is from Romania. What really hurts Catalina, though, is having forgotten her passport. U.S. Customs therefore holds Catalina, placing her in the border detention prison. Mitch is not a happy boy. He calls everyone, ready to blow down the doors of the Romanian embassy, the FBI, and any other federal body for which he can find a number. Ultimately, Catalina's identity is confirmed; however, no one makes any serious attempt to facilitate her release. Mitch goes home alone, furious.

The following day, Mitch is told that the Customs people are going to "work it out," and she'll likely get out in a few days—tops. I have about a week with Lynn, and I know I've got to step it up a notch with her, show her some fun, and spend some quality alone time with her. She and I decide to head up to Santa Fe. I quickly learn two things: first, Santa Fe kicks some serious ass; second, my body is disintegrating, or imploding, or something.

I feel so sick that, in addition to my steroids, I have to take Hydroxycut and GHB intermittently throughout the day to give me the boost of energy I so desperately need, as well as to improve my melancholy disposition. In addition, because I am so incredibly sluggish, Lynn gives me three or four Adderall a day just to get my ass moving.

Also, probably of equal (or greater) importance to Lynn, without Adderall I don't have enough energy for sex, but with it, I can't stop for hours. No fucking orgasm is possible, just immense sweat—the sex is killing me. (Okay, not really.)

I'm guessing that all the GHB and Adderall I'm taking aren't really helping my stomach condition, but I have accepted that compromise. Despite not feeling so great, I seriously enjoy Santa Fe: we go kayaking, tour the marketplace, buy a lot of excellent handmade jewelry, eat some quality ethnic food, and go horseback riding.

Upon returning to El Paso, our first stop is at Mitch's, to see how he is holding up and if he's gotten any definitive word yet on Catalina. We find him passed out, lying on his bed in an unmovable, snoring slumber. We also find empty bottles of beer, rum, and vodka—all strewn about chaotically and combining magnificently with the vomit all over the sink and surrounding kitchen area. This all works perfectly to produce the apartment's newly refinished "drunken-apathetic-slovenly-guy-without-a-girl" décor.

It's amazing how quickly a man can dissolve in the absence of a woman, I reflect.

After doing a little cleaning, and assuring ourselves that Mitch is in no danger, the two of us quietly exit. The following morning, after seeing Lynn off at the airport, I head back over to Mitch's to see if he's still alive.

"Dude, I'm a total fucking moron. Did you stop by yesterday?" Mitch asks.

"Yeah, you seemed totally fucked up, so we just left. Why, what happened?" I reply.

"Well, I guess shortly after you guys left, I woke up, still totally fucked up, and figured I might as well go play some blackjack."

"No, you didn't!"

"Yeah, man. I threw on some clothes, grabbed some beers, hopped in my Mustang, and headed toward the casino."

"Dude, you're a jackass. It's at least a forty-five-minute drive. And you must've still been fucking trashed!"

"Yeah, I was. And usually it is about forty-five, but I was driving ninety in the 'stang."

"You dumb ass. That's really stupid shit, bro. For you, and others, man. You don't want to fuck up some other people and shit. That would really suck."

"Yeah, I know. And I got mad lucky, too. Get this: some cop actually pulled me over going almost a hundred in a sixty-five."

"You fuckin' kidding me?"

"No, and what's more, Winder, he doesn't give me any sort of Breathalyzer or anything, and he just lets me off with a warning."

"You got to be kidding me, you lucky bastard. So he let you just drive home?"

"No, man. I'm not nearly that bright," Mitch says, laughing. "After he let me go, I just figured I might as well continue to the casino."

"You fucking . . ."

"Yeah, yeah. I know, I know. So, I ended up drinking and

gambling through the wee hours of the morning, and I just got back a couple hours ago."

"You fuckin' shittin' me? What about work, man? I mean, you're a freaking officer. You can't just not go, can you?"

I have the day off, but Mitch should've been at work hours ago.

"Ah, that's questionable."

"At best, man. At fucking best. Seriously, what are you going to do?"

"No worries, Winder, already took care of it."

"For real? What'd you do?"

"Ah, I'm just full of shit. Actually, I might be totally fucked," he says, laughing.

"You mean you've done nothing? You're just rollin' the dice? Dude, you're already on probation and trying to stay in the army and shit, man. What gives?"

"I don't know, man. I've just been so depressed about Catalina, so I'm thinking like an idiot. That fuckin' schnapps is wicked brutal, too."

"So, the plan is . . . ?"

"Well, there's not much I can do now. I'm just going to hope that since I'm not a real platoon leader, my absence will be a little less conspicuous."

"Really? Is that likely?" I ask, genuinely concerned. I really like Mitch and don't want to see him self-destruct.

"Yeah, Winder, honestly, it's probably cool. I mean, my staff position in no way excuses me from the army's expected compliance with duties and shit, but since I'm permanently excused from PT, no one will miss me there, and then, during the rest of the day, I'm usually running errands and shit around post. I think I can pretty easily make it through a day without my absence being noticed."

"Cool, man. I just don't want to see you get fucked."

"Ahh, wise ole Booneside [one of my many nicknames], giving the advice to Mitch, the drunk as a lazy-eyed monkey's tit son of a bitch. Now, let's get fucked up!" Mitch says, amid my laughter.

"You already are," I say, the two of us both laughing heartily now.

I help Mitch nurse his hangover by drinking with him throughout the rest of the afternoon. As night comes, we are resigned to slipping deeper into the shadows; that is, until the white angel shows herself, illuminating the darkness with all her possibilities. When Brian pops in, with that distinct crookedly mischievous grin, I know trouble is afoot. I am not surprised when he brings out an eightball of coke (3.5 grams), but I am taken aback when Mitch reaches for her wings for the very first time.

So pure, so breathtaking, he hopes he might be carried to heaven, I imagine.

After snorting it all, they still want more, so Brian goes out and buys another eightball with Mitch's money. The two of them finish the entire stash, freebasing all the way into the following morning.

Needless to say, Mitch doesn't make it in to work the following day, either. However, fortunately for Mitch, his luck takes a turn for the better. That afternoon, as promised, the FBI manages to get Catalina released from detainment. Good news for Mitch; he probably wouldn't have lasted much longer!

23

Pushing Through

July 2001

O verwhelmed by nausea and the sharp pains tearing through my upper torso, I am doubled over, spewing a steady stream of cascading vomit. Looking over my shoulder, back at the finish line, I see my instructor shaking his head; I have failed my final Army Physical Fitness Test (APFT) miserably.

In my age group, the passing time for the two-mile run is fifteen minutes, and I have flopped across the finish line in just under nineteen. I am painfully aware that getting a passing score is not hard; in fact, it's quite easy for anyone who's at all athletic or who runs more than just once a year. I know that no one should ever fail the APFT, especially if one is an officer, and even more so if one is (like me) an officer in OBC, taking the final physical training test, which one needs to pass in order to graduate. The whole scenario is just ridiculous.

It is mid-July, about two weeks after Mitch's alcohol-gambling-freebasing tour, which coincided with Lynn's departure and my own self-implosion. Since she left, my physical ailments have escalated at an alarming rate (even for me): I have graduated from being not only a regular at morning sick call but a familiar face in the emergency room as well. As my already poor health begins an even more rapid decline, I've started taking steroids again—this time at even higher dosages than before in order to compensate for my increased fatigue.

My instructor, a captain in the U.S. Army, is surprisingly understanding, simply telling me, "Well, Winder, looks like we'll just have to bust some ass so you can pass the retest in two weeks."

As I look at him, my strong feelings of anger and frustration at having failed are overwhelmed by my current state of physical collapse. He sees this and believes that I might actually be quite sick, so he sends me to be examined once again by the doctors at sick call.

I am not too optimistic, for I have been to the infirmary a million times (I'm barely exaggerating) since I've been in El Paso, and all that the doctors there have ever said is that I have sinusitis and a bad back. Although I have admittedly forsaken God's trust, on the way to the infirmary I begin to pray once again, asking for help once more, so that this time my checkup will be different.

I'm hoping that something is seriously wrong with me, because if the doctors once again find nothing, it will mean that I have no legitimate reason for failing, and I might not graduate OBC on time. After today's performance, I know that passing the APFT in just two weeks is a farce. I get my wish: I have mononucleosis, hepatitis, and anemia—the trifecta.

The doctors tell my commanders that I am to be put on immediate convalescent leave and may out-process from the post on my own time during the last two weeks of school.

It's a miracle! I am going to graduate, and on time to boot. No going to the field for the next week, no worrying about passing the APFT, no more bullshit. Fuck it. I am happy as shit; who the hell cares about a little sickness? I tell myself.

I am confident that the final two weeks of out-processing are a good start toward my own recovery. The doctors have said that it is dangerous for me to consume alcohol, but they mentioned nothing about LSD or G. Every day, alone in Mitch's apartment, I drink G, eat tabs of acid, write poetry, and, when my brain permits, do some reading. In light of my extreme fatigue and nausea, I also decide that it's prudent to stick with steroids indefinitely. Smart thinking. As for alcohol, I clock five solid days of abstinence—a new record!

I have no worries. As I drive away from Fort Bliss, my car fully packed, I reflect back on my recent experiences. I've left this Texas hellhole with a diploma. So much has happened in El Paso. It was a hellish abyss that I desperately yearned to be free of, each and every day. It seemed that I would never get out alive, but it's over. Soon I will be with my family and, more important, with Lynn, who is home for the summer.

SERVICE SCHOOL ACADEMIC EVALUATION REPORT				DATE	
For use of this form, see AR 623-1; the proponent agency is MILPERCEN.				27 JUL 01	

1. LAST NAME - FIRST NAME - MIDDLE INITIAL	2. SSN	3. GRADE	4. BR	5. SPECIALTY/MOSC
WINDER, MICHAEL		O-1	AD	14B

6. COURSE TITLE	7. NAME OF SCHOOL	8. COMP
ADA OFFICER BASIC COURSE 01-01	USAADASCH, FORT BLISS, TX 79916	USAR

9. TYPE OF REPORT	10. PERIOD OF REPORT *(Year, month, day)*	11. DURATION OF COURSE *(Year, month, day)*	
☒ RESIDENT From: 010312 Thru: 010727	From: 010312 Thru: 010727		
☐ NONRESIDENT 12. EXPLANATION OF NONRATED PERIODS			

13. PERFORMANCE SUMMARY	14. DEMONSTRATED ABILITIES
*a. ☐ EXCEEDED COURSE STANDARDS *(limited to 20% of class enrollment)*	a. WRITTEN COMMUNICATION ☐ NOT EVALUATED ☐ UNSAT ☐ SAT ☒ SUPERIOR
	b. ORAL COMMUNICATION ☐ NOT EVALUATED ☐ UNSAT ☐ SAT ☒ SUPERIOR
b. ☒ ACHIEVED COURSE STANDARDS	c. LEADERSHIP SKILLS ☐ NOT EVALUATED ☐ UNSAT ☒ SAT ☐ SUPERIOR
*c. ☐ MARGINALLY ACHIEVED COURSE STANDARDS	d. CONTRIBUTION TO GROUP WORK ☐ NOT EVALUATED ☐ UNSAT ☒ SAT ☐ SUPERIOR
*d. ☐ FAILED TO ACHIEVE COURSE STANDARDS	e. EVALUATION OF STUDENT'S RESEARCH ABILITY ☐ NOT EVALUATED ☐ UNSAT ☒ SAT ☐ SUPERIOR
*Rating must be supported by comment in ITEM 16.	(SUPERIOR/UNSAT rating must be supported by comment in ITEM 16)

15. HAS THE STUDENT DEMONSTRATED THE ACADEMIC POTENTIAL FOR SELECTION TO HIGHER LEVEL SCHOOLING/TRAINING?
☒ YES   ☐ NO   ☐ N/A *(A "NO" response must be supported by comments in ITEM 16)*

16. COMMENTS *(This item is intended to obtain a word picture of each student that will accurately and completely portray academic performance, intellectual qualities, and moral/professional skills and abilities. The narrative should also discuss broader aspects of the student's potential, leadership capabilities, moral and professional qualities. In particular, comments should be made if the student failed to respond to recommendations for improving academic or personal affairs.)*

2LT Winder is an excellent officer who achieved all course standards. He demonstrated a sound understanding of Army and Air Defense tactics and doctrine. He is a maturing officer with unlimited potential. He achieved an academic average of 91.6% and scored 240 on his record APFT. His written assignments and briefings were well prepared and presented in a logical and professional manner, resulting in a superior rating. 2LT Winder is a true team player who gave freely of his time to help others. He possesses the knowledge, aptitude, and attitude to be an outstanding FAADS platoon leader.

PASS 0701

74/201 YES

17. AUTHENTICATION	
a. TYPED NAME, GRADE, BRANCH, AND TITLE OF PREPARING OFFICER 0-3, AD, SMALL GROUP INSTRUCTOR	SIGNATURE
b. TYPED NAME, GRADE, BRANCH, AND TITLE OF REVIEWING OFFICER 0-4, AD, BATTERY COMMANDER	SIGNATURE

18. MILITARY PERSONNEL OFFICER	
a. FORWARDING ADDRESS *(Rated student)* WESTPORT, CT 06880	b. DISTRIBUTION ☒ STUDENT ☐ UNIT CDR *(P/S NCOES only)* ☒ STUDENT'S OFFICIAL MILITARY RECORDS

24

A Complete Mess
August 2001

H ey, lazy boy," Lynn says, with her trademark sass, as she hovers over me. "My lazy Winder-butt. Get up! Get up, get up!" she yells, as she shakes me with her hands.

"Aaaaahhhhhhhh! Please, just let me sleep," I say, pulling the covers over my head.

"Hey, I will, I promise. I just want a kiss good-bye," she says, teasingly, tugging on my shoulder.

Despite my extreme lethargy and general listlessness, I quickly turn over and smile, completely genuinely. There is no facade with her. I don't have to fake it—not who I am or how I feel. I sit up and kiss her good-bye.

"So, when you going to be home?" I ask. "The usual?"

"Yeah, hopefully I'll be back by around four-ish and then we can play! Yay!"

"I don't know how much playing we're gonna do."

"Yeah, 'cause you a lazy, crazy Winder-butt!" she says, giggling.

"Ha ha, funny girl!"

"Hey, so what are you going to do today, boy?"

"Well, girl, the same thing I do every day: try to take over the world!"

"Yeah, right, 'cause you're 'The Brain'!" she says, laughing heartily now.

"Yeah, and guess who that makes you: Pinky!"

"Naaaarrrrrrf!" she shouts, just inches from my face.

"Hey, honestly, have a great day, and I'll call you in a little bit," I say, grabbing her hands.

"Cool. I wish I didn't have to go-o-o," she whines charmingly.

"I know, but it'll just be a bit. And then we'll have fun, I promise."

"Okay, so honestly, whatcha gonna do until then?"

"Well, I really do need some sleep. But, if you'd really like to know, I'm gonna . . ."

"Wait, let me guess! You're gonna get up, do a shot of G, eat some acid, and then probably take some Adderall that you've secretly stolen from me. Oh, and then you'll read and write, of course."

"Ha! You think you know me so well! You're wa-a-ay off!"

"Really?" she asks, her curiosity seemingly genuinely piqued.

"Definitely way off. I'm thinking first Adderall, *then* a shot of G, *then* acid. Also, I plan to sit on your porch and get totally *blitzed* while I read and write. Seriously, Lynn: you got the order all wrong, and you left out some really important parts."

I quickly see that Lynn doesn't appear so amused by my sarcasm.

"Um, not cool. Mike, you know that annoys me. I mean, I don't mind you living at my place while my parents are away at our country house this month. I know you can't stand being around your parents right now. You're lucky that despite your being so sick and acting like a grumpy Winder-butt sometimes, I love having you here."

"'Cause I'm adorable!" I say playfully, trying my best to diffuse the unnecessarily tense situation I've created. *Dumb ass, why'd I have to go and blurt that out? Lynn's so good to me. Why don't I just try and be cool? Think about what she's put up with. I need to keep a few things to myself.*

"Mike, I'm being serious. You can do whatever you like, even though I don't totally approve, but no alcohol, all right? Honestly, I don't want to go to the emergency room again. Cool?"

She's really a great girl. Why the fuck is she still with me? She's right—I ought to do it for her. How many times has she been to the ER with me? Five, no, six times so far this year? Man, I suck.

"Uh, hello, Mike, are you in there?"

"Oh, I'm sorry. Really, I am. I wasn't ignoring you, I was actually just realizing how much of an ass I am," I say, honestly.

"Well, good work, Einstein!" Lynn says, now laughing again. Making fun of me is definitely one of her favorite pastimes. Situation diffused. I still feel bad, though.

"Lynn, can I ask you why you're still with me? I mean, what am I really bringing to the table?"

"Mike, you know the answer to that. Despite all your faults, and you have many," she says, giggling again, "you're also extremely bright, which I find very attractive, and you're a total sweetie. You've always treated me well, and you make me laugh. If you didn't, you stupid boy, you'd have been outta here awhile ago," she says, smiling, though quite serious.

Can my being bright and sweet and funny really be enough?

"So we're good?" I ask.

"Yeah, if you're going to behave."

"Of course I will. Look who you're talking to!"

"That's what scares me!" she says, as she kisses me one last time. "Be good, Winder-butt! I don't want to come home to another K Real episode," Lynn shouts, as she walks out her bedroom door. She's referring to a recent situation in which she came home from work to find me, Porter, and another friend (the notorious K Real) totally trashed, tripping heavily on acid, and cutting up lines of coke on her kitchen table.

"I will, I promise," I reply, quite disingenuously.

While Lynn is at work, since it's my last day here, I decide to stay true to my word and be a good boy. I spend the majority of the day lying in her bed, writing and reading, consuming GHB, Adderall, and acid until she comes home; without these drugs I don't have the energy to move. I am making the best of a somewhat bad situation, confident that my health will begin to improve, since I've recently decided that I am (almost) definitively done with alcohol, after learning in a recent medical exam that my spleen and liver are each 50 percent larger than they should be.

Regardless of my momentary abstinence, I still feel very ill, with harsh pains in my sides, severe disorientation, profuse sweating, and nausea. When these symptoms come on, I just take more acid, GHB, or Adderall, and usually I'm assuaged—temporarily, at least.

Taking these drugs isn't an option, it's a necessity—for Lynn. I have to look and feel good for her. What am I without drugs? Otherwise, she'll definitely kick me to the curb! It's all for her, I tell myself.

The following morning, much to my displeasure, I begin my trek south to Fort Stewart, Georgia, to rejoin military life. My convalescent leave is officially over.

Well, fuck it! I can handle this! Can't I? I question, as I drive despondently down the freeway, almost praying that an eighteen-wheeler will position itself between me and my unfortunate destiny.

Yeah, of course I can, I think.

After a few minutes, I reluctantly turn back to that three-letter word: *G-o-d.*

"God, I've been good lately. And, well, we both know that I am extremely anxious about reporting to Fort Stewart—scared of being back in army life and the responsibilities that will come with my first command. Moreover, my body's condition has not improved much lately. And, well, God, I know that I haven't always kept my promises in the past. But if you've been paying attention, you've noticed that I have greatly reduced my alcohol intake lately—I'm down to just thirty drinks a week. Well, almost. And although my drug use has continued unabated, I promise, honestly I do, that I will do no more drugs for the rest of my career. Um, wait! How about we make our deal realistic, something that we both know I can adhere to. I got it! If you help me out, just this one last time, and help me get better, and watch over me as I transition back into military life, I promise I will do drugs only if I am on leave," I say triumphantly, as tears start to form.

Moments later, there's a virtual flood flowing down my cheeks. *Get a hold of yourself, you fucking wreck!*

And so on, for 900 miles.

There are two words that can succinctly describe me (and my state of mind) when I finally sign in at Fort Stewart: *complete mess.*

After signing in, I am given a week to in-process. I already feel totally overwhelmed. Waking up before 6:00 AM and merely attending to simple administrative tasks is killing me. Previously, I had been taking GHB all day, every day. I can't handle the sudden lifestyle shift. Things are changing fast, and only for the worse; my body feels as if it's giving up. Thank goodness, Fort Stewart has one major saving grace: Parker and Pete, two of my closest friends from the Academy, are both stationed here as well.

Today is my last day of in-processing. Tomorrow it's time to meet the commanders. *Jesus, I'm fucked!*

As the night sets in, I grab my bottle of G and pour a hefty shot, which I mix with some orange juice for palatable flavoring. I don't even bother to measure carefully anymore; I just eyeball it. For a moment, I just stare at the glass.

I'm in a horrible cycle. I'm taking GHB with such reckless abandon that I no longer have any choice but to G myself out in order to get some sleep, however brief. There's no way that hard-core G addicts like myself can ever fall asleep naturally. Nevertheless, although I'll be completely unconscious during my GHB faux-sleep, I know by now that I won't actually receive any of the essential benefits of normal sleep that are absolutely critical for human physiology and psychology.

Don't worry. You're doing the right thing. The dose has to be large, dangerously large, otherwise there's no chance of sleeping.

I rapidly chug it all down, putting the kibosh on any further introspection.

"Ha! Yup, that's gonna be enough to knock your ass out!" I proclaim, reveling in my momentary euphoria. However, after a few minutes go by, I start to wonder: *Fuckin' A, this sucks. I better get to sleep. I really need some sleep.* Then, with no clear warning, I'm out.

Throughout the night I wake up twice, taking slightly smaller dosages in order to maintain my slumber. With tired, drooping eyes, I clumsily reach toward the premeasured shots, desperately trying to phase out the auditory hallucinations. The bells chiming, babies crying, and women screaming unsettle me to my core.

Quickly, Michael. Quickly, now. Let's get back to sleep. God damn the noise! Fuck, they're coming—I know they're coming. Quickly, now.

As the sun's rays shine through the windows onto what I imagine is an extremely weathered, haggard-looking face, I glance at my watch before pulling the covers tightly over my head. *So fucking early. God damn! Please, can't I just get back to sleep?* I pray, knowing full well that it's impossible.

Lying on the couch in Parker's apartment, I can't find the energy even to get up. My sides are killing me, I have a terrible headache, and I can't shake the unrelenting urge to throw up.

God damn, last night was fucking brutal! The sweats, the paranoia, the disorientation, and those fucking bells. Jesus Christ, I can't handle any more of those damn noises! How the fuck am I gonna end this madness? I wonder.

Suddenly my mind turns to something momentarily forgotten, which quickly consumes my body with fear: *Fuck! Why does it have to be today? Why today, of all days, do I have to freaking meet them?*

Now that I've completed all my in-processing, it is finally time for me to meet my unit leaders. Needless to say, I am terrified about what sort of first impression I will make.

The first person I go to see is my company commander, a captain in the U.S. Army. He appears outgoing, obviously bright and competent, and seemingly laid-back and cool. However, I quickly decide that most of his persona is an act; I peg him for a highly competitive, arrogant, narcissistic, self-absorbed, self-serving, anal prick.

Is this as obvious to others? I wonder.

As he talks to me, I hear nothing except my own overwhelming voice: *I hate people who serve up such bullshit! This guy is a freaking fake, all the freaking time, I bet. Is he ever real? Jeez, why do I dislike him so much? Ah, who the fuck cares! He sucks!*

I instantly decide that he's a man I can never trust—much as I'm sure he doesn't particularly care for his brand-new, sick-as-a-dog, seemingly worthless platoon leader.

My second introduction is to my battalion executive officer (XO), second only to our battalion commander. My XO is a major, who, unlike my company commander, is a very impressive individual. He is a sharp, intelligent man whose only apparent flaw is that he seems to think he's smarter, cleverer, and just that much more astute than everyone else around him. I find it interesting that a man who obviously relishes his ability to read other people is so poor at hiding any of his own thoughts or emotions. His long, narrow stare, stoic demeanor, exaggerated pauses, and subtle smirks make quite an impression on me. He strikes me as a man who takes great pride in his job and possibly even more joy in the art of making others feel uncomfortable.

All in all, I quickly size him up as the sort of man who ought to make the rank of general, or at least colonel, but probably won't because he doesn't kiss enough ass. Although I don't imagine that he shares the sentiment, I immediately respect him.

Standing in his office, in addition to still having my ongoing trifecta of diseases, I am crashing hard off GHB and don't care about showing it. I know I am way off my game. I'm aware that I've come to that point in a drug user's life when he's ceased to care about acting normal.

In fact, I already came to an important conclusion earlier that morning: *I am too sick, unhappy, and disoriented to start working a full-day schedule. If I look sick enough and appear unable to lead a platoon, then no one in his right mind will want me to come to work.*

I can tell that the battalion XO thinks I'm extremely sketchy.

I am a serious question mark for my commanders.

I have planted the necessary seeds. The battalion XO sends me to see the unit's physician.

The doctor cannot understand how I could have been allowed to graduate from OBC and sign in at Fort Stewart in such poor health. She finds me more than credible and gives me a full profile. This excuses me from physical training and morning formations and allows me to arrive at work at 9:00 AM; for the army, this is late—a real treasure. After I turn in my profile, my commander gives me ten days' permissive leave to find a place to live and become acclimated to the area. I plan to use my time wisely.

During my leave in the last weekend of August, I drive to Nashville, where Lynn has returned to school, to visit Lynn for her twenty-first birthday. When I give Lynn her gift, I'm confident that I earn a whole bunch of jazzy cool points: it's a poem I wrote for her, which to this day remains one of my favorites.

I love poetry. It's an essential outlet for my emotions and creativity. The poems I write are important to me not only because they capture events, people, and emotions but also because they're the means by which I keep from forgetting these things. Although Lynn's poem has a very basic rhyming scheme and would never be judged a work of any true importance, it has enormous value for me personally. It's a fine representation of our growing relationship, and it's also the only poem I've ever written for someone else. (And, of course, there's the jazzy-cool-point factor.)

I spend the weekend guzzling GHB, eating tabs of acid, and popping Adderall. My sides are hurting, and my auditory hallucinations are increasing. No problem, though. Overall, I feel fine.

PHYSICAL PROFILE
For use of this form, see AR 40-501; the proponent agency is the Office of The Surgeon General

1. MEDICAL CONDITION		2.						
Mononucleosis / Enlarged Spleen			P	U	L	H	E	S
			T3	1	1	1	1	1
						CODES		

3. ASSIGNMENT LIMITATIONS ARE AS FOLLOWS

No Physical Training, No APFT, allow soldier to report to work @ 0900

4. THIS PROFILE IS ☐ PERMANENT ☑ TEMPORARY EXPIRATION DATE: 4 Oct. 01

5. THE ABOVE STATED MEDICAL CONDITION SHOULD NOT PREVENT THE INDIVIDUAL FROM DOING THE FOLLOWING ACTIVITIES

☐ Groin Stretch   ☐ Thigh Stretch   ☐ Lower Back Stretch   ☐ Neck & Shoulder Stretch   ☐ Neck Stretch
☐ Hip Raise   ☐ Quads Stretch & Bal.   ☐ Single Knee to Chest   ☐ Upper Back Stretch   ☐ Ankle Stretch
☐ Knee Bender   ☐ Calf Stretch   ☐ Straight Leg Raise   ☐ Chest Stretch   ☐ Hip Stretch
☐ Side-Straddle Hop   ☐ Long Sit   ☐ Elongation Stretch   ☐ One-Arm Side Stretch   ☑ Upper Body Wt Trng
☐ High Jumper   ☐ Hamstring Stretch   ☐ Turn and Bounce   ☐ Two-Arm Side Stretch   ☑ Lower Body Wt Trng
☐ Jogging in Place   ☐ Hams. & Calf Stretch   ☐ Turn and Bend   ☐ Side Bender   ☐ All

6. AEROBIC CONDITIONING EXERCISES
☐ Walk at Own Pace and Distance
☐ Run at Own Pace and Distance
☐ Bicycle at Own Pace and Distance
☐ Swim at Own Pace and Distance
☐ Walk or Run in Pool at Own Pace
☐ Unlimited Walking
☐ Unlimited Running
☐ Unlimited Bicycling
☐ Unlimited Swimming
☐ Run at Training Heart Rate for ___ Min.
☐ Bicycle at Training Heart Rate for ___ Min.
☐ Swim at Training Heart Rate for ___ Min.

7. FUNCTIONAL ACTIVITIES
☐ Wear Backpack (40 Lbs.)
☐ Wear Helmet
☐ Carry Rifle
☐ Fire Rifle
☐ With Hearing Protection
☐ KPH Copping/Moving Grade
☐ Marching Up to ___ Miles
☐ Lift Up to ___ Pounds
☐ All

PHYSICAL FITNESS TEST
☐ Two Mile Run   ☐ Walk
☐ Push-Up   ☐ Swim
☐ Sit-Up   ☐ Bicycle

8. TRAINING HEART RATE FORMULA

MALES 220   FEMALES 225

MINUS (−) AGE
MINUS (−) RESTING HEART RATE
TIMES (x) % INTENSITY
PLUS (+) RESTING HEART RATE

50% EXTREMELY POOR CONDITION
60% HEALTHY, SEDENTARY INDIVIDUAL
70% MODERATELY ACTIVE, MAINTENANCE
80% WELL TRAINED INDIVIDUAL

9. OTHER Ongoing workup for hepatitis & extreme fatigue. Thank you.

TYPED NAME AND GRADE OF PROFILING OFFICER	SIGNATURE	DATE 14 Sept. 01
TYPED V	SIGNATURE	DATE 14 Sep 01

ACTION BY APPROVING AUTHORITY

PERMANENT CHANGE OF PROFILE	☐ APPROVED	☐ NOT APPROVED	
TYPED NAME, GRADE & TITLE OF APPROVING AUTHORITY	SIGNATURE		DATE

ACTION BY UNIT COMMANDER

THIS PERMANENT CHANGE IN PROFILE SERIAL ☐ DOES ☐ DOES NOT REQUIRE A CHANGE IN MEMBER'S		
☐ MILITARY OCCUPATIONAL SPECIALTY ☐ DUTY ASSIGNMENT BECAUSE:		
TYPED NAME AND GRADE OF UNIT COMMANDER	SIGNATURE	DATE

PATIENT'S IDENTIFICATION (For typed or written entries give: Name (last, first, middle); grade; SSN; hospital or medical facility)	UNIT B Btry 1/3 ADA
2LT	ISSUING CLINIC AND PHONE NUMBER SHC 737 762-9532
Winder, Michael	DISTRIBUTION UNIT COMMANDER — ORIGINAL & 1 COPY HEALTH RECORD JACKET — 1 COPY CLINIC FILE — 1 COPY MILPO — 1 COPY
DOB 04 Apr '77	

25

White Angel

September 2001

H ow can this happen to me? I'm too smart a person to have
something like this happen to me, aren't I? I wonder.

Things are getting worse—much, much worse.

My ten days' permissive leave are over, but I am not ready to go
back to work—not even close. As I lie on Parker's couch, contemplating those tiny things that to a normal individual would seem
so trivial, I feel immense despair. Getting sleep, getting out of bed,
putting on my uniform, and acting normal in front of my commanders all seem so incredibly daunting.

I wish I wasn't alone.

As my shaking hands pour myself an extremely large, unsafe
shot of GHB, I feel only unhappiness. Even GHB isn't enjoyable
anymore. All I'm looking forward to is that brief period of just a
few seconds, right after I drink such a nice-size dose.

I am almost always doing more G than is acceptable now so that
I'll get really high, really fast, and won't have to stay awake for
longer than absolutely necessary. Without GHB (and a lot of it),
I'm seriously unstable, although with it things aren't much better.

The nausea, the dizziness, and even the anxiety—I can handle all of
it, I am still telling myself. I just need some time to decompress or

something. This just shouldn't be happening—not to me.

A couple hours later I am awakened by the sudden sounds of loud bells, doors opening and closing, and voices from nearby rooms. As I pull the sheets up over my head to drown out the noise, I see bugs, primarily spiders, crawling along my arms and legs. I'm going mad. "You're not real," I tell them. I just need some sleep. I haven't had a real night's sleep in more than three months.

"What the hell am I gonna do?" I ask myself out loud.

The following morning, feeling completely despondent, my anxieties are suddenly eased by what I can only believe to be divine intervention. As I look in the mirror, I see my salvation: blood pooling up in the corner of my left eye.

Fucking God, man. Thanks, man. I mean, thanks, God. You're not just a three-letter word. I'll change. I promise, I say, trying hardest to convince myself.

My commanders see that something is wrong with my eye, so they give me approval to see the necessary doctors. Ultimately, I am sent to an outside specialist who tells me I need surgery—soon. The buckle in my left eye, surgically implanted three years ago to reset a detached retina I suffered in a drunken bar brawl, has become dislodged. Because of the profile I already have for my mononucleosis, hepatitis, and anemia; my pending eye surgery; and my visits to various doctors for sinus and allergy problems, I have more than enough calamity on my plate to keep me in complete limbo and thwart any of my commander's attempts to have me do anything remotely officer-like. To be honest, no one ever sees me; I am a ghost. My commander and I reach an agreement: we decide that the most prudent option is for me to hang back, by myself, while the rest of my company does their four weeks of training in the field. I am given one order: to take care of myself.

I am ecstatic. I have bought myself more time, at least until mid-October.

There are certain points in my life when I realize that I have lost all control or am in way over my head. Like many addicts, I often feel capable of conceding to either of these notions, but never both at the same time. Presently, I am willing to admit that things are growing more unmanageable by the day; however, I still think that I am in control of my devil. Things have gotten really bad, but I am not ready to take action.

Five days later, I am proved wrong. It is September 15, the day I decide I want my life back. Actually, to be more precise, it is the day on which—similar to my experience with heroin—I have a fleeting instance of unexpected, impulsive decision making that shows some sense of a survival instinct. The intelligent part of my brain takes control for a moment. I realize what I am becoming, and I hate myself. I feel extremely depressed and unstable. In a brief moment of clarity I even give Pete my bottles of GHB to dispose of. (Pete really impresses me. He actually cares enough to get involved, something I don't see in people very often.)

Quitting GHB cold turkey is the worst experience I have undergone, thus far, in my life. I want to die. In the first few days of quitting, I am constantly reminded of an axiom of drug addicts: "There are those times that you think you will die and pray you will live; and there are those times that you know you will live but hope you might die." Currently, I am experiencing the latter.

The first night of quitting GHB is very bad; I cannot sleep. Everything I am feeling, that I desperately want to get away from, is still here—only now it's just amplified. I try drinking a few beers and then taking a few Tylenol PM, but nothing helps. The second night is even worse. I am so edgy, disoriented, and miserable that I drink eighteen beers and take six Tylenol PM; still no sleep. I never knew I could be this unhappy. The sweating, shaking, severe depression, vomiting, hallucinations, and wild-eyed paranoia are all there. The third night I want to die.

Why didn't you do your research first, you fucking dumb ass? I ask myself.

I go on the Internet, and my blurry eyes try to focus as my shaking hands tremble across the keyboard. After several hours of brain-fogged reading, my anxieties are far from gone.

It appears that GHB withdrawal is characterized by symptoms of both alcohol and benzodiazepine withdrawal. Although the risk of death is extremely low, withdrawal from GHB elicits some of the most severe mental and emotional symptoms of any drug. Attempting to quit GHB cold turkey is apparently not a good move.

One article in particular says that, without constant medical supervision, one should gradually reduce one's GHB consumption over a period of at least two weeks.

Even in quitting drugs I am acting like a moron, I think.

Until the date of my scheduled eye surgery, I am basically on my own, lying on my bed at home, which for the moment is the spare room in the apartment of a woman named Emily, whose husband, a fellow West Point graduate, is deployed overseas.

Momentarily I am distracted.

"Shouldn't you be going in to work or something?" Emily asks, at one point.

"Yeah," I answer, completely apathetic to her, to my army responsibilities, to everything.

Looking back at the hazy screen in front of me, I am given reason for hope. The website I am looking at says that one of the most effective ways to deal with GHB withdrawal is taking a benzodiazepine, such as Valium. By some stroke of luck, I had purchased a large quantity of Valium several months ago—even though I've never done it, never cared to do it, and, at the time, didn't even need it. A dealer offered it to me, and I immediately said yes. It was as simple as that.

Thank God! I think, as I throw some clothes in a duffel bag.

"Where you going?" Emily asks.

"Nashville."

"Nashville? Don't you . . ."

I ignore Emily's queries. *I need to see Lynn; moreover, I need the eighty (10 mg) Valium tablets I hid in her apartment.*

I am aware that things between the two of us are distinctly changing. Lynn is a smart girl, so I am sure she has some idea of what is going on. The image of her cool, partying, drug-dealing, drug-addict boyfriend is quickly unraveling.

Less than five minutes after entering Lynn's apartment, I have already eaten two Valium tablets. It calms me down immensely, subduing my insane craving, delirium, shaking, and inescapable anxiety. I'm not sure what time in the afternoon it is, but I am already guzzling vodka.

"This is the only way I know how to deal with the withdrawal. It'll all work out in the end," I tell Lynn as her watchful eyes burn a hole through me.

"I didn't say anything!"

"I know. I'm sorry. I just can't imagine how wonderful I must look to you right now."

"Don't worry about it. I know everything will be back to normal soon."

Normal. Was there ever a "normal"?

"So, what have you been doing for the past week?" she asks.

I ignore Lynn's question. Even with the Valium, all I can think about is my craving for GHB.

"Mike, I asked you . . ."

"Oh, sorry. Lynn, I'm real sorry. My brain's just all banged up. I don't mean to ignore you," I tell her, sincerely.

"Have you been drinking?" she asks me.

"Um, so yeah, well, you're not going to love this, but over the past week I've been drinking one to one and a half liters of vodka a day."

"What? Mike . . ."

"Lynn, I know it sounds ridiculous. But I didn't have any Valium, and I was seriously messed up, and alcohol, in large quantities, is the only way to dispel the thoughts and cravings."

"Uh, okay, I guess. As long as this isn't something long-term or anything."

"No. Definitely not."

"So, you've just been drinking? By yourself?"

"Well, kind of. Lynn, I've been *really, really* messed up. And, as I previously mentioned, I didn't have to go in to work, so I was on my own, in my apartment, drinking, waiting till some of the other guys got home from work."

"Mike, I'm just worried for you, is all."

"I know, Lynn. And I appreciate it, seriously, I do. But, trust me, I'll be fine. I've got things under control," I say, knowing it's a lie.

Despite my statements to the contrary, I'm confident that Lynn sees the obvious: her boyfriend has an ever-deteriorating physical condition, along with newly faltering mental and emotional states.

Why does her opinion not bother me more? I ask myself.

My complete, genuine indifference toward her growing dissatisfaction is the only thing I find somewhat troubling, but I reflect on the irony for only a brief moment.

Lynn is meeting her friend, Crazy Kim, at Kim's apartment. I don't mind tagging along.

As Lynn and I walk into Kim's suite, the seven or eight hits of acid I secretly took on the way really start to take hold of me, reminding me instantly of how much it sucks to be on something with a group of people who aren't, and who mustn't even know.

I am sitting at a table in their living room, watching the madness unfold, as I drink my Puligny-Montrachet (always a French white!) with uncouth speed. I'm completely in my own world, not paying the slightest attention to anything that the girls are talking about. I am the only guy in the place, with five girls sitting around me, and for all I care they might as well be stuffed animals or hallucinations.

I am pretty rude, ignoring the girls as thoroughly as possible. I drink the entire bottle of wine in less than thirty minutes, and when I ask for the corkscrew in order to open the second bottle, I am well aware of the looks I am receiving from around the table, but there is no reason to care. LSD and my personal preference, wine, go marvelously together.

At a certain point Lynn and the rest of the girls decide it is time for a little smoke break. Lynn tells me they are going out for cigarettes and will be back in ten minutes. I realize after Lynn leaves that I haven't listened to a word she said.

Where the fuck did they go? I think they mentioned something about smoking. Is that right? I wonder.

After thinking about it for a moment, I realize that there is no reason to care. I am in my zone. As I watch the patterns on the wallpaper morph into various animals, it hits me—something is missing. And I quickly realize what it is: *more!*

Restless, I pour the rest of the bottle of wine down my throat and leave. No note. No nothing. I just leave. I walk out the building, find the nearest bar, and order a double shot of vodka.

As I play pool with a new friend, my cell phone is ringing off the hook. Lynn's number is flashing on the screen, and I can't stop laughing. My new friend is egging me on; he finds it hilarious that I've bailed out on some girl I am in town to visit, and even funnier still that she is calling me repeatedly. I just stare at the ringing phone and laugh with him.

"You gonna head back to your lady, or you wanna bolt?"

"Why? What's up?" I ask.

"Some of my friends are throwing a tight party nearby—trimmed with all the fixin's."

"Party favors?"

"Definitely. So, you in?"

"You fuckin' kidding me? Hell, yeah, I'm in!" I tell him.

"Cool. Let's bounce, then," he says.

My new friend (whose name I still haven't processed) and I leave the bar and head to someone's house. The party is pretty cool, but there is one problem. Actually, it isn't a problem, but it is definitely something that, given the fact that I am tripping my brains out on acid, is reason enough for me to be uncomfortable: I am the only white guy in a party of roughly fifty people.

Ah, whatever, I think to myself.

Of greatest importance, however, is that my new friend is quickly able to find what I have asked for: coke. Moments later, I am in the bathroom of some stranger's house, dead drunk, tripping on acid, with my phone incessantly ringing—but everything is cool.

Nice party favors—thank God, I am saved! I think to myself, glaring at the beautiful white powder before me. I stand before the mirror, staring at my immensely distorted image, anxiously flipping a razor blade in my right hand. A smile creeps across my face.

It is time to end it all, I decide, joyously.

I look at the razor. I can feel that part of me doesn't want to do this, but obviously a stronger part does. It is indeed time to end all the waiting—for Her. I roll a dollar bill, take a quick snort, and then it is over. The white angel grabs me, pulling me in tight; my throat clenches, anxious with expectation. "Don't worry—forget everything," she says, as she flies us high above the city.

I grow anxious, increasingly aware of a looming concern. *Do I have enough?* I wonder, with the utmost gravity. My uncertainty worries me even more.

One gram of coke simply is not enough, I decide. I buy another gram and answer my phone. "Hello?"

"Uh, Mike, I've been trying to reach you for three hours. Where the hell are you?"

"Oh, hey, Lynn, um, hold on a second. Hey, guys, where are we? Cool, thanks. Uh, Lynn, you there?"

"Yeah, where are you?"

"Well, it appears that I'm in Nashville."

"Really, no shit! I'm in Nashville, too, and you wanna know why? Because you're visiting me, jackass!"

Fuck! I think, as my evening quickly returns to me.

Upon realizing my mistake, I figure I might as well just continue down the same "dumb-as-a-drunk-washrag" path I've embarked upon.

"Oh, yeah, I knew that. So what's up?"

"You've been gone for three fucking hours. You just disappeared and then ignored all my phone calls. So where the fuck are you?"

"Oh, I thought I just told you, I'm in Nashville."

"No shit, but what are you doing?"

"I'm at a party with these guys I met."

"Well, you thinking of maybe coming back soon?"

"Oh, yeah, of course, I was just leaving. What's your address, again?"

"I'm at Crazy Kim's apartment, at the corner of Church and Fourth Street."

"Cool, sounds good. I'll grab a cab and see you in a few."

"Yeah, looking forward to it."

Well, needless to say, Lynn isn't exactly a cup of chamomile when I get back, especially when she finds out I have been doing cocaine. She makes me tell all her friends, perhaps thinking that I will be embarrassed or ashamed, but it doesn't faze me.

The girls are mortified, which I actually find pretty amusing. I can tell that my casual demeanor is seriously frustrating her. Lynn shakes her head. It is time to go home.

Back at her apartment, we argue for some time before she finally goes to bed, giving me the couch.

Maybe I screwed up—maybe, I ponder.

This night is the first time that Lynn and I have ever really argued. This makes me uncomfortable. I need her. I need my rock.

How can I fix this? How can I get my rock back? I wonder.

Ultimately, I decide I'll make it up to her by staying up for several more hours, powering through the coke, and finishing her math homework for her. She gets an A. I'm a good boyfriend.

READER/CUSTOMER CARE SURVEY

HEFG

We care about your opinions! Please take a moment to fill out our online Reader Survey at **http://survey.hcibooks.com.**
As a **"THANK YOU"** you will receive a **VALUABLE INSTANT COUPON** towards future book purchases
as well as a **SPECIAL GIFT** available only online! Or, you may mail this card back to us.

(PLEASE PRINT IN ALL CAPS)

First Name _____ MI. _____ Last Name _____

Address _____ City _____

State _____ Zip _____ Email _____

1. Gender
☐ Female ☐ Male

2. Age
☐ 8 or younger
☐ 9-12 ☐ 13-16
☐ 17-20 ☐ 21-30
☐ 31+

3. Did you receive this book as a gift?
☐ Yes ☐ No

4. Annual Household Income
☐ under $25,000
☐ $25,000 - $34,999
☐ $35,000 - $49,999
☐ $50,000 - $74,999
☐ over $75,000

5. What are the ages of the children living in your house?
☐ 0 - 14 ☐ 15+

6. Marital Status
☐ Single
☐ Married
☐ Divorced
☐ Widowed

7. How did you find out about the book?
(please choose one)
☐ Recommendation
☐ Store Display
☐ Online
☐ Catalog/Mailing
☐ Interview/Review

8. Where do you usually buy books?
(please choose one)
☐ Bookstore
☐ Online
☐ Book Club/Mail Order
☐ Price Club (Sam's Club, Costco's, etc.)
☐ Retail Store (Target, Wal-Mart, etc.)

9. What subject do you enjoy reading about the most?
(please choose one)
☐ Parenting/Family
☐ Relationships
☐ Recovery/Addictions
☐ Health/Nutrition
☐ Christianity
☐ Spirituality/Inspiration
☐ Business Self-help
☐ Women's Issues
☐ Sports

10. What attracts you most to a book?
(please choose one)
☐ Title
☐ Cover Design
☐ Author
☐ Content

TAPE IN MIDDLE; DO NOT STAPLE

FOLD HERE

Comments

26

Ward 3A

October 2001

As I poke my head out from under the covers, my partially shut eyes scan the room, searching—but for what? To say I'm disoriented is putting it mildly.

Where am I? I wonder.

Something is off, even wrong, perhaps. A dense chill runs through my body, and I am consumed by a relatively foreign feeling which tells me that today, October 3, 2001, is going to be an extremely important day in my life. I am not comfortable with this premonition at all.

Finally, it hits: *I'm in that hotel room.* I might know where I am, now, but my head is still so incredibly clouded. Looking around the room, all I see is alcohol, alcohol, and much more alcohol. The room is shocking. I feel like Nicholas Cage in a scene from *Leaving Las Vegas*.

"Jesus, could I really have drunk all this?" I ask myself out loud, looking at the impressive collection of empty vodka bottles.

My cell phone is ringing. Without even looking to see who it is, I throw the phone against the wall; there is no way I am speaking to anyone right now.

I am anxious and apparently unhappy with something, but I

still can't make heads or tails of it. As I lie in bed, I feel an even eerier feeling come over me; I am very afraid, but I have no idea of what. I don't want to move.

Five minutes after waking up, I make the initial connection to the previous evening, which starts a domino effect in my recall. I realize that my mind is not just foggy but awkward and clumsy as well, and moving at an extremely erratic pace. I recognize this weird state that my mind is in; there is no mistaking it, I have been there many times before. The day after consuming large quantities of LSD and alcohol is brutal on the brain. Things just barely start to make sense, when I start crying.

This is the worst, the absolute worst! I think. *I'm lying in a bed, in a hotel room, by myself, and I'm crying. And I don't even fucking know why.* However, I do know that I am very sad and that something is very, very wrong. *This is the worst, the absolute, motherfucking worst!*

I try to stop crying, but I can feel it inside me. A deep, sharp piercing pain is moving through my heart and my mind; there is no escape. Then, suddenly, I remember everything, all of it, in total detail, and all I can think of, as I pull the covers tight, trying to hide, is an intense desire simply to forget. All I want is to hide and forget. *Why can't I just forget?*

After my trip to Nashville, I had returned to Fort Stewart and Emily's apartment. One night I got really, really drunk and said some distasteful things to Emily, and she immediately told me to leave her apartment. As Pete tried to talk some sense into me, I couldn't help bursting into uncontrollable tears. I was a wreck, and Pete helped me to move my stuff to this hotel. *It doesn't matter,* I told myself, *a hotel is just as solid.*

Six days later, I am alone in the hotel, comforted by a blanket of my own misery. My friends call around 6:00 PM. and I actually answer, thinking it best to put their minds at ease. I've spent the last five days drinking, all by myself, ignoring my friends' calls, convinced that I am having fun, with no real plan to change the current protocol.

I play it cool, assuring them I am fine, and I decline their invitation for dinner. I am content in my hotel room and don't want to change anything. It is all too perfect.

One twelve-pack is already gone. I take a final swig from the bottle near my bed and go to the fridge to start on another twelve-pack. The phone rings again. I look and am happy to see that it is Lynn, so I gladly answer, but shortly after we start talking I realize that my mind is somewhere far away and there is nothing I really care to speak about.

"Lynn, I gotta go, I'll call you later," I tell her.

"Uh, okay, I was just checking to see . . ."

"Yeah, I know, thanks. I'll call ya later. Bye."

"B . . ."

Click. I am by myself again. *Thank God,* I think.

Eager to release myself from my melancholy chains, I rip an entire row off my sheet of acid, shoving the large chunk of paper into my mouth. It is around 8:00 PM when the LSD starts taking hold of me.

After two hours of feverish chemical-induced drinking and writing, I suddenly jump out of bed and walk into the bathroom. I'm standing in front of the mirror, feeling an uncontrollable urge to look at myself. I don't like what I see. "What's happened to you?" I ask aloud.

In my reflection I see a terribly unhappy young man who has consumed twenty beers, half a liter of vodka, three Valium, and ten hits of acid. Never have I experienced a bad trip on acid, but that doesn't seem to matter to the distorted, wavy, surreal image in the mirror. The discomforting image whispers his words, ever so softly, from deep inside me.

Michael. How are you this evening? Not so great, eh? Guess what? I've got some bad news for you: You're not real. You're a facade, a phony, a fraud. Do you think you earned anything you have? Do you think you should have graduated from West Point? Look around you. Look at yourself. Do you think you deserve to have any of your friends? Is there any way a girl like Lynn should be dating you? Michael, think about your mom. Think about her hard. Michael, tell me, what would she say if she saw you right now? What would she say, Michael? *One final question, Michael: Is there anything that makes you smile anymore? You're so unhappy, why are you even awake? Michael, don't you want to sleep? Let us put an end to all the pain.*

My mind is more than scrambled; it is my enemy, the very weapon being used to torture me. Relentless thoughts scream through my head; I can't handle it. I do the only thing I could think of: I lie down on the bed and start to write, ultimately producing my absolute favorite poem to date.

After a while, my words on the page start to wither under the overwhelming force of a much more intense voice resonating inside my head. *Is there any worse feeling than complete fear of yourself?* As the voices in my head yell, I punch the wall. I feel so helpless, worthless, and doomed. Both my own voice and the voice I equate with that thing in the mirror want all the pain to end.

Terrible thoughts come to my head again, only this time they are even more powerful, and clearer. I decide to retaliate. I go to the front lobby and grab a pack of cigarettes from the machine and a lighter from the desk clerk.

Back in my room, I light a cigarette, look toward the ceiling, and push the lighted end into my left forearm. I push the cigarette in deep, holding it there for a minute. I need to feel the pain; it doesn't faze me.

Pain, why is there so much pain? The whispers change, and now they are laughing. *Fear, why is there so much fear?*

I have to speak to someone, so I call Lynn. Although our conversation is brief, I try using the time to reconnect myself to something decent and good and wholesome, not letting her in on anything I am feeling, but giving her enough of a negative disposition to hopefully elicit some sort of comfort.

Lynn's not impressed. "You know, you really need to stop drinking. You know that?" She has no sympathy, nor does she understand.

"Lynn, I . . ."

"Bye, Mike, I'm going to bed."

"'Night." Click.

When the receiver is back down, the voice in my head starts screaming. *Fuck! God damn it all!*

I call my parents, but there is no answer. I call my younger sister, but there is no answer. I call Mitch, but there is no answer. There is no one. I am alone, with him, that thing I saw in the mirror.

The more I think, the more things don't make any sense. *Why me? How has this happened?*

There is laughter coming from somewhere—I'm sure I hear it. It is too much. I can't handle it. I can't be awake anymore. I don't want to be awake anymore. That is what *he* wants as well.

The problem is that falling asleep after taking ten hits of acid just hours ago is nearly impossible. If I stay up any longer, though, I fear I might lose this chess match. I care about nothing anymore, except not being awake.

I carry the bottle of vodka into the bathroom. I trust what I hope is the good, longing-to-be-alive voice. My body feels nothing. I grab six Valium and six Tylenol PM, washing them down with the bottle of vodka. I know I am walking a fine line. I want to make sure I take enough to fall asleep, but not so much that I don't wake up. However, I'm also acutely aware that I'm far more concerned with the former than the latter.

Lying in bed, holding the vodka bottle, I stare at all the empty bottles around me, and tears roll down my cheek. I've officially lost it. All I can do is laugh as my inescapable demons whisper their thoughts to me.

C'mon, what do you have to wake up for tomorrow? You fucking loser! You're doing jack shit tomorrow, probably just drinking, so why not just take a few more of each and sleep a bit longer?

I pop two more of each pill and drink as much as possible before falling asleep.

Now it's the next day. I've woken up (by some miracle), and

unfortunately remembered everything that occurred last night. I lie listless, as everything washes away. Suddenly, there is nothing. Forgotten are all the drugs, all the alcohol, all the fights, and all the gambling. They're all gone. The mad satchel, Lynn, everything and anything—forgotten. My family, coworkers, supervisors, and friends—forgotten. Work—forgotten. God—forgotten. Anyone who might be able to help me—forgotten. All is forgotten. This is where I am. There is nothing, and that is all I see this morning.

All I can think, see, and feel are that image in the mirror and those thoughts of not wanting to be awake. I pull the covers back over myself, trying to hide, but the darkness still finds me. It covers me from head to toe and holds me to myself.

No one will ever be able to understand me or relate to me, I think. I am the only person in the entire world, my world, and no one can ever help me; I am by myself. This is where I am. Alone. Completely and utterly alone.

Thinking of the previous night, or rather, what I had been thinking of doing, is completely overwhelming; it makes me feel so fragile, so vulnerable. I need to numb the pain, so I pop two Valium. The crying stops, but I am still lying in bed, motionless, staring at the wall.

I have always believed that everyone occasionally has unsolicited, seemingly uncharacteristic thoughts about very bad things; the difference, though, is how one's mind receives them. What usually happens is that, for the good of themselves and society, people discard the negative thoughts. They dismiss them as almost surreal, without merit, and not warranting any further inspection.

Furthermore, I have never understood how people can harm themselves and become the pinnacle of selfishness by hurting those close to them. That's how I've always seen things. I simply could not comprehend how someone could ever get to such a point. *How could this happen to me?* I question, with sincerity.

It's my previous mind-set that makes last night so especially traumatic. Last night the thoughts actually took shape and spoke to me: *Michael, we cannot be discarded, because we are real and we are alive!* This is the sort of thing one cannot easily forget.

My thoughts turn back to my mother and how badly she would be hurt if something ever happened to me. I feel so low to be living like this and having such thoughts, when I have so many people who care so much about me.

I feel even lower when I take inventory and become aware of how much I really have: a good family, a great girlfriend, friends, a good intellect, an education, a home, food, money, health (in the big scheme of things), and a profession.

Why am I thinking like this? Why can't I stop thinking about ending it all?

I feel even lower when I realize that I am also supposed to be an officer and a West Point graduate. *A leader? I am no leader!*

I take a break from things and finish reading Oscar Wilde's *The Picture of Dorian Gray*, which actually eases things immensely. The brilliance of books is their ability to transport you to another world, which is something I desperately need right now. This short novel quickly takes what I know will be a permanent place among my favorite books.

It doesn't matter that I have not eaten; I'm not hungry. I make a trip to the bathroom to throw up before sitting back down to give my problems some serious thought. *Par for the course,* I think. I've been drinking so much that I am now puking on a regular basis, although it is always the morning after drinking.

My issues with drug and alcohol abuse are not going away, and I need to do something to fix them—fast! The decision to go see my commander is an incredibly hard one to make, especially since I am the new officer in the unit, but I can feel the severity of my situation, and I know this is a time when I cannot afford to worry about how I will be received by others. I have to do what I have to do, to get the proper help—today!

The drive from the hotel to Fort Stewart to speak with my battalion commander, a lieutenant colonel, about all my current

problems feels like a never-ending, listless voyage through a night-
marish facsimile of my life. The same question keeps reverberating
throughout my mind: *How did someone like me ever get to such a
point?*

As far as I'm concerned, my decision to go see my commander
is crucial. Although I have an astounding propensity to do very
impetuous and often very stupid things, I am confident that this is
definitely not one of those times.

The battalion commander is unavailable, so I am forced to
speak to the battalion command sergeant major (CSM), an assistant to (and enlisted equivalent of) the battalion commander. The
CSM is highly receptive, showing a genuine desire to get me the
proper help; his father was an alcoholic, so he knows exactly where
I am coming from.

After we talk for a little while, the CSM and I go to see a substance abuse counselor. When I speak to the counselor I don't want
to come across as outlandish as I actually am, so I don't mention
any drugs yet, and I tone down my alcohol intake by about 50 percent. Despite the fact that I minimize my consumption, the counselor is still extremely concerned and orders me to be seen by the
emergency room doctors.

After asking numerous questions, the doctors put me on intra-
venous therapy, supplying me with nutrients that I've lost from all
my drinking, while they conduct numerous tests, one of which is a
urinalysis. I attempt to water down the urine specimen, but this is
not entirely effective, because the hospital performs an extended
test, screening me for almost every drug I can think of.

I come up hot for benzodiazepine, or tranquilizers, which
includes Valium. I am aware that Valium can produce a positive
result on a urinalysis for up to three weeks after ingestion, but this
is somewhat moot, since I've done it earlier today.

Fortunately, since the test was done in conjunction with
hospital care, the army cannot use it to court-martial me. After I
have been lying in the hospital bed for four hours, the shaking,

cold sweats, and terrible headaches really start setting in. The cravings rip through my mind and body, magnifying my unshakable feelings of being alone, unhappy, and scared.

In light of their conversations with me, in which I am noticeably emotionally unhinged, and given my positive result on the urinalysis, the doctors demand that I speak with the psychiatrist on call. "Yes, ma'am. Yes, ma'am. Yes, I have been drinking a lot lately. Yes, ma'am. Yes, I did come up positive for . . . No, ma'am, I don't know . . . Yes, ma'am. Yes, I did drink a lot last night, ma'am. Yes, that's correct, ma'am. I just drank twelve beers and took four Tylenol PM, ma'am. No, I don't mean it like . . . Yes, ma'am, I do know how dangerous . . . Yes, ma'am. Yes, but . . . Yes, ma'am."

Although I've reduced my previous night's intake to something I feel is quite reasonable, she orders me up to the hospital's psychiatric ward.

"Do I have any choice, ma'am?"

"In the military," she replies crisply, "soldiers are considered the property of the government. I am ordering you upstairs, and you have *no* choice in that matter. Understood, Lieutenant?"

Fucking bullshit. Fucking property? Fuck that shit! Freaking doctors able to make decisions as they please. Fuck that shit! I restrain myself from expressing my thoughts.

"Yes, ma'am," I reply.

Clack. The door swings shut with a purpose and locks automatically behind me. All I can think of are straitjackets, padded walls, pills, psychiatrists, and Jack Nicholson in *One Flew over the Cuckoo's Nest.* Crossing the threshold into Ward 3A is one of the most emotionally exhausting experiences of my life. I feel pathetic, miserable, betrayed, and alone—very, very alone.

I live in Ward 3A of Winn Army Community Hospital, Fort Stewart, Georgia, for two weeks, from October 4 to October 19, 2001. They put me on Ativan, an antianxiety medication; Antabuse, an alcohol-consumption deterrent that causes one to get extremely ill and throw up when even the smallest drop of alcohol is imbibed; and a healthy dosage of Prozac, an antidepressant. I also come to the realization that unloading one's emotional baggage on total strangers can be absolutely invaluable.

On October 12, 2001, I have my eye surgery. I am kept in the ward for another week so they can monitor my pain medication. I am then released to the custody of my commander, who puts me on convalescent leave until a bed opens up at rehab.

Leaving the hospital, I feel confident and optimistic. My time in Ward 3A was surprisingly productive, one of the most important experiences of my life.

I sincerely believe I've rounded a corner. I'm finally becoming healthy.

```
MTF: WINN ACH FT STEWART                    Nov 200101526   Page 1
                    PERSONAL DATA - PRIVACY ACT OF 1974

                    RECORD OF INPATIENT TREATMENT
REGISTER: 0228135  NAME: WINDER,MICHAEL H              FMP/SSN:
-----------------------------------------------------------------------
                         A D M I S S I O N

DATE/TIME: 04 Oct 200102110  SOURCE: ERA  CLIN SVC: PSY/AFAA
SEX: M                                     DOB: 04 Apr 1977

                         D I S P O S I T I O N

DATE/TIME: 19 Oct 200101231  TYPE: DUTY   CLIN SVC: PSY/AFAA
                             AGE : 24
-----------------------------------------------------------------------
                         D I A G N O S E S

DX 1.   Principal DX:  30390
        ALCOHOL DEPENDENCE WITHDRAWAL , MILD

DX 2.   29181

DX 3.   311
        MAJOR DEPRESSIVE EPISODE SECONDARY TO #1

DX 4.   3004
        DYSTHYMIA

DX 5.   4011
        ESSENTIAL HYPERTENSION, BENIGN

DX 6.   3619
        RETINAL DETACHMENT

DX 7.   4719
        NASAL POLYPS

DX 8.   4739
        CHRONIC SINUSITIS
-----------------------------------------------------------------------
                         P R O C E D U R E S

PR 1.   Principal PR:  9462   D  1 (P)  04 Oct 2001
        ALCOHOL DETOXIFICATION THERAPY
-----------------------------------------------------------------------
I CERTIFY THAT THE IDENTIFICATION OF THE PRINCIPAL AND SECONDARY DIAGNOSES
AND PROCEDURES PERFORMED IS ACCURATE AND COMPLETE TO THE BEST OF MY KNOWLEDGE.

ATTENDING PROVIDER
-----------------------------------------------------------------------

DRG: 901  ALC/DRUG ABUSE OR DEPEND, WO REHAB THERAPY AGE > 21 WO CC
-----------------------------------------------------------------------
REGISTER: 0228135  NAME: WINDER,MICHAEL H              FMP/SSN:

            REPLACES AF FORM 565, DA FORM 3647, NAVMEDCOM 6300/5
                    *** CONTINUED ON PAGE 2 ***
```

27

Winter Wonderland

November 2001

I t is the second weekend in November. I haven't seen Lynn since that ill-fated trek into the heart of Nashville. I need to see her. Back in a new hotel, awaiting my admittance into mandatory rehab, lying on the bed, I dial her number. Lynn is well aware that I've been in some bad places recently, and she knows that my sobriety is a fragile, unstable work in progress. Accordingly, she is positive that my visiting her before going to rehab is a very bad idea; however, I really need to see her. I need the comfort, security, and support she'll provide me. She is far from pleased that I bought a plane ticket without asking her first. She makes it clear that she does not want to see me right now, but she ultimately acquiesces.

Thank God, I think. *Now I just need to buy a ticket,* I reflect, grinning with delight at my sneakiness.

I am incredibly glad to see Lynn. It is a chance to relax, smile, and just forget about things for a while. Immediately on arriving, I make her a promise: I am abstaining from alcohol for the next year. She believes in my commitment to become more functional, and I'm confident that I've at least temporarily saved our relationship.

The next day, I am alone in Lynn's apartment while she's in class for the afternoon. I sit on her sofa, trying to concentrate on read-ing, but I am far too distracted.

I put down my book and start to work on my poetry. Although I love writing, I still feel an incredible void of motivation, energy, and focus. I need something. I need more.

I go to Lynn's bathroom, open her medicine cabinet, and find her bottle of Adderall. I pocket just two pills, which I am sure she will never notice. I swallow one and start working diligently on my poetry. About forty-five minutes later, I take the second.

I am simply trying to fill my time constructively, I tell myself.

Less than three hours after that first trip to the medicine cabinet, I am lying on Lynn's couch, staring at the ceiling, with one hand on my heart. The palpitations are nearly audible.

Why am I such a fucking moron? How could I have eaten six pills?

I find myself once again praying to some unknown entity, some-thing I know I don't believe in but nevertheless hope will deign to save me yet again.

Please, God, just one more time. I promise I'll change. Please help me!

About ten minutes later I am in the hallway, walking at a frantic unstable pace, when I meet Lynn coming out of the elevator. I am confident that I am having a heart attack, so when Lynn looks at me with such incredulous, skeptical eyes, I am quite irritated.

Without fully understanding the cause, Lynn escorts me to Vanderbilt University Hospital, a five-minute walk from her apart-ment in Nashville. On the way to the hospital I repeatedly drop to the ground, hold my heart, and gyrate every which way while Lynn stands by in amazement. She shows a bit of empathy, but mostly she's just completely embarrassed.

By the time we get to the hospital I am hyperventilating, unable to speak, and shaking immensely. I am brought inside, placed in bed, and given a few Ativan. The pills quickly calm me down.

"Drugs, Mr. Winder. Cocaine, perhaps?" one of the doctors asks.

"No, I don't do drugs. I'm an officer in the United States Army," I say, with misguided pride.

"Regardless, you have no heart condition. What you had was simply a panic attack. Now, what brought it on, we don't know, because we didn't do a urinalysis and . . ."

"I said I'm a United States Army officer. I went to West Point. I don't do drugs, okay?"

"Yes, Mr. Winder. I understand. You just had an isolated unprovoked panic attack, which is quite possible," the doctor says in a somewhat patronizing voice. "Just sign here and you're ready to go."

"Thank you," Lynn says to the doctor, as I quickly scribble my name. Her eyes follow him out of the room and then rivet on me; she is clearly not a happy girl.

I'm not happy, either. What I had thought was a heart attack was in reality my first panic attack. I thought only weak, pathetic people have panic attacks.

How could this happen to me?

I don't think anything compares to a panic attack's overwhelming feeling of anxiety and helplessness. Despite my visit to the emergency room, however, the next night I call a girl I met on a previous visit to see Lynn. I am looking for mushrooms, but all she has is Ecstasy.

That will do just fine, I think.

I am about to finalize the details, when Lynn storms over, forcing me to quickly hang up the phone. Lynn's clenched fists, shaking head, pursed lips, frenetic pacing, and heated complexion are so glaringly emphatic that I almost can't help but laugh. My obvious lack of concern for her feelings only causes further frustration.

"I just don't get it. Can you please explain to me what in God's name you're doing? Didn't you just go to an emergency room yesterday? Didn't you just get discharged from a mental ward? Aren't you about to go into freaking rehab?" Lynn says, as I sit quietly, letting her get it all out. "And wait, wait a second, didn't you just say yesterday that you aren't doing anything for a year? Well, didn't you?"

"Actually, no. I said I wouldn't drink for a year, and I'm not. I'm just doing some X, that's all."

"That's all. You make it sound like it's no big deal."

"You know, you're not being very open-minded."

"Open-minded? Are you freaking kidding me?"

"Well, my problem is with alcohol, not drugs. Drugs are a different story."

"Are they really? And what about yesterday?"

"What about yesterday? That had nothing to do with anything. I don't care what you or that doctor thinks, I just had a fucking panic attack. I've been crazy stressed out lately. You know, you ought to be ashamed of yourself for being so unsympathetic."

"You know what, I don't care—do whatever you want. I can't possibly comprehend what you're doing, but I don't care anymore, either," she says, obviously lying.

"All right," I say, as I take out my phone again.

Lynn's disbelief, which is actually more along the lines of disgusted mortification, is not nearly enough to sway my decision. It all makes perfect sense to me. I call the girl back and set up a time and place.

"Oh, and don't worry, my closed mind won't be mentioning it again, so go ahead and get all you want," Lynn offers.

"Cool, thanks for understanding," I say sarcastically as she walks away, shaking her head.

"Yeah, really cool!" she yells over her shoulder, her own sarcasm and anger inescapable.

Later that night, just before going to bed, she asks me how many rolls I've eaten. (So much for promising not to mention it again.) I tell her seven. She is not happy.

The next weekend I visit Lynn again, but this time things really feel all wrong. I am still annoyed about being chastised for buying Ecstasy, but I have another problem with Lynn: the fact that she has such a serious problem with my drug and alcohol consumption. Basically, she wants a functional boyfriend, and I'm clearly not that guy.

The irony is palpable. Here I am, a drug addict and a drunk,

going through a highly erratic and unstable period of my life, yet
somehow I find myself telling Lynn that I want to break up with
her. Luckily, I quickly realize that this is stupid, even for me, and
we work things out.

The next week I am home with my family in Connecticut for
Thanksgiving. It's November 30, 2001, the day after Thanksgiving,
and I am spending time with Lynn, who is also visiting her parents
for the holiday. I drop three hits of acid before going over to her
house, confident that such a low quantity will slip under the radar.
After watching a movie, Lynn and I hop into bed; she is tired, but
I am far from being able to fall asleep.

I'm not 100 percent sure why Lynn's parents don't have a problem
with my sleeping over. It's probably a combination of their being cool
and, more important, thinking that I'm good for Lynn. Although
they're presumably unaware of my sordid habits, they know that I treat
their daughter well and that the two of us really click. I suppose that
they probably see what we see: that, barring any unforeseen craziness,
our relationship will most likely last for quite some time.

Lying in bed next to Lynn, tripping, my intertwined thoughts
run rampant.

How nice it would be to have more, I think.

I get up, go to her bathroom, and rummage through her medicine cabinet until I find something with potential. Looking at the
back of the Robitussin bottle, I see what I'm looking for: dextromethorphan, or DXM. I know from experience that this drug, in
large quantities, sparks a dissociative trip characterized by extreme
dehydration and relentless scratching but no redeeming qualities
of which I'm aware. It's called "robotripping," and it's absolutely
miserable.

Nevertheless, I empty the bottle without giving it a second thought.

As I brush my teeth, trying to get rid of the disgusting taste in my
mouth, I suddenly notice the bottle of oxycodone painkillers in my
toiletry case.

Wow! I almost forgot about you guys. Perfect!

During a recent follow-up visit with my eye specialist just after my surgery, I stole a pad of prescription sheets from his office. I already had his signature on several prescriptions that he had given me for drops and such, and there was no problem replicating it. Three times in the past month I've donned my eye patch and gone into pharmacies to fill bogus prescriptions for Tylox, a combination of Tylenol and the painkiller Percocet; it was definitely worth the risk.

I pop a few pills and jump back in bed. Lying next to Lynn, I am wide awake and tripping on multiple narcotics; I feel total solitude in my mind's arena, absolutely alone with my thoughts. The past few years race vividly in front of my eyes. All the events and people swirl together, ultimately and paradoxically resulting in an awesome sense of newfound clarity.

I am quite thankful: for my family, for my friends, for Lynn, and, most important, for not being dead or in jail. It's somehow become clear to me that I am a fool. I'm an addict and a worthless charlatan. I feel sad that I have hurt many of those close to me. I do not want to be a walking facade anymore; I want to be real.

My situation envelops me, flooding my head with pulsating images and novel thoughts. The feeling is intense, overwhelming my emotions, but it is also much more. The same thoughts circle repeatedly through my mind: *How can I be such a fool? How have I brought myself to such a point? Why has Lynn stayed with me?*

My body shakes from head to toe. I am compelled to wake Lynn up.

"Lynn, Lynn, *Lynn!*" I say, shaking her.

"Yeah, what, what, Mike?" Lynn finally says, groggily, reluctantly turning toward me.

"I love you."

As soon as these words leave my mouth, Lynn jumps up and stares at me in complete awe, her eyes wide open; suddenly she is completely awake.

"Wait, what? What did you—did you just say what I think you said?" Lynn asks, shaking her head in total disbelief.

"Yeah, I did. And just so you know, this is the only time I've ever said those words to a girl, and actually one of the very few times I've ever said them to anyone."

"Are you kidding me?"

"Of course not. You know I would never say it unless I really meant it."

"That's not what I meant, but—wow! Just when I think one thing, then you go ahead and do this! Jesus, Mike, what's a girl supposed to do?"

"Nothing, Lynn. I just had to say it, because I've been lying here, contemplating the past year and how shitty I've been and how great you've been. You know, I just realized how lucky I am to have you. So I just had to say it, because I felt it—that's all."

"You're amazing."

"Thanks, I guess."

"Wait, hold on a second. I want to say something, too."

"Lynn, you don't have to say or do anything. I wasn't trying to elicit any response from you. I just . . ."

"Mike, shut up. You're absolutely amazing, you know that?"

"Well, not . . ."

"And I love you," she quickly spurts out.

"Seriously?" I ask, genuinely curious. Lynn just nods, as the two of us embrace and kiss each other passionately, before lying back down.

Then, before I fall asleep, she tells me how proud she is that I am going to rehab. I can sense she's a little skeptical, and to be honest, so am I. Nevertheless, nothing can ruin our wonderful, surreal moment, as we lie in bed, side by side, giddy with romantic feelings and fairy-tale thoughts, drifting into our own magical, private, two-person wonderland.

Three days later, as I am flying back to Savannah, I can't think about anything but what transpired between Lynn and me. Things have definitively changed. From the moment I spoke those three words to her, a large part of me would always resent her.

28

Clean and Sober
December 2001

I'm an addict who has come to the crossroads, and somehow, against all that feels reasonable, I've chosen to seek help. In the back of my mind, however, there is still that ever-looming voice, yearning to push me back out into the wild.

Michael, who are you kidding? You seriously think this is going to work for you? Ha! Honestly, why are you even here? We both know this isn't where you want to be. Couldn't deal? Guess some little boy wasn't quite as tough as he thought. C'mon, seriously now, we both know you're not going to stay sober, so why not save us both the time and the trouble and get the hell out of here?

Today is December 7, 2001: my fourth day of rehab at Fort Gordon's Eisenhower Army Medical Center in Augusta, Georgia. I have always been curious to see what one of these rehab facilities is like, but, just as with my previous stay in the mental ward, I never expected that I would ever become an actual patient.

My reflection smiles back at me from the mirror. *But is it real? Isn't it still drugs that cause my feelings, just now prescription antidepressants?*

I pull out my journal and quickly write my previous day's required entry:

The first several days have been somewhat surprising in that I found them much more interesting and worthwhile than I expected. Although my commitment to abstinence, especially from drugs, is quite tenuous, I have really tried to go into rehab with a positive attitude, so that I may actually get something out of the experience.

I think everyone has some idea of what goes on at rehab: movies, group therapy sessions, skill management classes, physical training, health classes, and various other emotional and social interaction workshops. As I have previously mentioned in group, the benefits from unloading my baggage, especially to strangers, is absolutely invaluable, but there is so much more.

I believe time is partly the key. I'm guessing (hoping) that twenty-eight days is just enough to actually start feeling the sobriety take shape inside me. It's four weeks away from enabling bad influences, spent surrounded by people going through exactly the same thing. I'm quite happy with the service provided here, how things are going for me, and moreover, I feel optimistic about my chances for a healthy future.

Another patient, Kevin, wanders over. "Can you believe this shit we have to write, man? Do they really buy this shit?!" he asks me.

"Yeah, mine's pretty fucking corny," I say, with sincerity.

"Dude, read what I wrote. You'll fucking love it!"

"A'right. Let me see."

Kevin hands me his journal, and it takes only a few seconds for me to realize why he's so excited to have me read his entry.

"Dude, Kevin, you really might not want to write this shit," I say, laughing, "I mean, calling AA (Alcoholics Anonymous) a cult and ..."

"Well, aren't they, man? I mean, come on Winder, we both know they're a bunch of crazy crackpot cult-worshiping nut-jobs."

"Yeah, I know," I reply, cautiously.

"And that fucking Serenity Prayer. Jesus, how freaking lame can it get? God grant me the serenity to accept the fact that I'm a fucking cult-worshiping loser," he says, laughing heartily now.

"True. True," I lie.

Actually, I kind of like that prayer, I think.

Less than an hour later, at morning sick call, I tell the doctor about my chronic back pain and intermittent spasms, which recently have become quite aggravated. A few minutes later, I am back in my room with seven muscle relaxants for the next week. It seems odd that they'd give me a whole bunch of pills in a rehab facility, especially because I've been admitted for polysubstance abuse in addition to my problems with alcohol. Anyway, beggars can't be choosers. It's probably purely psychological, but the moment I take one of the pills I feel as though I've satisfied some deep inner craving. My body immediately reacts with a sort of high, even though they're not even really painkillers. So of course I do what I am used to doing: I swallow the rest of the pills.

When I go to morning group therapy, where we have the chance to share whatever is weighing on our minds, I raise my hand and tell the group, which happens to include the program director, that I took all the pills in an attempt to get high. Based on this disclosure, I am given a warning and put on one week of probation, during which time, I am basically told, I will be kicked out if I even breathe wrong.

The next three weeks of rehab go smoothly; I actually start to give some credence to the novel notion that I am no better than any other addict. I am constantly being reminded that I use my intellect to justify my actions, so I am genuinely trying to humble myself to accept my numerous shortcomings.

It is Christmas Eve. All the staff is gone and I feel quite lonely. I am spending all my free time reading, but on this day that just isn't enough. Lying in my bed, alone with Dostoevsky, I feel the need to do something special. I walk down to the emergency room and tell them exactly how I feel: "My head feels like it's in a steel vice. I can't think or really do anything, for that matter. The pain is just too much; it's absolutely unbearable."

Thanks to my honesty, I am given a shot of Demerol and five Lortab painkillers to take back to my room. Again, I find this very odd. *This place clearly has a strange approach to addiction recovery*, I think. Lortab contains the painkiller hydrocodone, a powerful narcotic. Christmas Eve festivities are officially under way.

Lying on my bed, I call Lynn and then my parents, but there is no response from either. I am surprised by the sadness I feel when my parents don't pick up the phone. At this point, despite all their disappointment and undeniable shock at learning where I was, I would welcome a few words with my father. It doesn't really matter, though; I have my painkillers. After passing one of the five pills to a grateful fellow patient, I swallow the other four, putting myself in a dreamy state of artificial happiness.

I have been talking a lot during group sessions, listening during AA and NA (Narcotics Anonymous) meetings, and trying to give all the homework as much attention as possible. For all I've been through, I deserve to celebrate, and this is the perfect reward.

As I float off to sleep, everything feels great. I am more optimistic than ever about the coming year and my ability to live a healthy, clean, and sober life.

Part Four

THE BOULEVARD OF
BROKEN DREAMS

2002

29

That's Dog Shit!

January 2002

S hortly after I arrive in Nashville, Lynn and I are walking out of a local mall, and she starts giving me hell. "Yeah, but I'm not the one who failed out of rehab. You know that, right? You did fail out of rehab, remember?" she scolds.

I have no clue why I am visiting her. As I previously mentioned, a large part of me now resents her, and today I find her to be just a constant and ever-increasing irritant. "Yeah, I know, but like I told you, it was absolutely ridiculous, there were just two days left in the program."

"Yeah, but you failed, right? I mean, you did *fail*, didn't you?"

"Yes, Lynn, I failed, along with the rest of my group, which collectively decided that sleeping through a worthless one-hour afternoon discussion was no big deal, since there were no counselors present and it was just a couple of days before graduation."

"Yeah, I know, but you did fail; I mean, you did fail out of rehab, right?" Lynn is not just annoying, she is redundantly annoying and about as cool as a two-legged pig.

"You know you're just saying the same thing over and over again, right? Do you have anything new to add? I wanted to fail, I was looking to fail, and I am glad I failed. Now I'm getting out of the army,

206

and with an honorable discharge to boot. Everything's perfect."

This isn't entirely true. Although I am glad to be getting out of the army—with an honorable discharge, no less (a lucky break, because I sought help)—I had not been looking to fail, and when it happened, I actually had another minor emotional breakdown.

I am suddenly lost in thought as my mind drifts back to my final group discussion. Just hours after learning I was being kicked out of rehab, I was asked to share how I felt. For the first time, I disclosed my drug abuse; previously, I had attributed all my problems to alcohol. As I did so, I was immediately gripped by an overwhelming sense of terror, which I previously had no idea was lurking just below the surface. I found myself unable to escape from this feeling of dread or from the tears that relentlessly began pouring down my face.

Lynn and I avoid speaking to each other as much as possible for the rest of the afternoon. That night, she's doing homework in her living room while I am pouring myself a glass of vodka in the adjacent kitchen. It has been a little more than two weeks since I was kicked out of rehab and had stopped taking Antabuse. I figure that the medication is probably all out of my system by now. Lynn sees me, and she isn't impressed.

"Uh, what are you doing?" she asks.

"I'm having a glass of vodka."

"Interesting."

"What is?"

"I thought that the glass of wine you had earlier was going to be it. Wasn't it?"

"No, all I said was I wanted to have a glass of wine. I never said that was going to be it."

"Interesting. First you come here this afternoon asking for a drink, after previously going two months without a drink and having promised me you would stay sober for the next year, and now you're pouring yourself a glass of vodka."

"What? What's the big deal? I'm not doing any drugs, am I?"

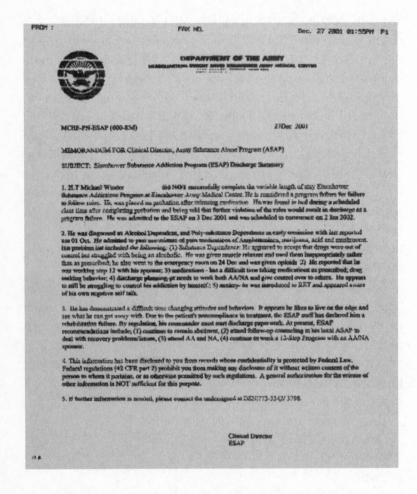

"Whatever. Do what you want; I don't care."

"Yeah, I know, I am."

It amazes me how quickly my image of a person can unravel before my eyes. A single chink in her armor, and it's all come apart. One moment I have Lynn on a pedestal, thinking she is just perfect for me, and the next, as soon as even a little part of me finds fault with her, the whole enchilada comes crashing down.

All I see now is a spoiled, critical, annoying, out-of-shape, immature girl who disrespects her parents by telling her addict boyfriend that it is cool to do drugs in their house. I am hard-pressed to find anything to like about her anymore, and I don't care if I upset her.

It suddenly occurs to me that the same thing might be happening that took place with Sarah: with the drugs gone, so are my feelings. I do like Lynn, but only as far as any lonely addict yearns for that girl nearby who might provide him momentary comfort from his anxieties, unhappiness, and fears.

As the hours pass, it isn't hard to let Lynn do her own thing, while I just drink and watch television; actually, it is quite refreshing. Eventually, though, I become bored. "Hey, I'm heading to bed."

"Uh, why don't you just wait a half hour and I'll go with you?" she asks.

"No, I'm too tired. I'm just going to go now."

"Um, okay. Whatever—do what you want."

"All right, good night."

"Yeah, good night."

About ten minutes later Lynn comes into the bedroom and gets on top of me, hoping (I'm guessing) that sex will basically make everything good between us again.

I try to ignore her.

"Are you just going to lie there and do nothing?" she asks.

She doesn't arouse me anymore. "Hey, I'm sorry, Lynn, but I can't do this right now. I just took four Tylenol PMS."

"You're kidding, right?"

"No, I'm not. The stuff makes me languid Jell-O."

"Whatever, this is terrible."

I know she is referring to our entire relationship, and although I don't say anything, I completely agree.

Lynn jumps out of bed and grabs Weenie, my pug, whom she has been taking care of for me since he was first purchased. She puts him in the middle of the bed, separating us both physically and symbolically, and then turns out the lights and goes to sleep.

She knows I hate sleeping with the pug; I've never heard anything snore so damn loud.

Around 3:00 AM, in a very confused and groggy sleeplike state, I feel something moving all over my legs, so I grab at it with my hand and then, with my eyes barely open, bring it to my face for examination. "Holy shit!" I scream.

It's shit, literally. I hurl the handful of pug poop at Lynn's window, jump out of bed, throw on the light switch, and run to the bathroom screaming like a teenage girl being chased by a psychotic killer in a bad horror flick. Lynn wakes up with a start.

"Jesus, what the fuck, Mike? What the hell's wrong with you?"

As I wash the crap away from my hands and legs, the moment passes.

"Weenie shit all over me. I felt something weird on my legs, so I grabbed it with my hand, and when I realized what it was, I threw it at your window and ran here to clean it all off."

"Wait, what? You threw shit at my window? What the hell is wrong with you, Mike?"

"What do mean what's wrong with me? It's not like I freaking shit all over Weenie. Look at him, he's not even a dog, he's like some weird space creature."

"Stop yelling at Weenie, he didn't mean it. Look, you're scaring him; he's hiding underneath the bed now. Apologize to him."

"I'm not yelling at him, and I'm definitely not apologizing to him after he pooped on me. I'm just pissed to be woken up at 3:00 AM with shit all over my body."

"Whatever, clean it all up and turn out the lights."

"Uh, no. I'll clean the window and myself; you clean the bed. You're the one that wanted shit monster sleeping with us, remember?"

"Whatever, it's on your side of the bed, you clean it."

"No, I'm cleaning myself and that freaking window; that's it. You're cleaning the bed."

"Mike, you're being a total jackass. You know that, right?"

"Listen, you do what you want, but as soon as I'm done

cleaning my stuff, which does not include your bed, I'm going into the other room and sleeping on the couch."

"Great, Mike, that's great. Do what you want, I don't care."

The following morning we say good-bye, and I grab a cab to the airport. I know inside that my relationship with Lynn is over.

Vincent
February 2002

I t's the first weekend of February, three weeks since I last saw Lynn. I find myself once again living in a hotel in Savannah. Uncertain about how long it will take for me to be officially discharged from the army, I am wary of signing a six-month lease on an apartment.

My buddies aren't cool with me staying with them anymore. I know I have crossed definitive lines when my friends, who are no light drinkers themselves, feel so uneasy around me. I wish I was home with my family.

I feel very alone and want someone nearby who actually seems to care about me, because I'm not sure that I even do. In addition to all my other concerns, my cash situation is going from bad to worse. I have spent so much money on drugs, plane tickets, hotels, and lavish dinners, not to mention the fact that I eat out three meals a day, that despite all the money I have made in the stock market ($30,000 from day-trading) and dealing drugs, my credit card debt is rapidly skyrocketing. Ultimately, I decide to ignore the money situation, figuring that I'll deal with this detail when I have to.

I have more important things on my mind; despite the Prozac, I am getting very depressed again. I am quite aware that my resumed heavy alcohol consumption is only making my emotional and mental states that much worse.

I need something else tonight. I search my room one last time, but to no avail; my last sixty hits of acid are indeed lost. Craving anything besides alcohol, I decide to robotrip once again, even though I have always disliked this experience.

As I pour bottle after bottle of Robitussin down my throat, summoning all my strength to keep myself from hurling, I feel so incredibly disheartened. I want consciousness to go away so badly that I'll do anything in front of me, even something I hate, which I had promised myself I would never do again.

About an hour after drinking three bottles of the foul liquid, I am already feeling quite unhinged; honestly, there is nothing cool about a DXM trip. Nothing. As I lie on the bed, my fingers shuffle through the TV channels, finally resting on what seems to be an interesting program: *The Life of van Gogh*.

I am aware that DXM can cause users to dissociate, or detach from themselves, transferring them mentally to an alternate reality where they feel as if they are somewhere far away and someone far different. However, I am still caught a bit off guard. I've never done so much of this drug.

I truly feel as if I am in the television with the host of the van Gogh documentary and that he is talking directly to me. There is no one else, just the two of us. I contemplate why he is telling me all about the famous impressionist painter, and I conclude that either I am Vincent's reincarnated spirit or that I am being shown a path I ought to consider following. I decide that the host is my spirit guide, and so I pay rapt attention.*

"Unfortunately, for many, van Gogh is most well known for being the painter who cut off his ear, which sadly is indeed true," the narrator states. "On December 23, 1888, van Gogh, in an irrational fit of madness, mutilated the lower portion of his left ear. He

---

*I have used the website www.vggallery.com to refresh my memory.

severed the lobe with a razor, wrapped it in cloth, and then took it
to a brothel and presented it to one of the women there."*

I want to cut part of my left ear off, but I have two problems: I
have no prostitute to give it to, and I have no energy to go out to
my car and look for my Swiss Army knife. DXM really makes one
unbelievably lazy (lucky for me!). So instead I focus back on my
personal conversation with the television narrator, wondering
what else he has to tell me.

"On May 16, 1890, Vincent van Gogh left the asylum and took
an overnight train to Paris, where he entered the care of Dr. Paul
Gachet, a homeopathic therapist living in Auvers-sur-Oise."

It is all starting to make sense now. The man talking to me is trying
to point out all the similarities between Vincent and me. How many
more times will I visit mental institutions? It seems all too likely that I
will find myself back behind rubber walls before too long. Is it my destiny, I wonder, to go mad? I wonder if I might ever have anything to
offer society that is remotely similar to van Gogh's contributions. I
decide that if I do, it won't matter if I lead a lonely and unhappy life.

"On the evening of July 27, 1890, Vincent van Gogh set out into
the fields with his easel and painting materials. There he took out
a revolver and shot himself in the chest, still managing to stagger
back to the Ravoux Inn and collapse in bed, where he was soon dis-
covered by Ravoux."

Yes! It all makes perfect sense: I am meant to suffer a similar fate.
I have already been to a mental institution; I wonder how long it will
be before I shoot myself in a field (or anywhere else, for that matter).

"Theo [van Gogh's brother] later wrote: 'He himself wanted to
die; when I sat at his bedside and said that we would try to help
him get better and that we hoped that he would then be spared this
kind of despair, he said, "La tristesse durera toujours" [The sadness
will last forever]. I understand what he wanted to say with those
words.'"

---

*www.vggallery.com.

And so do I.

"Theo was holding Vincent as he spoke his last words: 'I wish I could pass away like this.'"

And so do I.

"Vincent's longtime friend, the painter Emile Bernard, wrote about the funeral in detail to Gustave-Albert Aurier: 'The coffin was covered with a simple white cloth and surrounded with masses of flowers, the sunflowers that he loved so much, yellow dahlias, yellow flowers everywhere. It was, you will remember, his favorite colour, the symbol of the light that he dreamed of being in people's hearts as well as in works of art.'"

It all seems so beautiful, so incredibly beautiful and proper. I envy Vincent's dream, wishing it for my own. A few minutes later, the narrator is done giving me advice, and I turn off the television.

Inescapably unhappy and unable to think of anything better to do, I call Lynn's cell phone; there is no answer. I call Lynn's apartment, letting the phone ring until the answering machine picks up. I hang up and call Lynn's cell phone again; still no answer. I call Lynn's apartment again, but no one picks up. I call Lynn's cell phone a third time, again letting it go all the way through to her message. Then I call her apartment a third time, a fourth time, and a fifth time.

"What?" she says icily.

"Oh, hey, Lynn, you up?"

"What the hell is your problem, calling me five thousand freaking times? Dude, it's after midnight, so stop being an asshole!"

"Hey, I'm sorry, just feeling real depressed and wanted to talk to someone."

"I don't care. You're really getting on my nerves now!"

"Hey, I wouldn't have called if I didn't really . . ."

"Good-bye!" Click.

Overwhelmed, I resort to the only certainty I know: swallowing a few Valium and Tylenol PM. The pain disappears as I quickly fade into the darkness.

I know that things have gone badly, and the following day I find out exactly how much so. Lynn calls and tells me that she wants us to take a break in our relationship. Although this isn't anything unexpected, I am still taken aback for a moment. Perhaps I expected to be the "dumper" and not the "dumpee." I tell her that I'll call her later. Soon my pride sets in, however, and I write her in an e-mail later that day that I want to break up for good.

All in all, I am a little unhappy for a couple of days, but only because I feel more alone. I ultimately realize without question that any feelings I had for Lynn were purely arbitrary and would have been the same for any random girl who was in my life. Although I feel better, on another level I'm a little concerned at how quickly I've recovered from the loss. I try to care. I try really hard, because I know that deep down there must be something; I want there to be something. But I don't feel anything; I can't. There's simply nothing there—only a void that I know I need to fill.

DEPARTMENT OF THE ARMY
OFFICE OF THE STAFF JUDGE ADVOCATE
HQ, 3D INFANTRY DIVISION (MECH) AND FORT STEWART
60 MCNEELY ROAD, BUILDING T-53
FORT STEWART, GEORGIA 31314-5039

AFZP-JA (600-8-24)

MEMORANDUM FOR Commanding General

SUBJECT: Initiation of Elimination – 2LT Winder, Michael,

1. Purpose: To obtain approval to initiate elimination of 2LT Winder, Michael,   . D
Battery, 1st Battalion, 3d Air Defense Artillery, Fort Stewart, Georgia, for failure to respond to
alcohol or drug problem rehabilitation efforts in a reasonable length of time.

2. Background:

   After graduating from Officer Basic Course at Fort Bliss, Texas, 2LT Winder PCS'd to
Fort Stewart in September 2001. He was assigned to his current unit in October 2001. He had
medical problems including hepatitis and detached retina, and he was on convalescent leave for
approximately two months. When he returned to work, he self-referred to ADAPCP. Based on
his self-referral, he was enrolled on 3 December 2001, in the Eisenhower Substance Addiction
Program (ESAP) at the Dwight David Eisenhower Army Medical Center, Fort Gordon, Georgia,
for a one-month comprehensive in-patient treatment. There, he admitted to using drugs on 1
October 2001. He was diagnosed as alcohol dependent and poly-substance dependent. While
there, he failed to follow the program rules. He was placed on probation for misusing prescribed
medication. He was also found in bed during a scheduled class time. He also sought out, and
obtained, opioids which he misused. According to the ESAP clinical director, he demonstrated a
difficult time changing attitudes and behaviors and that he liked to live on the edge and see what
he could get away with. Because of his failure to abide by the program rules and continued
misuse of drugs, he was declared a rehabilitation failure.

3. Recommendation: The chain of command recommends that you initiate elimination
proceedings and notify 2LT Winder of his rights under AR 600-8-24. I agree with this
recommendation.

22 Feb 02

Encls
as   COL, JA
                                      Staff Judge Advocate

31

Back in the Saddle
March 2002

W hat a surprise: just about the only person I am getting along with is my new supervisor. He is a captain, the battalion's supply officer, and I am his new assistant. Apparently rehab failures are not fit to be platoon leaders. But until the army can officially get rid of me, I've been sent to bide my time doing inventory data entry. I really lucked out: he is an excellent officer, a competent man who gets the job done.

He has a good rapport with everyone in his shop. He feels comfortable having very laid-back conversations with everyone, but he still demands quality work—a pretty good balance, I think. I feel all alone. He's almost all I have, and he doesn't even know it.

With Lynn out of the picture, and Pete and Parker really distancing themselves from me, I decide to take a few days' leave to visit Eric and Chad at their new school in Florida. I am excited to see them because they are two friends who actually have no idea of the negative events that have recently transpired in my life. The last they knew of me I was a happy, drugged-out loon. Around them I feel like my old self again—an identity I still prefer, even if I'm not really that person anymore.

I tell the guys some bits and pieces of my story, but only those scraps that do not portray me as a loser—which isn't much. In the edited version, I never actually have any drug or alcohol problem at all, but I ask to go to rehab because I know I can get an honorable discharge if I fail out. Everything, I maintain, has gone perfectly according to plan.

Both Eric and Chad are quite bright—especially Eric, whose enormously high intellect is almost too much for his own good; he appears to believe that he can always get away with anything. Ironically, I sense that his incredible mind was the main reason for his crazy behavior at West Point. I genuinely get the impression that he plays on a completely different playing field, with a thoroughly different set of rules, from everyone else.

Chad, on the other hand, is more like me: he is bright, but instead of using his brain he prefers to rely on his inner jackass. It is because both guys are so bright that I am certain they must see holes in my story—particularly in light of the disjointed, hesitant way I tell it and the fact that when they pull out the GHB I am noticeably wary, telling them I have been abstaining from that particular drug for the last six months.

As soon as they put the bottle of G in front of me, though, I am instantly overtaken by emotion. All my bad memories immediately return: all those sleepless nights, hallucinations, tremors, anxieties, and fears. Nevertheless, as strong as these negative feelings are, they are no match for one simple thing: my desire to be high on GHB.

Chad measures me a shot, and moments later I am reunited with my old flame. In the back of my mind I tell myself that moderation is the key—and at least I'm not using cocaine again, which is readily available as well. Waves of joy crash through my body. It is sweet bliss; the void is filled.

Two days later, back at Parker's new home in Savannah, where I am now living (I moved in, much to his chagrin, shortly after my recent robotripping experience), I order a shipment of GHB from Holland. I need it to help me with the depression and feelings of worthlessness that are actually only getting worse living with Parker.

Parker and I were good friends at West Point; I spent more time around him than I did with anyone else. Now Parker is a Ranger. It didn't surprise me that he took on the challenge of Ranger School or that he never quit (as so many do). More important, he is just a constant reminder to me of how incredibly low I have brought myself: he represents the path well chosen, and I, the exact opposite.

Two weekends later, back in Florida, I break down and buy an eightball of coke. The saddle feels even more comfortable than when I left it.

32

Over the Hill and Through the Woods . . .

April 2002

I t's great to be home, I think.

As I walk through the front door, I couldn't possibly be happier. I haven't seen my family for five months, not since Thanksgiving. I am extremely excited that my unit has a three-day weekend and that I am able to visit Connecticut.

"You know, I was telling your mother to prepare herself for the worst. But you really don't look so bad. Glad to have you home, Mike. Come here," my father says, pulling me in for an awkward hug.

You're obviously not looking hard enough, I want to say.

"Thanks, it's good to be home," I reply. Moments later, my mom is rubbing my cheeks, then squeezing me tight; I don't want to resist, but I feign apathy to avoid the tears.

My father's right, I am too sensitive, I think, as I anxiously walk away.

"So, any word yet on your discharge?" my father asks amid a surprisingly relaxed dinner.

"No, nothing yet. Honestly, you never know what to expect from the army. No one in my chain of command seems to really know, either. Could be a week from now or a year from now. I've got no idea."

"Well, that's got to be really rough on you. I mean, it's been almost four months since rehab. Mike, you should just know that your mother and I are a hundred percent behind you. If you need anything, just let us know," he says.

"Thanks," I mutter. Lately it's been getting harder and harder for me to dislike my father. I'm confident that the heart and brain surgeries have been the catalyst for a very positive change in him, which I really don't like, because I'd grown quite comfortable with my fundamental aversion to all things him.

Could any of my past problems with him be due to me?

My parents are clearly quite worried about me, but they are happy to see that I at least look fine. Dinner is basically a running question-and-answer period, during which time they dig for clues about rehab, my discharge, how I am feeling, and most important, if I am still drinking or doing drugs. I feel obliged to bend the truth slightly (for their sake, of course): "Absolutely not. I'm done," I say.

After dinner I head over to Porter's new place. He has the top two stories of a three-bedroom house in South Norwalk (aka "SoNo"), which he is sharing with two other guys. I enjoy being around Porter because he is someone who can always find a way to make himself smile and get pleasure from life.

Last summer, after graduating from college, Porter took most of the money he had made from selling drugs his senior year and traded it in for an incredible five-month European vacation, visiting just about every country on the continent. After coming back home, he accepted a sales job for a pharmaceutical firm and moved in with Chuck, a mutual friend from high school. Just as things are falling apart for me, they seem to be coming together for him. I am quite envious.

More important, since I am the black sheep with both my unit and my friends back in Georgia, I am glad to be home in Connecticut, around my family and Porter, who, though quite bright himself, is the sort of person I can count on to just go with the flow. He simply won't bother to try poking holes in my story.

Upstairs in Porter's house, the two of us smoke the opium that my younger sister Vanessa has just given me. I love it. The high feels so much better than marijuana. It replaces all the anxiety of weed with a jazzy, dreamlike feeling of floating above the ground. Vanessa reveres me. Although she knows all about my stint in rehab, I tell her I have no real problem with drugs, an idea that she immediately embraces.

That night, as we drift around the room, Porter opens up the closet door and finds a brand-new, custom-made sign, still snuggly wrapped in its original plastic sheet: THE BOULEVARD OF BROKEN DREAMS. With great amusement, we mount the sign above the window, christening this room as our drug haven. Our laughter is uncontrollable as we lose ourselves in the absurdity of this ominous harbinger of things to come.

Several hours and several shots of G later, I am at the bar with Porter, Vanessa, and her friend Lisa. Nothing eventful happens: I drink and I do G, over and over, until finally it is time to go home. As we're leaving, Vanessa asks me if I want to go back to Lisa's grandmother's house; Lisa is house-sitting and says we are all welcome to spend the night. Most enticing, though, is the fact that the two girls have a big bag of coke with them, which means that very soon I will be in a much better place.

As soon as we get there we cut up some lines and start throwing back vodka shots, and I also down a couple more shots of GHB. A few hours later the girls call it a night and head off to bed; I tell them I am going to stay up just a wee bit longer. I take another shot of GHB and walk into the downstairs bathroom; to my delight, the medicine cabinet contains Ativan and Percocet.

"Excellent!" I announce, with great satisfaction.

I pop a couple of tablets of each and flop back onto the couch in the den. About fifteen minutes later I'm starting to feel loopy, so I wander upstairs, looking for more trouble. I spot a few more lovely names in the medicine cabinet of Grandma's upstairs bathroom: Demerol and Ultram.

"My lucky day!" I proclaim triumphantly.

I pop two of each. My brain is rapidly becoming a nonpartici-
pant. Watching from the sidelines, I stand in the bathroom for an
indiscernible amount of time, making faces at myself in the mirror.
As the chemicals rush through my bloodstream, the house begins
swirling around me.

I stumble back down the hall, but instead of finding the stairs, I
wind up in Grandma's bedroom. I walk into the middle of the
room and start spinning in a circle, with my arms stretched out
parallel to the floor. I'm a human helicopter, watching the room
swiftly fly by my eyes. Extremely dizzy now and unable to find my
balance, I feel as though I am floating on clouds in a semiconscious, drunken stupor.

I fall down and grab the edge of the bed to help me back up,
only to realize that I'm not able to feel anything anymore in my
extremities. I have turned into marshmallow fluff. Everything is
quickly getting quite blurry. Staggering around the room, I accidentally collide with the closet, and relying on my finely honed
instincts, I decide that it's time to try on some clothes.

I hate to say it, but I don't make a very pretty grandma.

As I bounce around the room in my new ensemble, snooping
around here and there, I suddenly notice a whole lot of shiny
things staring back at me. Unable to resist, I put on a necklace, a
few bracelets, and a brooch. I strut back and forth in front of the
mirror; I now decide that I look pretty damn good.

Quickly surpassing enjoyable levels of being high, I toss the
grandmother's apparel on some empty hangers and put my black
leather jacket back on, but when I return to the jewelry box, I
decide to go with that inner voice that never fails me. I grab two
large handfuls of lucky charms, stuff them in my jacket pockets,
and, with my eyes barely open and my hands holding the wall for
navigation and balance, I slowly stumble back downstairs and
onto the couch.

As I lie there, I notice that my breathing is becoming quite shallow and my heart rate has slowed to a virtual standstill. Very anxious and nauseous, I decide there is nothing I can do if I am overdosing, so I just close my eyes and hope for the best.

The next morning, in a very foggy, half-asleep state, I can hear the girls' voices from the kitchen. Although I think I remember just about everything from the previous night, I'm shocked to find my pockets bulging with jewelry. I know what I have done but can't believe I've actually done it. Hearing someone call my name, I hurriedly pull the blanket over me. Vanessa walks into the room.

"Hey, you up? Lisa has to get going, so we're going to take off now. Cool? We'll get breakfast at the diner or something."

"Yeah, that's fine, just give me a sec."

I hastily take off the last few pieces of jewelry that I am still wearing, shove everything in my jacket, stand up, and walk into the kitchen. Everything is happening too fast, and I am too scared to tell the truth. I decide that maybe I can figure out a way to return the stuff later.

I have no clue where we are, and on the way home I am too nervous and tired to pay attention to any landmarks that might help me get back later in the day. But I'm too embarrassed to tell the truth, so I say nothing, and Vanessa drops me off at home. Shortly after lunch I am sitting in my bedroom, staring at the jewelry that I've laid out on my bed, when my parents call me from the other room: "Mike, we're running late."

"Yeah, I know, I'm coming."

My plans for returning the goods bear no fruit. I decide to keep the stuff near me until I think of what to do, so I throw it all in my suitcase and head to the airport. A few days later, when I am back in Savannah, my sister calls me, asking me bluntly if I have stolen the jewelry; things are not looking good.

Since returning to Savannah, I have come up with no plan, except possibly to fence the jewelry—I'd be lying if I said that doesn't constantly pop into the back of my head. This frankly seems to be the easiest and most profitable solution. However, although I have definitively decided that I am not going to pawn the jewelry, I simply do not want to admit what I've done.

"Mike, honestly, just tell me the truth, I won't be mad."

"Vanessa, listen to me, I'm telling you the truth. I would never do something like that."

Later, after talking to Lisa and again denying what I've done, I realize that it has to end—regardless of how terrible it looks. So I call my sister and tell her the truth. The next day I ship all the jewelry to her overnight, praying that the police will be left out of the situation. They are, but that does not diminish the fact that in addition to everything else, I am now a thief as well.

33

Me Love You Long Time
May 2002

D ude, I don't fucking believe that shit," I say, as we walk down the dark, crowded Atlanta sidewalk.

Porter is in Atlanta for the week, attending the beginner sales training course for the pharmaceutical company that hired him one month earlier. I am visiting him. I still can't believe he got the job.

It is 2:00 AM, my last night in town, and the two of us are restless. I recently popped several of the pure ephedrine pills that used to be sold in gas stations. Ephedrine can drastically increase one's libido. Coupled with my endless guzzling of GHB, which is also known for making one extremely frisky, suffice it to say that I am quite the nonsensical, horny freak. I can sense that more bad decisions are in my near future.

Recently, on this same trip, Porter visited the local massage parlor we are now standing before. Despite his being the idea man for this jaunt, having given this place such high kudos, when we arrive at the establishment, he waits outside; I am undeterred.

Walking into the massage parlor, I am confronted by two distinct sets of people: sketchy, lowlife undesirables; and scary, dirty-looking, scantily clad Asian women. Quickly realizing that I'm not the latter, I place myself in the category of the fine gentlemen. After paying the hostess my initial fee, I drink another capful of G and wait for my name to be called.

I'm not sure how much time has passed, because I know that, depending on how much of an overdose of G one takes, a G coma can last anywhere from a few minutes to several hours. I've felt these symptoms numerous times before. The sleeplike state often hits with just seconds of warning and almost always results in a very disoriented, unaware, and hazy condition upon awakening. It usually takes several minutes for things to begin to process again, as you attempt to clarify where you are and what has happened. Being on the brink of falling asleep can be even worse, because your head bobs in all directions and your eyes open and close like a shutter box; you hover in a state of limbo that lies somewhere between conscious and unconscious, desperately trying to remain awake.

This is my current situation.

Twenty minutes later, I'm lying on my back as my eyes swirl in and out of consciousness. I'm struggling to stay awake and focus on an anorexic-looking Asian woman in her mid-thirties. Her jagged yellow teeth, dirty hair, unsettling makeup, and long black press-on nails all conspire to make a frightening image indeed.

I remember having to lean on the Asian woman for balance as we walked back to her room. It was all I could do to keep from falling to the ground. In her room, as I swayed back and forth, I remember that she told me to just lie down as she undressed me herself. Then she straddled me, and although I never came, she soon stopped, complaining, "You no participate." I had become more unconscious than awake.

I mumble the words "How much?"

"No worry. Already taken care of," she responds.

As I get dressed, things rapidly begin clearing up, and my mind becomes reattached to what is actually going on around me. Since I never completely passed out, the recovery is relatively quick. On my way outside, I stop in the bathroom and do another small dose of G, which does nothing to soften the coming blow. When I tell Porter I had sex with one of the girls, he responds, "Damn, you actually had sex with one of those girls?"

Wonderful. My one solace had been that Porter had done the exact same thing—that my friend was just as disgusting and pathetic as I am. Apparently, in my messed-up ephedrine and G-ridden state, I had misunderstood. Now there is no escaping it: I am a scumbag. Moreover, to add icing to the cake, I soon realize that while I was passed out, the woman cleaned out my wallet—to the tune of more than $300. It's a great day to be me.

34

The Green Fairy

June 2002

I stare up at the sky, entranced by the horizon but even more so by the clouds, which dance before me, calling for me to do one thing and one thing only. *"Paint us!"* they scream.

"Man, I love that shit," I say, chuckling.

A few months ago, with out-processing rapidly approaching, I had started to think about how I would approach life back in the civilian sector. First and foremost, I had to determine what sort of job I would look for. Unsure of any interests besides writing and art, I made only weak, half-assed attempts at finding a new job, going through the motions but completely apathetic to the whole venture. After my experience in February with the van Gogh documentary, I had become enthralled with the artist, reading everything I could find about his life.

As my fascination with Vincent grew, so did my desire to try absinthe, which I had never tried but which seemed to have been a van Gogh staple. Shortly thereafter I received my first bottle of absinthe: a vintage, distilled, $250 bottle from the Czech Republic. Absinthe and I were a perfect match.

Well-known for its endemic use around the turn of the twentieth century in Western Europe, the drink was extremely popular with some of the most famous artists and writers of the era. The alcohol, predominantly emerald in color due to the fact that it's distilled from wormwood leaves, turns a milky white hue after cold water is added. It is also extremely bitter, which explains the traditional custom of adding sugar. Thujone is the psychoactive chemical responsible for absinthe's renowned reputation.

For those unacquainted with the liquor, strong absinthe has psychedelic effects, which put one in a very jovial, trancelike state in which shapes, colors, and patterns all seem to magnify themselves with surprising intensity. However, unlike the effects of other drugs, the effects of absinthe are in many ways more intense in the days following its use; the sky, hillside, and rivers all seem completely surreal, like a beautiful impressionist painting. It also grants an incredible boost to one's imagination and creativity.

The downside of (strong) absinthe can be enormous, however: the banned liqueur is notorious for inducing madness. Having ordered several bottles with the highest thujone content ever available (even in the late 1800s), I am fully prepared to embrace the absinthe experience. At a time when I know that I want to focus more on my creative side, the visual and artistically enhancing effects of absinthe fit me like a glove.

The green fairy is becoming my most trusted companion. Bar none, absinthe is my all-time favorite drug of choice, I think, staring at the breathtaking scenery around me.

35

Final Out

July 2002

I t's July 15, 2002. I'm officially done with out-processing. I sign out of my unit for the last time, and after a brief excursion to Florida for a quick farewell drug romp, I head back to Connecticut.

I served a total of one year and seven months as a commissioned officer. Including my time at the Academy, I have been living in a military environment for a little more than six years. To be honest, based on my current condition, I have no regrets about leaving.

With my car fully packed, I am driving on Interstate 95—the same highway that took me to Fort Stewart almost one year ago. However, things feel much different this time, because both my car and my life are heading in the opposite direction.

Alone, with so much concrete to cover, I am lost among my thoughts. I reflect on the past year and try to make sense of it all. *Fuck rehab. Things happen for a reason; this all happened for a purpose. The army simply isn't where I am meant to be right now. I am better off without the army, and it is certainly better off without me!*

A few moments pass. "Fuck!" I yell, as I slam my hands against the steering wheel. *If all this was for a reason, then why can't I escape the overwhelming feeling that I failed?*

"God damn it all!" I scream. *I could have been a good officer. I know I could. My commander knew I could've. He even gave me a good Officer Evaluation Report. It's all bullshit, isn't it? He was just being a good guy. My review doesn't mean anything, does it? God damn it, Michael, why the fuck do you care so much?* Assuming that I could have been a good officer, I wonder what it would have been like to be responsible for a large group of people who actually respected me as their leader. *Another time, another place; who knows, it might've actually been kinda cool!*

If it would have been anything like my West Point experience, which in retrospect was the best and most rewarding time of my life, I imagine that my stint as an officer would have been extremely arduous, exhausting, and at times miserable—but also the sort of experience that I'd always keep close to me, as a defining aspect of who I am, for the rest of my life.

I pause for a few moments. My thoughts are once again scattered, pulled in too many directions for me to focus. There are simply too many things to think about. I try to step back, calm myself, and deal with them one at a time.

Well, if anyone asks, I'll just tell them I got a medical discharge. That's almost the truth. After all, I do have chronic back pain, back spasms, a herniated disk in my neck, and that nerve damage shit.

During the past six months I've been making the rounds of the doctors again, hoping to find out something concrete about my ever-increasing neck, shoulder, and back pain. Although I saw numerous physicians at West Point and during OBC, it wasn't until two months ago that someone finally suggested I get an MRI. Two weeks later I was told that I had a herniated disk in my neck, which apparently I'd been living with for quite some time. Based on these results, a neurologist sent me for an electromyogram (EMG), which checks for nerve problems by sticking needles in key areas up and down one's body. My EMG revealed that I have cervical radiculopathy, a problem with the nerves in my left arm that causes loss of feeling in my hand and fingers, shaking and twitching, and shooting pain throughout my neck and shoulder. Quite a mess.

In light of these new developments, my judge advocate general (JAG) lawyer told me that I was legally entitled to submit paperwork asking for a medical discharge in lieu of the pending honorable discharge. The deciding factor for me was the time it would take—roughly an extra six months for the medical discharge (assuming it was even approved). Ultimately, I decided that my desire to be out of the army far exceeded any of the admittedly considerable advantages that a medical discharge might offer, such as easier employment, monetary benefits (which always accompany a service-connected disability), and guaranteed health coverage for life. Another time, another place, six months in the military would not be an issue; however, right now there are too many other variables. I am rapidly coming apart, with chemicals pouring out at the seams. I need to move on.

After several more moments pass, I ask myself another piercing question. "Jesus, how did this all happen? I didn't even do any drugs before West Point. Is the army to blame? Would I have been fine somewhere else?" *That's horseshit,* I think.

A few minutes go by before my mind turns back to thoughts of much greater gravity. It used to be just rumors, but by now everyone knows that my (former) unit, along with almost the entire post, is getting ready for deployment to Iraq. I have very conflicted feelings. *No one should want to go to war; and if they do, they're morons. Want to defend your country—yes. Want to honorably fulfill your duties—yes. Want to go to war—no.*

Although I do believe that a soldier is honor-bound to defend his country if called upon to do so, I am still glad not to be training and fighting in the desert, in gas masks and scorching hot heat, for the better part of the next year. However, I do feel less deserving of my West Point diploma when I think of all my friends being sent to fight, while I use my time primarily for hedonistic purposes. But make no mistake about it: I am happy to be out of the army, happy to be avoiding a war that I believe is an egregious mistake, happy to be going home, and happy to be reentering civilian life.

Yes, I am finally getting my life back on track. I stare off down the highway, part of me happy, part of me wondering what's to come. *Where the hell am I really going? Do I even have a plan?*

A few minutes pass as my mind tosses around different ideas before settling on something it likes. *Sound body, sound mind.*

Disregarding the pain I am feeling in my neck, back, and shoulders, I decide it is time to start taking steroids again, to jump-start my reimmersion into weight lifting and fitness. Exercise will be a key aspect of my mission toward rebuilding a healthy, well-rounded self.

What else, though? I think. After another several minutes, I latch onto another aphorism. *Work hard, play hard.* I decide that balance is important. Since I plan to devote a significant amount of time to writing and exercise, I will not begrudge myself a little relaxation and partying, if it's kept in control. *All things in moderation, including moderation,* I conclude.

My current routine (the basics of which I plan to carry with me to Connecticut) has included doing cocaine every other weekend with Eric and Chad in Florida, absinthe daily, and GHB only at night and no more than five times a week. In line with my decision to use drugs, but only sparingly, I've prepared for my discharge from the army by having Vanessa purchase mushrooms and opium for me (both of which will be awaiting my arrival in Connecticut), and by ordering a shipment of various drugs (Ultram, Xanax, Ambien, and Valium) off the Internet. Besides moderation, another key component I want to ensure is variety; together, these two guidelines will surely keep any repercussions in check.

"It's about time, Michael. It's about time. Everything's falling into place. I'm going to start living life again, on my own, and, even more important, on my own terms." My future is locked and loaded.

OFFICER EVALUATION REPORT
For use of this form, see AR 623-105; the proponent agency is ODCSPER

SEE PRIVACY ACT STATEMENT
ON DA FORM 67-8-1

PART I - ADMINISTRATIVE DATA

a. NAME (Last, First, Middle Initial)	b. SSN	c. RANK	d. DATE OF RANK	e. BRANCH	f. PMOS
WINDER, MICHAEL, H.		2LT	2000 12 22	AD	14B

g. UNIT, ORG, STATION, ZIP CODE OR APO, MAJOR COMMAND
HHB, 1st Battalion, 3d Air Defense Artillery, Fort Stewart, GA 31314   FORSCOM

h. REASON FOR SUBMISSION
04   Change of Duty

i. PERIOD COVERED						j. RATED MONTHS	k. NONRATED CODES	l. NO. OF ENCL	m. RATED OFFICER COPY (Check one and date)		n. PSC INITIAL	o. CMD CODE	p. PSC CODE
From Year	Month	Day	Thru Year	Month	Day	7		0	X	1. Given to Officer		FC	FS08
02	01	04	02	07	12					2. Forwarded to Officer			

PART II - AUTHENTICATION (Rated officer's signature verifies officer has seen completed OER Parts I-VII and the admin data is correct)

a. NAME OF RATER (Last, First, MI)	SSN	RANK	POSITION	SIGNATURE	DATE
		CPT	Battalion S4		

b. NAME OF INTERMEDIATE RATER (Last, First, MI)	SSN	RANK	POSITION	SIGNATURE	DATE

c. NAME OF SENIOR RATER (Last, First, MI)	SSN	RANK	POSITION	SIGNATURE	DATE
			Battalion Commander		

d. SENIOR RATER'S ORGANIZATION
HHB, 1st Battalion, 3d Air Defense Artillery
Fort Stewart, GA 31314

BRANCH: AD

SENIOR RATER TELEPHONE NUMBER

e. SIGNATURE: Timothy.Polaske@stewart.army.mil

f. This is a referred report. Do you wish to make comments? ☐ Yes   ☒ No   Yes, comments are attached

PART III - DUTY DESCRIPTION

a. PRINCIPAL DUTY TITLE Assistant Battalion Logistics Officer

b. POSITION AOC/SSI

c. SIGNIFICANT DUTIES AND RESPONSIBILITIES. REFER TO PART IV, DA FORM 67-9-1

Assistant Battalion S4 for a rapid deployment Forward Area Air Defense (FAAD) Battalion assigned to the 3d Infantry Division (Mechanized), with a mission to respond to worldwide contingencies with 18 hours. Assist with the training, welfare, and readiness of three soldiers and their family members as well as managing the accountability of battalion property valued in excess of $140 million. Assist with executing and maintaining a battalion operating budget of approximately $2.8 million; arrange and coordinate all contracting operations with sources external to the battalion; serve as the assistant Battalion Deployment Officer.

PART IV - PERFORMANCE EVALUATION - PROFESSIONALISM (Rater)

CHARACTER Disposition of the leader: combination of values, attributes, and skills affecting leader actions

a. ARMY VALUES (Comments mandatory for all "NO" entries. Use PART Vb)

	Yes	No			Yes	No
1. HONOR: Adherence to the Army's publicly declared code of values	X		5. RESPECT: Promotes dignity, consideration, fairness, & EO		X
2. INTEGRITY: Possesses high personal moral standards; honest in word and deed	X		6. SELFLESS-SERVICE: Places Army priorities before self		X
3. COURAGE: Manifests physical and moral bravery	X		7. DUTY: Fulfills professional, legal, and moral obligations		X
4. LOYALTY: Bears true faith and allegiance to the U.S. Constitution, the Army, the unit, and the soldier					X

b. LEADER ATTRIBUTES / SKILLS / ACTIONS: First, mark "YES" or "NO" for each block. Second, choose a total of six that best describe the rated officer. Select one from ATTRIBUTES, two from SKILLS (Competence), and three from ACTIONS (LEADERSHIP). Place an "X" in the appropriate numbered box with optional comments in PART Vb. Comments are mandatory in Part Vb for all "No" entries.

b.1. ATTRIBUTES (Select 1)

X MENTAL Fundamental qualities and characteristics	☒ NO	2. PHYSICAL Maintains appropriate level of physical fitness and military bearing	☒ NO	3. EMOTIONAL Displays self-control, calm under pressure	☒ NO

b.2. SKILLS (Competence) (Select 2) Skill development is part of self-development; prerequisite to action

1. CONCEPTUAL Demonstrates sound judgment, critical/creative thinking, moral reasoning	☒ NO	X INTERPERSONAL Shows skill with people; coaching, teaching, counseling, motivating and empowering	☒ NO	X TECHNICAL Possesses the necessary expertise to accomplish all tasks and functions	☒ NO
		4. TACTICAL Demonstrates proficiency in required professional knowledge, judgment, and warfighting			☒ NO

b.3. ACTIONS (LEADERSHIP) (Select 3) Major activities leaders perform: influencing, operating, and improving

INFLUENCING Method of reaching goals while operating / improving	X COMMUNICATING Displays good oral, written, and listening skills for individuals / groups	☒ NO	2. DECISION-MAKING Employs sound judgment, logical reasoning and uses resources wisely	YES ☒	3. MOTIVATING Inspires, motivates, and guides others toward mission accomplishment	☒ NO
OPERATING Short-term mission accomplishment	X PLANNING Develops detailed, executable plans that are feasible, acceptable, and suitable	☒ NO	5. EXECUTING Shows tactical proficiency, meets mission standards, and takes care of people/resources	☒ NO	6. ASSESSING Uses after-action and evaluation tools to facilitate consistent improvement	☒ NO
IMPROVING Long-term improvement in the Army; its people and organizations	7. DEVELOPING Invests adequate time and effort to develop individual subordinates as leaders	☒ NO	8. BUILDING Spends time and resources improving teams, groups and units; fosters ethical climate	☒ NO	X LEARNING Seeks self-improvement and organizational growth; envisioning, adapting and leading change	☒ NO

c. APFT: PROFILE   DATE: SEP 01   HEIGHT: 74   WEIGHT: 180   YES

d. JUNIOR OFFICER DEVELOPMENT - MANDATORY YES OR NO ENTRY FOR RATERS OF LTs AND WOs.

WERE DEVELOPMENTAL TASKS RECORDED ON DA FORM 67-9-1a AND QUARTERLY FOLLOW-UP COUNSELINGS CONDUCTED?   ☒ YES   ☐ NO   ☐ NA

DA FORM 67-9, OCT 97   REPLACES DA FORM 67-8, 1 SEP 79, WHICH IS OBSOLETE, 1 OCT 97   USAPA V2.01

NAME WINDER, MICHAEL, H.   **SSN**   **PERIOD COVERED** 020104 — 020712

PART V - PERFORMANCE AND POTENTIAL EVALUATION (Rater)

a. EVALUATE THE RATED OFFICER'S PERFORMANCE DURING THE RATING PERIOD AND HIGHER POTENTIAL FOR PROMOTION

| ☐ OUTSTANDING PERFORMANCE, MUST PROMOTE | ☒ SATISFACTORY PERFORMANCE, PROMOTE | ☐ UNSATISFACTORY PERFORMANCE, DO NOT PROMOTE | ☐ OTHER (Explain) |

b. COMMENT ON SPECIFIC ASPECTS OF THE PERFORMANCE AND POTENTIAL FOR PROMOTION. REFER TO PART III, DA FORM 67-9 AND PART IVa, b, AND c DA FORM 67-9-1.

While serving in the Battalion Logistics section, 2LT Winder successfully performed all duties asked of him, and consistently improved his performance through his demonstrated initiative and dedication to the section's success. From his first day with the section, Mike expressed an eagerness to learn, when he was trained and assumed the responsbilities for managing the battalion's daily expenses. Mike's efforts in this area directly contributed to the battalion meeting its annual spending projections.2LT Winder demonstrated initiative by working with the division's contracting office to negotiate purchasing contracts for over 100 pieces of equipment valued at over $110,000.00. His professionalism in coordinating and developing relationships with agents from several officeswas essential to the battalion receiving key vehicle components in time for a contingency deployment in May 2002. Due to his efforts and the base of respect he had developed between our battalion and all companies involved, Mike was able to arrange for equipment manufacture and delivery in one quarter of the normal lead time. In supporting the two short-notice contingency deployments since his arrival in the section, Mike's ability to react to unexpected problems and identify feasible solutions contributedto both deployments' success. His efforts proved valuable to overseeing correct completion of all predeployment requirements, and meeting the support needs of the soldiers being deployed. Mike is an intelligent, artriculate, and loyal individual whose efforts to date have left the Battlion Logistics section a more efficient and capable organization. These attributes will benefit any organization 2LT Winder serves with in the future.

c. IDENTIFY ANY UNIQUE PROFESSIONAL SKILLS OR AREAS OF EXPERTISE OF VALUE TO THE ARMY THAT THIS OFFICER POSSESSES. FOR ARMY COMPETITIVE CATEGORY CPT THROUGH LTC. ALSO INDICATE A POTENTIAL CAREER FIELD FOR FUTURE SERVICE.

PART VI - INTERMEDIATE RATER

PART VII - SENIOR RATER

a. EVALUATE THE RATED OFFICER'S PROMOTION POTENTIAL TO THE NEXT HIGHER GRADE

I currently senior rate ____5____ officers in this grade

X compared DA Form 67-9-1 was received with this report and considered in my evaluation and review ☒ YES ☐ NO (Explain in c)

| ☐ BEST QUALIFIED | ☐ FULLY QUALIFIED | ☒ DO NOT PROMOTE | ☐ OTHER (Explain below) |

b. POTENTIAL COMPARED WITH OFFICERS SENIOR RATED IN SAME GRADE (OVERPRINTED BY DA)

c. COMMENT ON PERFORMANCE/POTENTIAL

2LT Winder is being removed from the service under Chapter 4, AR 600-8-24.

☐	ABOVE CENTER OF MASS (Less than 50% in top box; Center of Mass if 50% or more in top box)
☐	CENTER OF MASS
☐	BELOW CENTER OF MASS RETAIN
☒	BELOW CENTER OF MASS DO NOT RETAIN

d. LIST 3 FUTURE ASSIGNMENTS FOR WHICH THIS OFFICER IS BEST SUITED. FOR ARMY COMPETITIVE CATEGORY CPT THROUGH LTC, ALSO INDICATE A POTENTIAL CAREER FIELD FOR FUTURE SERVICE.

36

The Boulevard of Broken Dreams

August 2002

Today I am moving in with Porter, Chuck, and Paul, who live on the top two floors of a three-story house in Norwalk, Connecticut. Norwalk is a diverse, growing community bordering Westport, the town where I grew up.

Looking at the place from the street, I see a ten-foot-wide driveway separating the house from its neighbor to the right, about ten feet of grass between it and the home to the left, and roughly twenty feet of grass that separates the metal fence bordering the sidewalk from the steps of the dilapidated home.

Approaching closer, I see two doors. The one to the left opens onto a staircase that brings visitors to the second floor of this worn-down, faded white house, and the door to the right leads to a one-bedroom apartment on the first floor that is inhabited by the owner's sister—a friendly, outgoing, average-looking, and slightly overweight Greek woman in her mid-thirties.

Before bringing my stuff in, I decide to take advantage of the rest of the guys' absence and take a look around. At the top of the staircase, I come to the door to Paul's bedroom—without a doubt the messiest, most cluttered bedroom of any adult I have ever seen, inhabited by one of the messiest slobs I've ever met.

Making a left in front of Paul's door, I immediately pass his bathroom—a dirty, disgusting display that no human being (besides himself) would ever contemplate using. A few short steps past the bathroom, I come to the kitchen, also in frightening and sloppy disarray. Everyone seems to have left their dirty dishes for someone else to clean.

Just past the kitchen is the den that I've been told no one ever uses—except to smoke, drink, and do drugs.

Heading back the way I came, I pass Paul's bedroom door again and walk into the living room of the house. It has a couple of old couches along two walls and connected in an L shape, a large glass coffee table, and a television against the wall on the other side of the room. Past the living room I come to a door on the right, which opens onto another staircase, which leads to the third floor.

At the top of this second staircase, the small, reasonably clean bathroom used by Chuck and Porter is on the right, and Porter's bedroom is on the left. I know not to go into Porter's room unless I want to be recorded: his hidden camera is set up on sensor mode, secretly videotaping the unsuspecting girls he brings back late at night.

Walking past the bathroom, Chuck's bedroom is on the right; it's a normal, well-kept room, appropriately belonging to the only normal individual living in the house. Finally, at the end of the ten-foot hallway, is another bedroom, an extremely small alcove, roughly eight feet by fourteen feet, with a low, sloping ceiling. It's the same room where Porter and I partied back in April, where we found the ominous sign THE BOULEVARD OF BROKEN DREAMS.

It doesn't take me long to settle in and make the Boulevard my own. Although I have no money coming in, I do have three platinum credit cards, so one of the first things I did when I moved back to Connecticut was buy a reasonably nice mattress for $1,000. I now set it on the far side of the Boulevard, parallel to the far wall it is pushed against, underneath the room's sole window. I also hang a beaded window curtain, imprinted with the beautiful butterfly I see as the sun shines through the window onto my face. The infamous plaque and namesake of the room stays mounted above the window, just where Porter and I had placed it originally.

To the left of the door I place a two-by-three-foot desk, on which I put my laptop, a few toys and trinkets, and a West Point beer pitcher on top of which I keep one of my prized possessions, my "Say No to Drugs" soccer ball, signed by all the patients and staff that were with me in rehab the day I was kicked out.

Between my desk and the bed I place a very small dresser and two old white bookcases, which house my books and my large collection of toys. To further augment my "boy who never grew up" persona, I have more toys hanging from the windows, sitting on my bed, strewn against the walls, and even hanging from the light cord in the middle of the room. (What can I say? I like toys.)

On the wall above the head of my bed I hang a Jim Morrison poster, and on the wall adjacent to my bed, next to the window, I hang postcard-size replicas of works by Vincent van Gogh, Pablo Picasso, Joan Miró, René Magritte, Claude Monet, Salvador Dali, Jackson Pollock, Wassily Kandinsky, Roy Lichtenstein, Henri Rousseau, and Giorgio de Chirico. Above the foot of my bed I put a Jimi Hendrix poster, and across the room, above my desk, a Pink Floyd tapestry.

I am eclectic, to say the least.

After finishing the main layout of the room, I turn my attention to my other necessities. Between the second bookcase and my bed is just enough room for my toiletry case, which contains bottles of Xanax, Prozac, Valium, Hydroxycut, and Ambien, all appropriately labeled.

On the bottom shelf of the bookcase closest to my bed, concealed by one of my stuffed animals, I store a bag containing my four bottles of Vicodin—720 (10 mg) pills in total. I've recently acquired these from an online pain clinic, whose doctor was more than willing to fill my prescription after I faxed him the medical records describing my back problems.

In the back of my top dresser drawer I stash my bottle of GHB, and on the floor of my closet, still in the box it came in, is a large magic mushroom growing kit, also recently purchased online. Finally, on the small shelf above the clothing rod in the closet, I hide my cocaine in a box pushed all the way to the back.

On moving in, I know right away that this house is going to have an interesting dynamic. We are four young men in our mid-twenties who all party reasonably heavily, three of whom actively use illegal drugs. Several hours later, after I'm all moved in and the guys are all home, I meet Paul, the only one of my three room-mates whom I don't already know. I quickly come to realize why I've been warned that there is so much tension so often.

"So what're your plans?" asks Paul, a five-foot-eleven former personal trainer and amateur bodybuilding competitor.

"Gonna get banged up!" I say, laughing.

"Ah, I like you already. Was a little worried about you, since you're friends with that piece-of-shit Porter, but I think you're okay, Winder," he replies. Paul's genuine, unwavering hatred of Porter amuses me greatly.

"Thanks, man. Yeah, I know Porter can be a pain in the ass."

"Dude, no offense, but he really fucking sucks. Honestly, I've almost killed the fucker a couple times."

I'm not surprised. But I'm also guessing that you have a bit of a tem-per, my friend. Regardless, Porter probably wouldn't be worse off for a little "reality check," I think.

Paul is telling me nothing new. I'm well aware of the fact that Porter is completely oblivious to everyone and everything around him unless there is something in it for him, so it doesn't surprise me that he would prove to be such a pain in the ass to live with. As an only child, he is used to being the center of attention. Furthermore, having never received any real discipline, he is quite prone to tantrums, very selfish, always looking out for himself, and often rude; if he is questioned about his behavior, he immediately lashes out and becomes extremely combative. In general, he's got a very alienating personality.

"Yeah, I know. But you gotta stick by your boys."

"I guess—you're a better man than me, Winder. I'd have ditched that clown years ago."

"Chuck's cool, though, right?" I say, referring to our other room-mate. Although Chuck and I played on my high school basketball team together, he is two years younger than I, so I don't know him all that well. What I do know is that he's six feet three, clean-cut, and athletically built—the classic frat-boy type.

"Oh, yeah, he's hell cool. Easy to get along with, usually in a good mood and smiling, and really just loves drinking and having a good time. Plus, unlike Porter, he's actually respectful, cleans up after himself, and is considerate of others."

"Yeah, although we went to the same high school, I don't really know him that well. But he always seemed like a good guy."

"Yeah, definitely. And we need him, Winder," Paul says, chuckling.

"Oh, yeah, why's that?"

"He's the only sane individual living here!" Paul replies, highly amused.

"Oh, yeah, 'cause he doesn't do drugs, you mean?"

"Exactly. The rest of us are all just twisted fucks," he jokes. "So, back to my first question: What are you going to do? Are you look-ing for a job or something?"

Hmmm . . . I wonder why Porter and Chuck have such issues with him. They paint him as a liar, schemer, and manipulator. I'm usually so good at sizing people up right away, but I just don't see it. He comes across as genuine to me. Hell, I'm pretty sure we'll get along damn fine.

"Well, right now I'm just trying to settle into my new life here," I say. "I'll kind of take it as it comes and see what happens."

"Sounds good."

"I'm also planning to go to law school next fall."

"Cool."

Yeah, I guess. But maybe you can tell me why I'm applying again?

"Yeah, that's my main focus. I've already registered for the December LSATs, so I'm gonna be spending a significant portion of my time the next several months just prepping for that shit."

"Yeah, definitely. I've heard it's some hard shit."

"Yup. It'll either make ya or break ya. I'm even thinking about doing a Princeton Review course or something. Gonna run it by the folks."

"Good stuff, man."

"Thanks."

"So, what about flow? What's your cash situation like?"

"Well, as far as money is concerned, I've already nailed down unemployment—that's $380 per week."

"Fuck, yeah, bro!" he says, slapping my shoulder.

"Yeah, total bonus."

"Definitely. So how long does that nice cushion last?"

"Well, I'll continue to get checks as long as I am 'actively seeking full-time work'—which, when coupled with the large credit line still remaining on my three credit cards, is more than enough to sustain me for the near future."

"Ha, ha, ha—that's great financial planning!"

I think he thinks I'm joking. Yeah, I definitely dig him. Good dude. No doubt.

"Hey man, great meeting you," I say. "I'm gonna get ready and then go meet your boy to pick up the good stuff."

"Excellent, man. Sounds like a plan. Catch ya in a bit," he says, as he walks away.

"Definitely, and get your legs ready for some early snow, bro," I shout back, as I head outside to meet his connection, aware of his laughter in the background.

God damn! What's their problem with him? Am I missing something? I mean, I could give two shits that he's the resident drug dealer of the house, regularly cooking up ketamine in the kitchen's oven. The only problem I can see myself having with Paul is his uncleanliness. Even conservatively speaking, Paul's hygiene is seriously terrible.

A few hours later, with a few lines of cocaine up my nose and a couple of capfuls of G in my stomach, I'm once again staring at myself in the mirror. I seem to be doing this a lot lately. I feel a great sense of optimism. *Things are falling right into place,* I think.

I expect that I'll probably get along with all three of my new roommates. My only worry is whether my constant drug and alcohol consumption will eventually wear thin on any of them. I doubt it. If anyone, maybe Chuck—but I doubt it. And anyhow, it'll soon start tapering down. I'm just blowing off a little steam for now.

I snort another line off the table in the Boulevard, before walking back to the mirror in the bathroom.

"Good work, Michael. Maybe you fucked up here and there. Failing out of rehab, losing Lynn, and all the rest, but now you're doing good work. Things are falling into place for you, and they're only going to get better! Be proud of yourself," I say, convincingly, effortlessly conjuring a seemingly perfect smile.

37

The Routine
September 2002

MY DAILY SCHEDULE
(August, September, and October)

11:00 AM   Wake up and move straight into proper revelry (on Saturday and Sunday, this starts at 1:00 PM.)

11:05 AM   Take twelve Hydroxycut, one-half bar Xanax, and two Prozac

11:10 AM   Shower and shave

11:30 AM   Dress, do hair, and (Monday or Thursday only) inject steroids

11:45 AM   Eat breakfast, watch television, and "actively seek full-time work"

12:30 PM   Leave house and "actively seek full-time work"

12:45 PM   Head to local park on waterfront and take one Vicodin

1:00 PM   Find open bench and begin working on poetry or "actively seek full-time work"

2:00 PM   Take twelve Hydroxycut and one-half bar Xanax

2:30 PM   Leave for lunch or "actively seek full-time work"

2:45 PM   Eat lunch at local restaurant

3:15 PM	Leave restaurant and take one Vicodin
3:30 PM	Go back to park bench and begin studying for the LSAT or "actively seek full-time work"
5:00 PM	Take twelve Hydroxycut, one-half bar Xanax, one Vicodin, and leave for gym or work on book
7:00 PM	Pick up take-out food from local restaurant
7:15 PM	Have dinner back at house and watch television
7:45 PM	Take two Vicodin and drink three glasses of absinthe
8:15 PM	Read in bedroom; on a good day, eat mushrooms or smoke opium
9:15 PM	Do first line of coke, take one-half bar Xanax, and get ready to go out
9:30 PM	Start drinking vodka
9:45 PM	Do second line of coke
10:10 PM	Do third line of coke
10:30 PM	Do fourth line of coke, take two Vicodin, and walk to local bar
10:45 PM	Arrive at bar, continue drinking
11:00 PM	Do a bump of coke and one-half bar Xanax
11:30 PM	Do a bump of coke
midnight	Do a bump of coke
12:30 AM	(Monday–Wednesday) Do a bump of coke and head home; take one Valium and one Ambien and go to sleep
	(Thursday and Sunday) Do a bump of coke and head home; at home, smoke weed and continue drinking (or throw in some K and coke); eventually take one Valium and one Ambien and go to sleep
12:30 AM	(Friday and Saturday) Do a bump of coke Friday and Saturday night activities continue as follows:
1:00 AM	Do a bump of coke
1:30 AM	Do a bump of coke, one-half bar Xanax, and head home or to club in Portchester, New York

1:45 AM	Arrive home or in Portchester
2:00 AM	If at home, smoke weed or do K—or continue coke and drinking; if in Portchester, continue coke and drinking
3:30 AM	If in Portchester, head home
4:00 AM	At home, smoke weed or do K—or continue coke and drinking
?:?? AM	Take one Valium and one Ambien and go to sleep

My Monthly Budget
(August, September, and October)

Income	
Unemployment Benefits	$1,520
Total Income	**$1,520**

Expenses	

Fixed Expenses

Rent	$450
Car	200
Insurance	150
Gym	60
Subtotal	**$860**

Variable Expenses

Food	$900
Credit Card Payments	300
Phone	60
Gas	60
Other	40
Subtotal	**$1,360**

Drugs & Alcohol

Cocaine	$1,000
Vicodin	200
Xanax	300
Valium	200
Ambien	200
Steroids	250
Hydroxycut	100
Absinthe	600
Alcohol	2,100
Subtotal	**$4,950**

Total Expenses	**$7,170**

Summary

Total Income	$1,520
Total Expenses	$7,170
Net Income	**–$5,650**

The King of Drama Queens
October 2002

I t is the evening of the third Saturday in October, a typical
Saturday night, with the typical routine. Following my normal
schedule of drug and alcohol consumption, I walk to
Amberjacks—one of the local SoNo watering holes, a jazzy restaurant and bar with great music and beautiful staff, where my sister
Vanessa works as a waitress. This is a huge bonus for me, in terms
of drink discounts and introductions to gorgeous waitresses.

I always look forward to my evenings. They're a repetitious blur
and inescapably redundant, but they never seem to last long
enough. I always want to get just a little bit more fucked up. On
this particular night, the bar closes at 1:30 AM, and, as usual, I start
walking home. When Porter calls me on the way, telling me that I
should meet him at some club in Portchester, it's an easy decision.

Day in and day out, I never give myself a break. To be honest,
I'm not able to do so. It is out of my hands. The cycle is too out of
control to stop it without crashing. I am living a balancing act.

Hydroxycut and cocaine compensate for my chronic fatigue from
drinking, giving me the energy to get started in the morning and to
go out at night. Xanax takes care of the shaking and anxiety that's
due to the Hydroxycut and cocaine and aggravated by my constant

dehydration. Prozac keeps my depression, which is exacerbated by my daily drinking and cocaine use, in check. Steroids give me the energy boost and motivation to exercise, which keeps me looking good despite the heavy alcohol consumption. Vicodin gets rid of any pain and is really just good old-fashioned fun. Valium and Ambien allow me to get a decent night's rest in spite of the drugs and alcohol in my system. Absinthe ensures that I am always a bit off-kilter, thus keeping any hope of sanity in check.

Because I'm far too drunk and messed up on cocaine, painkillers, and Xanax to drive, I order a taxi to meet me outside our house. I also grab a fresh gram bag from the Boulevard while I wait for my ride to arrive. Although I do a line right before getting in the cab, I still need a little bump on the way to Portchester—after all, it's a twenty-minute ride. I'm completely apathetic about the fact that the driver's eyes are watching me through the rearview mirror.

I am trapped in an unrelenting, unforgiving cycle of constant, unyielding consumption: I always want to keep going, want to keep doing more, *need* to do more to counteract the effects of something I've already done. I have an answer for everything, and I'm sure that as long as I can maintain my routine, all will be fine. Despite all my efforts, however, there is one area I know I can never stabilize: my emotional makeup. I'm coming apart at the seams.

Walking from the cab, I check my pocket to make sure I still have my bag, but to no avail—it's gone. I descend into a frantic, angry fit as the cabbie drives off with my bag of cocaine resting neatly on his backseat. Without my bag, I am nothing. I feel as though my world and definitely my evening have come crashing down.

"Dude, we gotta go! We gotta get outta here, man!" I tell Porter, after finding him in the club. He ignores me. I tell him again that we have to leave, but he just keeps on dancing, totally unrespon-sive. Furious at having lost my stash, and even more so at being ignored, I grab his shoulder and, desperate to get his attention, start screaming about how I have just been mugged at gunpoint and want to go home.

"Dude, I just got fucking jacked outside at gunpoint! Stop being a fucking asshole, and let's get the hell out of here!"

Despite my ranting and raving, Porter pays me little or no attention, which is normal for him. Realizing that nothing I do will get Porter to pay attention for more than two seconds, I ask for his cell phone, because mine is dead, and I very much want to call another cab so I can just go home to sleep (or do more coke): *"Dude, you're really a fucking prick, You know that? Just give me your damn phone, man, mine's dead."*

Even though Porter pulls out his cell phone, he actually refuses to give it to me, claiming that he is low on minutes. Pushed past any limit of self-control, I grab it from him.

"What the fuck, you fucking prick. Fuck you, bro, fuck you, you fuckin' asshole!" Porter shouts, obviously extremely angry that I took his phone. He grabs my hands, determined to wrestle the phone away from me.

Further irritated at Porter, I do the only rational thing I can think of: I hurl his phone to the ground. It shatters.

I storm out of the club and call a cab from a pay phone.

Upon returning to the Boulevard, I am left with no choice but to take my Valium and Ambien. I am experiencing another minor emotional crash, unable to stop crying until I finally fall asleep.

I slowly wake up to a loud banging noise. "Yo, what the fuck, bro! Where the hell's my phone! Yo, Winder, wake up. I want my phone, bro! Wake the fuck up!" Porter demands, as he pounds on my locked bedroom door the following morning.

Porter has succeeded in at least part of his mission, having actually managed to wake me up. However, he's not getting any phone from me.

"Dude. Get the fuck out of here, man. I don't have your fucking phone."

Apparently he didn't notice me throw it on the ground, or, more likely, he just forgot and never picked it up. Porter often blacks out, forgetting many of our nights, so it isn't a surprise that he doesn't remember much about our argument.

I let loose. *"Fuck you, man! Fuck you, you fucking prick! You don't remember shit, do you? I was fucking mugged last night, bro! Fucking mugged, at fucking gunpoint, and all you care about is your fucking phone! Your fucking phone is on the fucking floor of that fucking club in Portchester, because your sorry ass was such an asshole and wouldn't let me use it. Dude, I don't want anything to do with you! Get the fuck out of here, you piece of shit!"* I scream from my bed.

"Wait, what?" Porter queries, clearly having no idea what I am talking about. *"Fuck that! Fuck you, bro, fuck you! You're such a freaking asshole, bro. You know that? Fuck you!"* he adds, extremely irritated and angry. Porter hates to be reproached.

As I hear him walk away, part of me wants to jump out of bed, run after him, and apologize. But I don't. I can't. And what makes things even worse is that I know it has nothing to do with him and everything to do with me.

The thing that really upsets me is that last night was just par for the course. My lifestyle is wreaking havoc on my nervous system, and since I'm already an emotional person by nature, it's a guarantee that at least a couple nights a week, toward the end of the evening, with all the drugs and alcohol in me, I'll have created completely unnecessary drama. I have been in numerous arguments, most often with Porter, about everything and nothing—and although he is gifted at being a major prick, I have to admit that the arguments are almost always my fault. I am an emotional powder keg: the king of drama queens.

When I left Savannah I envisioned a work-hard, play-hard lifestyle. I wanted to get it all out of my system, but I fear I've gone too far. I'm already feeling like a zombie, and I see things only getting worse. During the course of the past three months I have done more than just succeed in getting it all out of my system; I have also pushed to the breaking point my already seriously unstable, vulnerable, and highly erratic mental, physical, and emotional states. So along with my decision to quit (some) drugs, I decide that I need to move out of the Boulevard—not just because of Porter, but because of me. I simply can't go to bed and wake up under that terrible sign anymore. Even removing it wouldn't matter; it will always be there. The sign is more than just a whimsical decoration; it is the incarnation of the room itself: the Boulevard of Broken Dreams.

Drugs, the Boulevard, anxiety, and unhappiness are all a blur now. Before the incident with Porter, there was no way I would have been able to move out of the house without looking incredibly sketchy. Moving into a house with three guys and then leaving after just two months, without any legitimate reason, would make me look like an insane asshole, and I never would have gone through with it. However, the Portchester situation gives me the excuse I am looking for to leave this hellhole.

The next day I tell Chuck and Paul that this will be my last month. I finally have an excuse—not only to leave, but to be as sad as I have already been feeling. I have felt enough to know that I am done testing my limits with drugs and alcohol. I am done with living a self-destructive lifestyle. With a little more than a week to go before my moving-out date, I become extremely lucky and find an available apartment. I had dreaded the prospect of moving back in with my parents, who surely would have been a nuisance in my life. I certainly don't need anyone monitoring my daily activities or inhibiting my drug and absinthe consumption. Although I'm certain that I'm on the right track and making all the right decisions, I'm also aware that my lifestyle still isn't in accordance with what the general public believes to be proper.

It is time for me to start making some long-overdue adjustments to my life. Things are going to change, and for the better, I think, as the Boulevard slowly disappears from my rearview mirror for good.

Adderall

November 2002

Having just woken up and tended to my magical fungi forest, it's time for me to take care of the rest of my business. I pop ten Hydroxycut and a couple of Vicodin and throw both bottles into my backpack.

Today is November 8, 2002. A week ago I moved into this beat-up, one-bedroom apartment in an area of Connecticut called Black Rock, which is on the outskirts of the city of Bridgeport, bordering the town of Fairfield. I'm subletting the place from a friend's older brother for the remaining seven months of his lease. I've quickly settled into my new routine. I am rarely in the apartment. When I am there, I am almost always in my bedroom—to sleep, to look after my 'shrooms, and to take the necessary pills.

With its cracked, plastered-up walls and weak, uneven wooden floors, this new place in Black Rock is another step down for me, in many respects. The building, a dilapidated brownstone, is drab, cold, and coming apart at the seams (just like me, I reflect!). It isn't glamorous by any stretch of the imagination. Then again, neither am I.

The door of the second-floor apartment opens onto a small hallway, with the apartment's bathroom almost immediately on the right, and the kitchen on the right at the end of the hallway. Continuing through the kitchen, you come to the living room, which contains a couch, table, and television. Past the living room is my bedroom, which I quickly set up similarly to the Boulevard, the only real difference being that now I have one very large machine growing mushrooms in the middle of the room and two smaller ones in the closet. All three are in active use.

Damn, do I have a lot of pills! What timing—another 720 pills arrive right when I decide to go healthy. These are virtually innocuous, though, and will definitely ease the transition. I pop one of my Valium and throw the remainder in my bag alongside the other two bottles. I'm counting on tapping into all three bottles quite regularly throughout the course of the day. *Thank God I received this shit when I did!*

I pause for a moment in front of the mirror, lost in conflicted reflection, as I look myself over, the chemicals rapidly making their way through my bloodstream. *Jesus, Winder. Morning to bedtime. Morning to freaking bedtime. Am I fucking up again?* I wonder.

I pause briefly. *Nah, I mean, who the fuck cares about all that shit? I mean, I don't go out anymore, and I spend my nights reading books, watching television, or just going to the movies. So there's no problem, right? Hmmm . . . but, morning to fuckin' bedtime? God damn it, Winder, you're fucking up again. Aren't I?*

"Fuck you! Fuck you! So what if I've increased my absinthe, Vicodin, and Valium consumption. So fucking what! I'm doing everything right—for the most part. I mean, c'mon, there's been no more alcohol, cocaine, GHB, or Xanax, right? And the Valium— that's just pragmatic thinking. No way I'm going to make the same mistake I made in quitting GHB; this time I am prepared," I say with assured confidence.

I sling the bag over my shoulder and head toward the door before stopping to look back at the mirror. "What?" I ask, unnerved. "Forget it," I whisper, disgruntled. The door can't close fast enough behind me.

Gotta look good. I look good, right? I think, as I look at myself in my car's vanity mirror.

"Yeah, too pretty. No way they'll know what you're on," I say, smiling. *And remember to sound good. Gotta say the right things*, I think, before getting out of my car and walking into the attention deficit/hyperactivity disorder (ADHD) clinic.

"This is a no-brainer. C'mon, it's you. And, anyway, I'm certain that I have ADHD, so it's an easy sell," I say out loud, prepping myself, as I walk toward the building.

Located in a medical complex no more than a few minutes from my parents' home, surrounded by numerous other medical offices, the office I'm visiting (a collaboration of three psychiatrists and two psychologists) comes highly recommended as the preferred ADHD clinic of Westport. Today is my first visit. I have an appointment to see the psychologist responsible for seeing all new patients. His job is to evaluate patients and explore nonmedical treatment if feasible, referring only those patients who need medication to the psychiatrist. My goal is to get that referral.

Sitting in the waiting room, I feel great satisfaction as I ruminate over everything that is currently going on in my life. With my December LSAT rapidly approaching, my drastic lifestyle change could not have come at a more perfect time. Since the LSAT is counted quite heavily toward law school admission, and even though I'm a notoriously good test taker, I am nevertheless taking my preparation as seriously as possible. I'm doing everything right, focusing in on what I know are my two key success factors: taking an LSAT prep course and seeing a psychiatrist about my ADHD. I'm intent on getting Adderall to help me study. It's all positive. All good stuff. My parents are even totally on board and have agreed to sponsor both efforts.

For a few minutes, I'm lost in thought, growing increasingly anxious as I stare at the wall and contemplate going out to the car to get another Valium.

Why do I feel like I'm doing something wrong, then? I wonder. *Fuck!*

While I wait for my name to be called, I skim through the ADHD leaflets scattered around the waiting room. It turns out that

there are actually two types of ADHD: inattentive type and hyper-
active type. I'm amazed at how generic the symptoms are for either
one.

Inattentive Type	Hyperactive Type
• Fails to give close attention to details or makes careless mistakes • Has difficulty sustaining attention • Does not appear to listen • Struggles to follow through on instructions • Has difficulty with organization • Avoids or dislikes tasks requiring sustained mental effort • Loses things • Is easily distracted • Is forgetful in daily activities	• Fidgets with hands or feet or squirms in chair • Has difficulty remaining seated • Runs about or climbs excessively • Has difficulty engaging in activities quietly • Acts as if driven by a motor • Talks excessively • Blurts out answers before questions have been completed • Has difficulty waiting or taking turns • Interrupts or intrudes upon others

Source: www.adhd.com

On one level I'm quite shocked by the universal applicability of
most of these symptoms. It seems to me that *everyone* suffers from
many of these issues. I mean, seriously: "loses things"? Then again,
who am I to second-guess the psychiatric profession? In general,
it's great that the clinic puts this literature out in the waiting room;
it helps take some of the guesswork out of my sales strategy.

"Mr. Winder," a woman calls.

"Yes," I reply.

"Dr. Langston will see you now."

"Thank you," I say, as she shows me to his office. *Game on,
Winder, game on.*

Moments later I'm in the doctor's office; he's sitting across from
me, clearly sizing me up. *Ha! Don't bother—I'm smarter than you,*

bro. This is what I do for a living. You're out of your element, I think, with genuine, ruthless confidence.

"So, what brings you here?"

"Well, I'm currently studying for the LSATs, which I'm taking next month, and I'm just finding it extremely hard to study."

"Law school, that's impressive. And the LSATs are definitely no slouch."

"Thank you."

"Has this always been a problem for you?"

"Well, yes. I've had documented problems since my childhood, ones that have constantly brought me social and work-related troubles throughout my life but that I've struggled to overcome. It was hard, but I managed. I got the best grades I could in high school and graduated from West Point."

"You went to West Point?"

"Yes," I reply, with great satisfaction. *Good work, Mike—the Academy seed has been planted. Ha! Academy grads aren't drug seekers!*

"So, you've had problems that you say have been going on since your childhood, which I will get to in a moment. First, though, I'd like to know how your parents feel about this. I would like to get their input, if at all possible."

"Well, actually I wasn't totally sure about coming down here, but it was my parents who asked me to come down, and they even offered to pay. They seem genuinely concerned," I reply, with slight sincerity. *Man, I'm good,* I think.

"That's good, because I always like to speak with the family when possible. Plus, any documents they do have from your youth will be quite helpful in formulating a correct diagnosis."

No doubt, I think. I then go on to describe what I know are all the symptoms of the ADHD inattentive type. It is easy to show how my life has been negatively impacted: I have had obvious problems with school, home life, relationships, work, and depression. However, I make sure to leave out substance abuse as well as my current use of Prozac, because I know that both are probably instant disqualifiers for the medication I am seeking.

After I finish my tale of woe, the only thing left is to show that even though I have never been diagnosed with the disorder, ADHD is indeed a problem lingering from childhood; this is all too easy to do. My parents have kept all my old teacher evaluation reports from kindergarten through middle school, which show that from a very early age I have been labeled by many teachers as having distinct social problems, failing to interact well with my peers or my instructors, and describing all the symptoms I expressed to the psychologist. It doesn't hurt that I had actually been forced to see an outside psychologist by my elementary school.

It's a slam dunk. After receiving a positive verdict from the psychologist, I stop in to see a doctor at the local walk-in clinic down the street. He calls the psychologist for verification before giving me my first prescription for Adderall: a two-week supply of extended-release tablets. Dosage: one 20 mg tablet per day. In addition, I'm given a referral to see their resident psychiatrist, Dr. Elionder.

Do I have ADHD? I ponder, after popping my first pill.

"Fuck if I know. Ha! Fuck if I care. Mission accomplished!"

Hmmm . . . do I, though? Ah, whatever. I don't know. Ha! What I do know for sure is that with just a little preparation, just about anyone could convince both themselves and their doctor that they have this disorder.

After a few moments, as the fast-acting medication starts to take effect, a genuine, unbridled smile creeps across my welcoming face. *Thank you, God! Thank you! I almost forgot how much this shit rocks!*

I loved Adderall right from the start, back when I was stealing it from Lynn. I know that Adderall will have an immediate and profound impact on my studies, giving me that extra something that I need to sit down and concentrate for the long, incredibly boring task of studying for the LSAT. In addition, I'm also pleased to note that Adderall totally changes my personality for the better, making me extremely outgoing, confident, and almost always in a good mood.

Everything is better. I am better.

40

Frida

December 2002

Two weeks after receiving my first prescription, I make an appointment with Dr. Elionder at the ADHD clinic. I tell him that my current regime, two 20 mg Adderall tablets per day (a lie), isn't working well for me due to unsettling highs and lows. I propose a new prescription for two 30 mg tablets of Adderall per day. Although he tells me that I should be careful because this is an increased dosage, he agrees and gives me the prescription.

That afternoon, in a thoroughly joyous state, reveling in my new acquisition, I head to the library to do some intense, Adderall-focused law school research. Later in the day, on my way out of the building, I'm walking past the racks when my eyes are suddenly captivated by a beautiful book jacket in the middle row, about six books in. Intrigued, I walk over and pick it up. It's *The Diary of Frida Kahlo: An Intimate Self-Portrait.*

Something strikes a chord in me, so I briefly skim through the book, faintly remembering a discussion from high school English class about the doomed Mexican surrealist painter. Such a beautiful person she was, driven to produce such beautiful things, but who unfortunately (and seemingly unfairly) experienced so much pain. I think of van Gogh and that they seem similar. I put the book back in its place and go grab something to eat before my LSAT review class.

A couple of hours later, during class, our teacher gives each of us a handout containing one sample reading from a previous LSAT, which we will use to prepare for the reading comprehension portion of the test; unbelievably, the selection is about Frida Kahlo. Spooked, I cannot see this as just a coincidence. Unable to find any deeper meaning, however, I reluctantly put it to the side for the moment.

Toward the end of this class, because I am again experimenting with larger dosages of Adderall, I have my second panic attack following that first time with Lynn. My heart starts racing so incredibly fast that I feel sure I am having a legitimate heart attack. *Fuck! Where's my Valium when I need it?*

With my instability rapidly increasing, I need to get to the pills I've left in my car. Consequently, I am forced to hastily leave the class in an anxious, sweaty, and highly erratic, hyperventilating fit.

At home, after calming myself down (with a little pharmaceutical help), I am left with conflicted thoughts. *They definitely all noticed. Definitely. No doubt about it. There's simply no way that everyone didn't notice me flipping out when I left. You know, I'll bet they probably even all started laughing the moment I was gone. Fuck! God damn it! There's no way I'm going back. But then, there is always a chance that they didn't all notice. I mean, from what the doctors told me and what I've read, part of the terrible thing about panic attacks is that you always think everyone is watching you, that you are consumed with the idea of how weak you look. And typically, this is all in the panicked individual's head. Hmmm . . . what to do, what to do. Jesus, I'm a jackass.*

Regardless of any embarrassment, I am back in class the following week. Just as I refuse to be dissuaded from returning to class, I will not let this minor hiccup influence my Adderall consumption. It is back to business as usual.

There is one minor change, however. Much to my chagrin, I am forced to move back in with my parents. My new landlord found out that his apartment was being illegally sublet, and I was given one week to pack up and move. I am not overly concerned, though, because I'm confident I've gotten things under control now. Along with my hopes for the coming year, my spirits are soaring. I am definitely glad to have escaped my destructive, drug-infused lifestyle unscathed.

Part Five

ANYA, JESUS,
AND EVERYTHING AFTER

2003

41

Flip the Switch
January 2003

I t's the first week of 2003, around 8:00 AM, and I'm standing alone with my mother in the kitchen. We're the only two awake.

"So, how'd you sleep last night?" she asks, with genuine concern.

I could care less for your genuine concern, I'm going crazy over here, and none of you seems to believe me! Why the fuck doesn't anyone believe me? They're everywhere!

"Damn it, I need some fucking sleep. I haven't slept for more than four freakin' hours—max—over the course of any single night during the past three weeks, Jesus, I just . . ."

"Listen, it'll get better. Don't worry. I'll take you to the doctor later, if you like. But the VA didn't think it was lice. And I'd appreciate you not using that kind of language around me. It's really not right."

"I know. I know. I'm sorry, Mom. It's just that I wish I had some Valium or Ambien or something to help me sleep. I just need some freakin' sleep. It's just driving me nuts. They're driving me nuts."

I'm definitely glad to have escaped my destructive, drug-infused lifestyle unscathed, but I just wish these darn lice would disappear so that I can properly enjoy my return to normality.

"Well, I don't know much about that stuff, but aren't those prescription items? We could go to another doctor and see if he'd prescribe something like that for you."

Jesus, no, you don't know shit. I can order that shit from just about anywhere and have it delivered to our front door by tomorrow morning. A fucking doctor, ha! God damn it! I certainly chose the worst possible time to stop taking those two drugs. What the fuck was I thinking?

"God damn, the fuckin' itching is driving me nuts," I say, to my mom's obvious displeasure, although I can tell she's somewhat wary of reproaching me in my current, wild-eyed state.

"Michael, please," she says, meekly, without directly looking at me, as she goes about her business in the kitchen.

"Yeah, I know. Fine. But you're not the one going absolutely bonkers with freaking lice all over your body."

"I know, and I'm sorry for you. But it'll all go away soon. I promise," my mom says, with obvious empathy, although I still can't tell if she believes me.

Does anyone believe me? Fuck the doctors; they don't know shit. This has to be freaking real!

"Lice, God damn it! Lice! Who the hell my age has freakin' lice?" I shout, as I frenetically pace our relatively small kitchen floor.

"Michael!"

"I'm sorry. I am. Honestly. But I'm going nuts over here. You get that? I'm gonna freakin' lose my mind if I don't do something soon!"

"All right. I understand. Lice can be quite horrible. But you already tried the lice shampoo and . . ."

"What? What were you about to say? What are you thinking over there? You think I'm just making this stuff up? 'Oh, look at Michael, he's having a grand old time over there not sleeping and scratching himself like a goddam madman . . . all freakin' day long!'" I shout.

"Michael, I don't know what to say. You know I care and you know that's not what I think, so I'd appreciate it if you would speak to me . . ."

"Yeah, I know. I *know*. I'm sorry, but it's really driving me crazy, Mom, and I need to do something."

"Okay, well, maybe we should go back to . . ."

"No, screw that; I've got my own plan. Game on! The man has spoken," I proclaim, with enthusiastic intensity and optimism.

"Do you mind if I ask what that is?"

"Well, I've tried the lame, conventional approach. Yeah, I've tried it *their* way. Now it's my turn."

"Okay," my mom whispers, nervously.

"Yeah, I'm doing things my way now."

"What exactly does that mean?"

"Oh, you'll see. Ha! You'll see!" I say, chuckling.

"Would you mind giving me some idea . . . ?"

"All right, already. It's really no big deal. Where do lice live? Hair, that's where! So, now it's time to take the fight right at 'em!"

"And what does that mean, exactly?" my mom asks, her anxiety noticeably increasing.

"Everything gone. I'm shaving the whole enchilada."

"Michael, maybe you had better just go to another . . ."

"No, Mom. This makes sense. I don't know why you don't see it. Lice live in hair. Without it they are nothing. So I'm just going to shave my entire body. I already tried that worthless lice shampoo, and it did nothing. This is the logical option. I don't know why you don't get it."

"You're not going to shave everything, are you?"

"Yup," I say, smiling, triumphantly.

"But Michael—everything?"

"God damn it, Mom! I just need some support here. Besides the total lack of sleep, you know this thing is driving me bonkers. I mean, all day, crawling, and all night, more crawling! You know this!"

"Yes, I know . . ."

"You know that I'm incessantly shaking and scratching myself and that I'm unable to sit still, constantly gyrating in all directions.

Just look at me right now," I reply, as my fingers recklessly scrape my tense body and I squirm to and fro.

"Yes, I know. Maybe, though, stress is playing a factor, and . . ."

"*Wait! God damn it! Wait a freakin'* . . ."

"Michael, please. Please don't talk to me in that tone of voice. I understand that you're having some significant health issues, but please speak to me in a proper manner. I am still your mother."

"Yes, all right. But you're implying that this is all in my mind, and it's not," I say firmly.

"That's not what I meant, and if that's what came across, I apologize. However, I do think you should explore other options before . . ."

"Mom, I've already got the clippers ready in the bathroom. And FYI, I'm not asking for your approval. I'm *telling you* what's going down. I just wanted to keep you in the loop."

"Well, thank you for that. But I do think that maybe you should wait to get your father's opinion," my mom replies, in clear desperation.

"Yeah, whatever. See you in an hour. Yup—smooth as a crazy baby!" I say, chuckling, as I turn to walk toward the bathroom.

"Michael."

"Yes?"

"You're not shaving everything, are you?"

"Oh yeah! It's all gonzo!"

"What about your eyebrows?"

"Gone."

"No. Now listen, you can go ahead with shaving the rest of your body, but I won't have you shaving your eyebrows. Understood?"

"Yeah, fine. I'll appease you on that one. I'll keep the eyebrows. You happy now?" I say, over my shoulder.

"No, not really. But I am glad that you're at least listening to me about your eyebrows."

"Don't want the world to know your son's a freak, do ya?" I yell, as I close the bathroom door and grab the clippers.

I spend more than two hours in the bathroom, meticulously

shaving every square inch of my body—excluding my eyebrows, of course. However, none of this gets rid of the disgusting bugs. Accordingly, I lather my head with shaving cream, virtually forcing my extremely reluctant mother to use a razor to shave it even closer. With the bugs still running rampant across my entire body, I ask my mom to shave my eyebrows, but she is adamantly against this.

"Why? I don't get it? If you don't do it, I will" I say, with the utmost conviction, as I grab the razor from her hand.

"Michael, just talk to your father."

"What? What's the big problem?"

"Honestly, Michael, just take a moment and think about this. Does shaving your eyebrows really make any sense? Do you think it'll really make the difference and put an end to all this?"

I pause, giving my mom's questions some legitimate thought as her unavoidable sense of gravity urges me to reconsider my actions.

"Well, I've shaved everything else, Mom! So, they've got to be, like, using the eyebrows as a home base or something!"

"Michael, please. This doesn't make any sense."

"All right, damn it!" I say, throwing the razor to the floor.

"Ha! Damn, I look good!" I say, sardonically, as I look at my bald body in the mirror. My gym shorts, the only piece of clothing I'm wearing, are the only reminder I have that I'm truly human.

"Mom," I say, with tears forming in my eyes.

"Yes, I know, Michael. I know it's bad right now."

"Mom, why won't they just go away already? It's making me so sad."

"I know, I know. And I feel terrible. You know that, right? And you know that we do believe you?" she says, although I can't tell if she's serious. Her German heritage gives her the distinct privilege of unparalleled stoicism, granting her the ability to often conceal her true emotions.

"Mom, it's just that I know they're there. I do. Because I feel them—all day long and all night. They're relentless—relentless and unforgiving," I say, despondently.

"I'm so sorry," my mom replies, hugging me.

"I'm sorry that I yelled earlier, it's just that . . ."

"I know, I know. Don't worry about it."

"Cool, 'cause I like my mother."

"And she loves you. And she wants you to be well."

"I know. It's just that *I feel like I'm losing my mind!*" I say with renewed intensity, as I pull away from her. Clenching my fists tightly, I raise and shake them vigorously.

"Michael, just try to calm down."

"All right, now's the time for you to leave," I say, rather bluntly.

"Fine, just before you go doing anything else, I'd really appreciate it if . . ."

"If what? *If what?*"

Over the course of the past month, leading up to this massive infestation, I have become increasingly anxious, erratic, and just plain off-kilter. No one's arguing that I am messed up something fierce, but I'm starting to get the impression that everyone thinks it's all in my head.

"Well, you just started taking all that Adderall; maybe . . ."

"Bullshit!"

"Michael, please!"

"Sorry, but it is! I mean, you don't know how ridiculous you sound. I know what's going on here, and I'm going to take care of it!" I say, as I storm out of the bathroom and head toward my bedroom.

So what! They don't know anything.

Granted, I just recently started taking Adderall, but I'm confident that absinthe is the real culprit behind most of my strange behavior in the past month—although none of this explains the fucking bugs.

God damn 'em, I think, as I punch the wall. "Fuck!"

All right, I'm calming myself down. No way I'm gonna go crazy over here. Let's look at this objectively. Absinthe was part of the problem, and I eliminated it because driving had become a true challenge—that part was definitely due to the absinthe.

The absinthe would actually cause me to forget that I was behind the wheel of a moving vehicle. I barely avoided countless accidents, my eyes fixed upon the brilliance above me: magnificent beams of sunlight shining across picturesque clouds, creating beautiful paintings in the sky around me. Besides all the questionable driving scenarios, I was also having strange thoughts again—lots of bad, borderline psychotic thoughts, which I really didn't appreciate. So I did the right thing, and on New Year's Eve, I drank my last glass of absinthe.

"So what am I doing wrong? Why can't I just catch a freakin' break? Please, God, please. Please just get rid of these freakin' crazy fucking bugs, damn it!"

"Michael, you all right in there?" my father asks, through my closed bedroom door.

Shit! Either Mom told him something or he heard the wall getting hit; or worse, he just heard me talking to myself—or all of the above. Great!

"Yeah! I'm fine!" I shout back, rather disingenuously.

"All right; well, if . . ."

"I said I'm fine!" I yell back, clearly the catalyst for the footsteps that soon move away from my bedroom door.

So what the fuck am I gonna do now? Jesus, this sucks. I know they're there. And I've already gotten rid of all the bad drugs, including absinthe. What do I do next?

A smile suddenly creeps across my face. *The green fairy—that seductive, sensual dominatrix. I will miss her so . . .*

For a few moments, I'm lost in a blissful trance. Unfortunately, the moment doesn't last. I realize that I need something to counteract whatever it is that is going on inside my brain, so I dig into my toiletry case. I pop a few Adderall and Vicodin, and after a moment, a few more.

Nothing wrong with this. Tough times call for tough measures. Who's counting, anyway? These are the only two drugs that I'm still using, besides antidepressants. I'm definitely all good.

Feeling no calmer than before I popped the pills, with the lice still scurrying across every inch of my body, I drive to the drugstore and pick up a couple more bottles of lice shampoo. Upon returning to the house, I pour both bottles all over me, covering myself head to toe with the fiery liquid.

God damn, this sucks! This shit burns like hell!

I'm suddenly extremely dizzy. The fumes are overwhelming. I limply examine the box, my eyes scanning the ridiculous list of toxic chemicals and warnings. Nothing should be able to survive this formula, yet the itching and crawling persist.

Not for long, though, I think.

I pause, looking in the mirror, my eyes half glazed over.

"Ha! You lice must be just a bunch of perfectly indestructible little creatures," I say, smiling mischievously.

Despite the nausea from the fumes and the fact that I'm on the verge of passing out, when I reach the suggested time limit on the shampoo box, I keep going. *If I keep my body lathered up twice as long, there will be no way any lice can stay alive,* I think.

A few minutes later, though, the fumes become unbearable. Having become quite sick and overwhelmed by anxiety, I find myself having trouble breathing normally. Nearly hyperventilating, I wash the chemicals off as quickly as possible. Walking from the bathroom, I realize that I am extremely light-headed. I desperately try to maintain my focus and, moreover, my balance. Dizzy, shaking, and covered in sweat, I struggle to catch my breath.

I must be having an allergic reaction, I think. Unsure of what to do, I fast-step it to the kitchen, grab a bottle of white wine, and pour myself a tall glass.

"Ahh," I announce to nobody in particular. It tastes divine.

"My ol' pal," I voice, with sincere zeal. *Yes, thank God I brought you back when I did. New Year's might have marked a sad farewell to absinthe, but at least it signaled a fond homecoming for you, alcohol, my loyal old friend.*

After downing the first glass, I pour another, then another, and then a fourth. Despite my efforts to purge myself of anxiety and light-headedness with alcohol, my situation ultimately only worsens. Yet even as my brain becomes saddled with a foggy distortion, my thoughts remain glued to the wine.

Yes, just lovely. I know I'm doing the right thing. I've committed to stick with wine only, keeping liquor and beer out of my routine indefinitely. It's a formula for success, and I know I've gotten it exactly right.

Seriously hyperventilating now, and barely able to keep my balance, I stagger into the den, lie down on the floor in front of my family, and announce I am not feeling well. After a short period, while everyone unsuccessfully waits for me to get better, I turn on my "Look at me! I'm flipping out!" switch, adamantly maintaining that I am having an allergic reaction and my heart is going to explode.

My family takes me to the emergency room at Norwalk Hospital, which is only ten minutes away. The doctors give me Ativan and charcoal, discharging me after a couple hours of rest with a surprising diagnosis: panic attack. This is the third time I've had one of these lovely experiences.

After this latest experience, I promise my parents I won't use any more lice shampoo. Moreover, I actually manage to start functioning again, having finally convinced myself that the lice were just a figment of my imagination. Literally the day after the attack, another blessing arrives, in the form of a package of pills that I had previously ordered over the Internet. It's Paxil, an antidepressant that is also used for anxiety disorders.

Always thinking ahead, Michael. Thank God you ordered this shit when you had that panic attack last November! Things happen for a reason.

My Prozac had been running out and, combined with the Adderall, it was making me far too hopped up anyway. I realize now that I was *meant* to have those panic attacks so that I'd buy the Paxil. Yes, Paxil is going to be the key. It's going to fix everything.

It is amazing how quickly the change inside me takes place. After just a couple of weeks I feel immensely different. Although

I'm sure that part of my newfound serenity is due to the departure of absinthe and any withdrawal symptoms associated with it, I place Paxil on a pedestal. I decide that it's nothing short of a miracle drug. With just a single pink 25 mg pill, all my anxiety melts away.

"It's beautiful," I tell myself, in giddy delight. *Yes, without a doubt, Paxil is my favorite drug—or, at least, my favorite prescription drug, besides Adderall.*

Feeling like a new man, I see my psychiatrist again and petition for another increase in my Adderall dosage. He bumps me up to 80 mg per day. I also reason that if one pill is good, two pills must be better, so I double my Paxil dosage to 50 mg per day. Sensing victory, I immediately order an additional three-month supply. Nothing can stop me now.

42

Rez

February 2003

W ow, that's great! That's just excellent! You hear that,
darling?" My father is clearly excited.

"No, what?" my mom asks.

"Well, I'll let Michael tell you. He's got great news."

"Hey, it's really not a big deal," I interject.

"Of course it is. You know, I don't think any of Jason's friends
did nearly as well."

"Could someone please tell me what the good news is?" my
mother asks, in her typically mild, genuine voice.

"Go ahead, Michael, it's all you," my father says, looking at me
with the amazing smile of a parent who's immeasurably proud of
his child.

*Yeah, I saw that smile once. It was on December 22, 2000, when I
graduated from the Academy.*

"Well, Mom, it's really not that big a deal, but I got my LSAT
score back, and I got a 166."

"And that's good, right?" my mom asks, looking to my father,
with her endearing naiveté.

"Of course it's good, dear. Don't be ridiculous! He scored 166 out
of 180. That places him in the 95th percentile for all prospective

275

law students in the entire United States. With that score, there's no way he won't be admitted to one of the top twenty-five law schools in the country."

"Well, then, that deserves a big hug," my mom says, as she squeezes me tightly.

"Jeez—it's really not that big a deal, Mom. You guys don't need to go all crazy on me," I reply, quite disingenuously.

"Way to go! Way to go! That's our Michael!" my mom exclaims, as she breaks from squeezing me to rub my cheeks relentlessly.

"All right, all right, everyone calm down now," I say, as I pull down my mother's hands and go grab some juice. I need my space.

"So what do you have left to do, for the applications?" my mom asks.

"Well, dear, I think that all he has left is the essay—right, Mike?" my father offers.

"Well, I also still need to submit three recommendations. But with the one I have from my last supervisor in the army, the amazing one that I still can't believe I just got from the assistant dean of West Point, and the one that's en route from Jason's New York City assistant district attorney friend, I should be all set."

"Wow! Those three ought to do quite nicely," my father says, still smiling from ear to ear.

"Yeah, I hope so."

"And then you've just got the essay left?"

"Yup, that's it. And then I'm good to go!"

"Hey, need any help?" my father asks. His concern is transparent.

"No, I think I got this one covered."

"All right, but I would love it if you would give me the chance to read it before you submit it," my father says, somewhat beseechingly.

"You got it," I say, focused now on figuring out a way to exit the room.

"Hey, you know, with that score, you've just totally leveled the playing field with all the upper-echelon candidates. The personal statement is the deciding factor now," my father says, with the earnestness I've grown to expect from him.

"I know, I know. Okay if I go now?"

"Sure, sure. Of course."

"Hey, bye, guys," I say, as I turn to head out the door.

"Michael."

"Yes, Mom?" I reply, turning around reluctantly.

"Congratulations again! We really are so very proud of you!" she says.

"And I couldn't agree more. Great job!" my father chimes in.

"Thanks!" I say, turning to leave once again.

"Hey, so when are you going to start that paper?" my father asks.

Man, does he ever stop? "Tomorrow morning. I'm going to head to the library first thing, when it opens, and try to bust it out."

"Well, good. Sounds like a plan."

"Later," I shout, as I walk outside. *Free at last!*

"Bye!" I hear from both my parents, through the closed door.

The next day, as promised, I am at our local library the moment it opens.

"Man, how in the hell am I gonna write this? Where should I start?" I whisper to myself. The task seems daunting.

After a few minutes of staring blankly at my laptop screen, I pop yet another Adderall. *Maybe I really do have ADHD. I am much more functional these days.*

In another example of excellent timing, a few weeks ago my doctor increased my Adderall dosage to the recommended maximum of 90 mg per day. In less than three months, I've gone from the lowest to the absolute highest prescribed dosage. Adderall is definitely my most favorite drug ever, and I also dearly love Paxil, if for no other reason than that without it, I wouldn't be able to take such large doses of my beloved Adderall—at least not without repercussions. (In passing, you might have noticed that I have had many favorites. To be honest, there was always one absolute favorite: whichever one was coming next. I just always thought I could feel a little better with whatever lay ahead.)

Things are really starting to fall into proper place for me. I'm becoming a totally different person, the person I'm supposed to be and a guy I love: a confident, energetic, and virtually always happy extrovert.

I'm invincible! I think. "It's just a match made in heaven," I whisper to myself, smiling now. Adderall is my savior. Popping the medication like Pez candy, I begin writing like a man possessed. It's almost physically impossible for me to stop scribbling. There is just too much to say. My pen rarely comes up from the page, and I pause only occasionally to flex my sore wrist.

When the library closes, I move this process back to my house. Time has no bearing. I write without care, without concern, and without any organization. *The structure will come later,* I tell myself. *I shall give my pen full rein until it tells me I'm done!*

When the writing stage is over, I take all my papers and divide them up by subject, placing all the paragraphs into their proper categories. Then I take all the neatly categorized paragraphs and type them all into my computer, yielding what I am confident will be hailed as the Best Entrance Essay Ever. *My method is flawless!*

Then I am finished. After only sixteen hours, my essay is complete. Reading over my completed personal statement, I am again certain that I have written one of the best personal essays that will ever be submitted anywhere. I smile, proud of my incredible accomplishment.

No stone has been left unturned; everything I want and need to say is there. There's absolutely no way that any entrance review board can look away from such brilliance. Everything, down to each and every word, is utterly perfect. In fact, only one minor problem remains: how to whittle my master treatise down from thirty-eight pages to the maximum allowed length of two pages.

I pause for a brief moment, momentarily unsure of myself. But the answer is obvious. *I need more Adderall!* So I call my psychiatrist and tell him that I lost my bottle of Adderall. This immediately allows me to increase my daily dosage by 30 mg per day, to 120 mg.

It occurs to me that manipulating my psychiatrist is easier than I had ever imagined. I vow to use that same "lost my pills" trick again in the future, and I also take a moment to brainstorm a few other maneuvers. I wonder if I can ask for one-month prescriptions every three weeks instead of four. Will he notice? I doubt it. *What a joke! It's too easy!*

Back at home, after swallowing a few Adderall, my satisfaction is palpable. I review my success: law school, Adderall, Paxil, quitting absinthe and all that other shit, keeping the Vicodin down to six or seven a day, and trying to keep alcohol consumption down to just a bottle (or two) of wine a night. I'm doing everything right, everything just right. My parents seem fine with my drinking because they are unaware of exactly how much I am consuming and that I am still using Vicodin. Moreover, they truly believe that I am well into recovery. "*Salud!*" I say, raising a glass, as I toast myself.

43

Corpse Pose
March 2003

I am in the kitchen, eating an omelet, as I carefully flip the
pages of one of my newest books. Lately I have confined my
reading to nonfiction books on Buddhism. I've been gaining
a great sense of self-awareness, which in turn has resulted in an
intense newfound curiosity into my spirituality. I am discovering
an essential, powerful component of myself that I had neglected
for far too long, thanks to ideas that I'd always dismissed as frivo-
lous propaganda for the weak.

I close the book and look up with genuine contentment, smiling once again. *Yes, I am changing, inside and out, and for the better*,
I think.

Everything is coming together, and it all started on New Year's
Eve. Thanks to my three-hour workouts and Adderall, which just
by itself helps to burn a great deal of fat (due to an increased
metabolism and suppressed appetite), I am rapidly becoming
more fit-looking than I ever was on steroids. In less than three
months I already look and feel like a new person—literally.

My body, all twisted and misaligned from my scoliosis, is making gradual, but very noticeable, changes. I am confident that my
new weekly regimen is stimulating nerves long since ignored,

slowly encouraging bones and muscles to reposition themselves. Everything is snapping into place.

In addition to quitting absinthe, my other New Year's resolutions were to start yoga, Pilates, cardiovascular exercises, and acupuncture, while continuing my weight lifting. I haven't let myself down. Without fail, since the start of the year, each week I've been doing yoga four times, Pilates twice, acupuncture once, weight training five times, and cardio three times. All I have to do is pop a 30 mg Adderall tablet before my workouts, and nothing can stop me. I always have the supplemental energy boost to keep going. Admittedly, however, this amphetamine rush doesn't help so much with yoga—which, much as with Pilates, I find to be much, much harder than it looks (to put it mildly!).

"You're a changed man," I say out loud to no one in particular, as I hop out of my chair and swallow some more Adderall and Paxil. I am immediately reenergized. I head to the bathroom and, after brushing my teeth, look at myself for a moment with reverence, smiling with intense satisfaction. *Definitely a changed man*, I think.

I have always had very bad scoliosis. As I mentioned earlier, the stabilized curvature of my back is still thirty-one degrees, which is quite high. Virtually every damn night of my high school years I was forced to sleep in a Milwaukee back brace, which is a form-fitting, custom-molded piece of padded hard plastic that starts below the hips and extends over the chest in the front and the shoulder blades in the back. In my case, due to my high thoracic curve, the brace went all the way up my back to the top of my shoulders, with a graphite and metal plate extending up behind my neck, and metal rings on either side of my ears that connected the plate to the front of the brace.

This torture device, constricting me in every direction, obviously made it impossible for me to sleep on my side or stomach. I was forced to lie on my back, which was miserable, but I simply can't describe how painful it feels to have an extremely twisted spine and to have one's upper back and neck forced into a straight line. Getting a good night's rest was virtually out of the question. I felt brutalized, victimized, and inescapably helpless. For a long time tears had been a staple of my nightly routine. I remember every night, as I lay in bed desperately trying to fall asleep, I would imagine that I was eighteen and about to head off to college, which would mark the end of my nights of torment. Consummating what had become an exceptionally vivid fantasy, I would take my back brace into the backyard, pour lighter fluid all over it, set it ablaze, and watch it and my pain slowly burn and melt away.

The worst part is that the doctors often told my parents that they expected I was going to need surgery unless I started wearing the brace all day—including at school. That wasn't an option.

Now I am lying on the soft carpet of my parents' bedroom floor, in the final pose of my yoga workout: Savasana, or the corpse pose. I'm lying on my back, shoulder blades tucked under, arms close to my body with palms facing up, legs shoulder width apart and turned outward, with feet also allowed to fall outward, and eyes closed. It's a pose of perfect and total relaxation.

I am addicted to yoga. During my free time at home I regularly go into my parents' bedroom to work on poses I am having trouble with, as well as others that I think are most applicable to my torso's realignment. I am determined not only to realize the greatest benefit in myself but to become the best in my class. *I'll be the best. Who cares if this goes against the whole philosophy of yoga?*

Lying on the floor, I'm letting my body go, sinking into the carpet, when I suddenly feel as if I have truly released myself from my physical being. I am watching like an observer as gravity takes control of me, melting me into the floor. It is then that I feel something rising inside me.

I lie motionless, lacking feeling anywhere in my body, when suddenly I feel my limbs start moving on their own, stretching in all directions, before slowly pushing past resistance points and repositioning themselves in a new, more proper place. As if on autopilot, my body is making changes that I am confident are meant to realign not only my physical self but my spiritual self as well.

After about fifteen minutes of this incredible experience, I go next door to my own bedroom to lie down. I am completely overwhelmed. I never use a bed frame—so, just as when I lived in the Boulevard, I've placed my mattress on the ground against the far wall of the room. Annoyed at having spent so much time over the past couple of years packing and unpacking, I have yet to get around to taking my things out of their boxes and making this room my own. As such, my space is an irritating hodgepodge of filing cabinets and boxes that my father uses for storage, decorated with random pictures of him with business colleagues on the walls.

There is one saving grace: hanging on the wall directly across from me is a very large, framed reproduction of one of Marc Chagall's paintings, *Le Champ de Mars*, which my eyes are always unavoidably fixed upon when I lie down. It's an almost entirely blue expressionist piece. It has a bird in the lower right-hand corner, the Eiffel Tower and the moon in the upper right-hand corner, and, most noticeably, a woman with two faces on the left side. Her angelic face stares straight out at me while her motherly face gazes to the right, seemingly watching over the right side of the painting.

I'm still feeling strange from what has just taken place next door—and not quite myself—but as I stare at this captivating image, she begins to move. I close my eyes and shake my head, confident that the hallucination will go away, but as I open my eyes, the opposite happens: The picture springs fully to life. The bird flies up to the motherly figure's outstretched hands, winks at me, then soars across my room and out my bedroom window. I look back at the woman, and she looks so incredibly beautiful, comforting, and pure.

What is she trying to tell me? I wonder. I realize that this is without a doubt connected to what just transpired in my parents' bedroom. I decide that if this is really happening, which I am certain it is, the woman in the painting must be from "the other side," an angel sent to guide me.

I take a couple of minutes to reflect on this incredible realization, examining its significance. I recall reading about something like this somewhere in one of my Buddhism books. I wonder if my spiritual core, my soul, belonged to someone else in a past life and if perhaps this ancient persona has finally been acknowledged and allowed to show itself.

As I reflect upon whose soul I might have, whose spirit is channeling itself through me, only one name appears—one name, whose captivating presence gives me chills all over when I think about it.

Frida Kahlo.

When I look back at the painting, both heads of the angelic, motherly woman turn themselves toward me and glide out of the painting. They float in the middle of the room above me, smile, and nod in reaffirmation, and then they are gone.

I immediately go on the Internet to learn as much as I can about the life of this incredible woman who graced me with her presence. As I read, I become more and more enraptured. I immediately process her story, internalizing all the important pieces of this fascinatingly unique individual's life.

Frida Kahlo was born in Mexico City on July 6, 1907. At age eighteen, on September 17, 1925, she was involved in a serious bus accident, which would prove to be without a doubt the most pivotal point in her life. She was left with a broken spinal column, a broken collarbone, broken ribs, a broken pelvis, eleven fractures in her right leg, a dislocated and crushed right foot, and a shoulder out of joint. For the following month she was forced to lie flat on her back, encased in a plaster cast and enclosed in a boxlike structure.

Although she made a remarkable recovery, Frida would spend most of her days in severe pain. She'd be hospitalized and bedridden for long periods of time, and forced her to undergo dozens of operations over the course of her life. But albeit the cause of debilitating health problems, this event also sparked the beginning of her renowned career in painting. Turning to the canvas during her recuperation, art became her lifelong passion.

Within a couple years of her accident she met Diego Rivera, Mexico's most famous artist, and on August 21, 1929, she and Rivera were married. Their marriage was a rocky, tumultuous relationship. They had a genuine, passionate love for each other, and a powerful creative connection; but they also had affairs with many other people, and at times great anger and hate—culminating in a divorce in 1940 that lasted for only one year.

Frida used the canvas for expressing all her unsavory emotions, including her anger and hurt over her stormy marriage, the pain she felt over several miscarriages, and, most often, the chronic physical suffering she was always forced to live with because of the childhood accident. In 1953, the same year as her only exhibition in Mexico, Frida had her right leg amputated below the knee due to a gangrene infection. She became severely depressed and suicidal, and on July 13, 1954, she died—officially from a pulmonary embolism, although it has often been suspected that she took her own life.

"Maybe I do have something beautiful inside me, after all!" I say, half seriously, before a wave of clarity washes over me. "Yes, of course. It all makes such perfect sense," I proclaim, with undaunted confidence and gravity.

I am Frida Kahlo. That is to say, her spirit is inside me, guiding me. We both wore a back brace to deal with chronic back pain; this is a decisive link to who she was, physically. It also seems reasonable to imagine that in reincarnation she would pick up in the general vicinity of where she left off, keeping some basic characteristics and traits, but not exact specifics. It's crystal clear to me now! Her spirit has revealed itself to me to help me make things right, and with her presence in my life, I know that my body will eventually correct itself totally; my hips, shoulders, and spine are bound to align themselves perfectly.

The following day I go back to the Westport public library and check out the book that had so distinctly captured my attention last November: *The Diary of Frida Kahlo: An Intimate Self-Portrait* by Sarah M. Lowe (New York: Harry Abrams, 1995). I begin to read it.

> *Frida Kahlo's amazing illustrated journal documents the last ten years of her turbulent life. This passionate, often surprising, intimate record, kept under lock and key for some forty years in Mexico, reveals many new dimensions in the complex persona of this remarkable artist. Covering the years 1944–54, the 170-page journal contains Frida's thoughts, poems, and dreams, and reflects her stormy relationship with her husband, Diego Rivera. . . . Frida's childhood, her political sensibilities, and her obsession with Diego are all illuminated in witty phrases and haunting images.*
>
> *The fact that Kahlo included artwork in her diary makes it almost unique among* journaux intimes *(private records written by women for themselves). Yet it differs from the typical artist's sketchbook, which is usually a place for preparatory drawings or working out solutions in a small format to be applied to large works. Only once did Kahlo transform an ink drawing from the diary into a full-scale painting. And unlike the classic intimate journalist, Kahlo is inattentive to day-to-day goings-on, and uses her journal as a repository for feelings that do not fit anywhere else. Thus, these pages must be approached with some trepidation; the portrait Kahlo paints here, with color and lines, with prose and poetry, is an image of the artist unmasked.*

Even before I realize that there is a translation of her entries in the back of the book, accompanied by explanations of her artwork, I find her diary extremely captivating and telling. This is because her artwork alone makes the book more than worthwhile, for her illustrations are unique, dynamic, and thought provoking. When I finally notice the translations, I am even happier; I find the manner in which she writes her journal, primarily poetic prose, also enjoyably easy for me to relate to.

Inspired by Frida's diary, I immediately begin my own comprehensive journal, adding at least twenty pages per day. For the next three months, Frida's diary will rest upon the desk in my bedroom, beneath Chagall's *Le Champ de Mars*, opening itself to me every night, as I set aside ample time each evening to peruse a new entry.

44

Diego

April 2003

I am sitting in Amberjacks drinking wine, riding an incredible high of ever-increasing confidence and serenity. It is overwhelmingly empowering to know that I am channeling Frida Kahlo, a rush only further augmented by the Adderall and Vicodin rushing through my system.

I truly feel wonderful with where I am. I've had an empowering spiritual awakening, and for the first time in my life I stand on solid ground.

As I wait for my sister to get off work, I reflect over my recent birthday trip to Niagara Falls. Eager to avoid the same old cliché birthday cake with my family, and with my credit cards all maxed, I borrowed a credit card from Vanessa and went to the Canadian side, just over the border from Buffalo, New York. I used this four-day excursion to create a contract with myself for how I want to live the rest of my life.

The way I see it, your birthday, at its core, should be a celebration of self, an ongoing benchmark you can use each year to evaluate where you've been, where you currently are, and most important, where you are going.

Despite its touristy reputation, Niagara Falls was far from a letdown;

it was an unexpected treat, really, because there is much more to the area than just a large waterfall. Overall, the trip was a major success; I'd definitely go back. I loved the view, I completed my contract with myself, and I once again seized the opportunity to practice what is becoming by far my most reliable line: "So, how much for one hour?" (Sorry, Mom.)

Scanning the bar, I see Anya, a beautiful cocktail waitress. Anya is about five feet seven, with curly black shoulder-length hair, a good body, and one of the most beautiful faces I've ever seen. In addition to admiring her obviously good looks, I like how Anya dresses. She has a good sense of style, and, more important, she seems genuinely nice and easygoing, like someone who can easily get along with anyone. From the first moment I see her, I am captivated by her natural beauty. *You're beautiful,* is all I can think of saying.

Several bathroom bumps, Vicodin, and glasses of wine later, I feel good—really good. I cautiously approach my quarry, and somehow I find the courage to ask Anya if she'd like to do something sometime, to which she makes a Mexican surrealist's day by promptly saying yes and giving me her phone number. A few hours later, as I lie in bed, staring at my beautiful angel, the world around me feels perfectly surreal.

A few days later I decide to give her a call. The fact that Anya seems amenable to the idea of us getting together, however, does nothing to soothe my nerves. I am far too anxious and, moreover, far too sober to give her a call. Turning yet again to my clutch savior, I pop a few Adderall, and then, craving just a little extra edge for the phone call, I chug a few glasses of wine and finally decide I am ready to give her a call. When I hear her voice, I'm still caught totally off guard, because I'd secretly prayed for no one to answer.

Fuck! Now what, jackass?

"Hey, Anya, this is Mike."

"Oh, hey, what's up?"

"Well, I was, uh, wondering if you'd like to do something later this week."

"Sure," she replies; again I'm completely dumbfounded.

"Cool. So, how's Friday work for you?"

"Well, why don't we do something Sunday? Friday is Anya's night to get drunk."

Disregarding her suggestion of Sunday, I get extremely flustered and upset at her putting getting drunk over going out with me, so I tell her, "No, Friday's fine."

"Well, I'm kind of going out with my friends and already have plans."

"Fine! You have to get drunk? This is ridiculous! I'll just go out with you guys Friday, then. How about that?"

"Uh, sure. Hey, I gotta go. Later."

Click. And that was that. It was all over.

Wow! That call didn't go quite as well as I'd have liked. Jesus goddam Christ! God fucking damn it, you stupid fucking loser! Do you have any idea what a shithead you just were? Yeah, she's gonna talk to you again! Fuck, fuck, fuck!

"All right, settle down, Mike," I say, as I feel myself coming unhinged. *All right, I'm calm. But God damn! Wow, did she give herself a quick exit once she realized any reasoning with me was probably going to fall to the wayside. Ha! Smart girl. Well, why the fuck was she talking to me to begin with, anyway?* I wonder.

I pause for a few moments to formulate a new plan and pop some more pills. After that, the brilliance comes rapidly. *All is not lost. No, not at all. Yes, all I have to do is roll on into Amberjacks later, make my presence known, and smooth things over. Of course! Hmmm . . . maybe this is stupid? It is, isn't it? What reason on planet Earth do I think I can do this? Ahhh, forget that! Of course I can. I know I can. I'm supposed to. I can feel Frida telling me so. Yes, I am able to feel my inner spirit, Frida, guiding me toward Anya for some reason. Why, though?* I think, as I pop another pill—which one, I don't know.

Several minutes later, after showering and getting dressed to go out, my thoughts feel even clearer. *Yes, that must be it! That is why I've been so attracted to her! It's been out of my hands the whole time; it was never my choice to make. Of course not! Anya and I are star-crossed lovers or something, soul mates, and, at least as far as Frida is concerned, we're meant to be together.*

(For any aspiring stalkers and/or lunatics out there, please feel free to go ahead and borrow some of these ideas.)

As I look in the mirror, giving myself a final look-over before I head out, I can't help but feel confident in my determination.

"Yes, indeed, Winder! You might sound like a freaking nut job, but who the fuck cares?"

It does all make sense now, doesn't it? However, to the outside "normal" folk, all this would probably be a bit lost on them. "Fuck that! And damn, I look pretty darn good!"

Several days later, I am back at Amberjacks to find Anya, hoping to apologize and make things right. Even though I've already taken 120 mg of Adderall, on the way in I chew up another 45 mg. Unfortunately, this doesn't help, and things go pretty darn poorly indeed. I'm surprised that Anya doesn't want to speak to me.

Despite her obvious displeasure with my presence, I persist, following her around the bar, determined to get out what I need to say—although I really have no clue exactly what I'm trying to say. With each step and each word, anyone (including myself) can see from the expression on Anya's face how much worse I am making things.

Completely unnerved and irritated, she finally stops and puts down her drink tray to speak with me. Normally a very laid-back individual and someone who obviously shies away from being mean or insulting, she loses her cool a little, telling me in no uncertain terms that she has a boyfriend and wants me to leave her alone.

Does she really have a boyfriend? Who the fuck knows? I think, as I walk out of the bar, a beaten man.

By the time I get home and am lying in bed, things really start setting in for me. *I am "that guy." It sucks to be "that guy." "That guy" doesn't go out to dinner with beautiful women. No, "that guy" actually*

scares women away from the whole notion of eating. And if "that guy"
is stranded on a deserted island with a jazzy, attractive woman, and he
is cooking up some fish he just caught, well, she'll pass on dinner and
take her chances waiting for a boat.

Depressed and embarrassed at how the situation transpired, I'm
desperate to make things right between us and in the universe. I am
sure I knew her in a past life, and so I begin writing her an apolo-
getic love letter.

Yes, of course! Anya is Diego Rivera! This all makes perfect sense.
Frida and Diego's notoriously tumultuous relationship is just carrying
over into us, which, much like my back, is meant to improve until things
are eventually completely right, as they are supposed to be, so our souls
can be set at peace.

It's amazing how quickly fifty pages go by after I've chewed up
another 30 mg of Adderall. My standard since the beginning of this
month is now 150 mg per day, thanks to the simple tricks I mentioned earlier. I fake lost prescriptions, I pick up monthly prescriptions every three weeks instead of four, and I routinely ask for
several months' prescriptions in advance so that I can later get
duplicate prescriptions for the same months. As far as the other
two drugs in my life are concerned, Paxil and Vicodin, I have
increased my Paxil dosage to 75 mg a day (more has to be better)
while I am actually (halfheartedly) weaning myself from Vicodin
(which I guarantee you is no cakewalk, especially when one has
hundreds of tablets remaining).

I began my letter by apologizing to her and making excuses for
my behavior, blaming it on medication or something. I then
moved into a lengthy, detailed analysis of who she is, based on
who I am, and who she used to be (Diego). I made it clear that I
knew her better than she knows herself, even though I'd never had
a conversation with her that lasted longer than thirty seconds. I
even gave her career advice; the irony is palpable. After making my
wild claims and assumptions about her, I moved into a bio of
myself, in which I lie a bit—but Frida made me!

For those who imagine that all this can't possibly have occupied more than fifteen pages, max, and are wondering how I could have possibly filled up the other thirty-five, don't worry; I'm mystified as well. I remember going off on numerous tangents, including a discussion on philosophy and spiritual awareness, a version of one of the favorite poems I've written (changed slightly to include her name), and a discussion of the writer Marcel Proust and how his ideas might help her. I also recall making several metaphors in which I compare myself to dogs (or possibly puppies), ice cream trucks, and flowers.

All in all, this is a wonderful collaborative piece: vintage Winder-Kahlo. The following week, on a night when Vanessa is working with Anya, I make my sister deliver the letter.

The final week of the month, with the house to myself for the evening, I rent *Frida*, starring Salma Hayek. My expectations are not that high, for I don't envision Her Sexiness playing a believable Frida or capturing her true essence.

I disagree with the critics who find it superficial; I think one honestly gets a good feeling for who Frida Kahlo was and what she was all about. I think the movie gives a really good overview of her life, especially for anyone unacquainted with her. I sincerely respect Salma's efforts to use the screen to bring this beautiful figure—who, I've read, is her heroine (and heroines don't get much better than this)—to the greater masses. Millions of people who might never have known this brilliant woman will now be exposed to her beauty.

When the movie is over, I feel incredible, buoyed by an enormous newfound sense of pride for who I used to be. Drifting off to sleep, I am more confident than ever in who I am and who I'm destined to be.

45

The Rich Housewife

May 2003

As I sit at my computer, my eyes scan the pages feverishly, consuming the knowledge before me with ardent hunger.

I have been learning as much as possible about Adderall, my wonder drug, from Internet sources. I find it quite interesting that even though Adderall and Ritalin are both meant to achieve the same desired outcome of a more focused, calm individual, the two medications work quite differently, hitting different receptors.

I don't get it! It makes absolutely no sense to me that the two drugs have never been combined to create the definitive ADHD supermedication!

I immediately order several hundred Ritalin tablets online. Just days later, my package arrives. Along with an increase in my Adderall dosage to 180 mg per day, I begin snorting Ritalin throughout the day. Almost immediately I begin noticing certain changes in myself. Along with my spiritual connection with Frida, I find that I also have some heightened awareness.

A combination of yoga, Pilates, acupuncture, healthy nutrition, and Adderall has stimulated my nervous system in such a fashion as to harness an inner spiritual connection that each and every one of has but that rarely gets touched. By tapping into my nervous system and spiritual core, I have opened the door to my third eye. *Yes, of course! That has to be it!*

I am confident that I can find anyone or anything, anywhere, by pulling my eyelids back into my head as far as they can go, holding my body perfectly still, and allowing Frida to guide my right index finger like a human divining rod. It is all quite simple, really.

I believe that I've finally, truly slipped into my groove. Having found the perfect routine, I feel extremely comfortable as I settle into my new lifestyle, which I am thoroughly enjoying. Thus begins my quest to become the perfect rich housewife: Winder-Kahlo.

CHECKLIST FOR A RICH HOUSEWIFE

Yoga:	3× per week
Pilates:	2× per week
Weight training:	5× per week
Cardio training:	3× per week
Acupuncture:	1× per week
Tanning:	4× per week
Breakfast (egg white & turkey sandwich):	7× per week
Lunch (sushi & a wheatgrass shake):	7× per week
Dinner (local restaurant):	5× per week
Haircut (local salon):	1× per week
Manicure and pedicure:	1× every 2 weeks
Antidepressants:	Every morning
Massage (foot or back):	1× per week
Facial:	1× every 2 weeks
Shopping (clothes, sunglasses, whatever):	2× per week
Piano lessons (breaking the mold):	2× per week
Sleeping with the pool guy:	Thank God we don't have a pool!

Yes, if I were actually a rich housewife, I'm sure I would do it better than most, I think, smiling with peculiar satisfaction.

During the second week of May I have my first run-in with Anya since Vanessa gave her my infamous letter. I am aware that I am trapped in a hopeless cycle: do something stupid, do something embarrassing to try to fix it, then do something stupid and embarrassing to fix that. I'm not quite sure when I will stop trying to (unknowingly) outdo myself, but I have stayed away from Amberjacks for the past three weeks, hoping that by keeping myself from seeing Anya I can pretend that the whole situation never happened, protect myself from doing anything more stupid, and keep both of us from feeling needlessly awkward.

Despite my efforts to avoid Anya, I finally run into her at a dance club around the corner from Amberjacks. She is surprisingly friendly to me, which I attribute to her being a little tipsy. Although she does protest certain parts of my assessment of her, it appears, amazingly, that some of my "insights" were actually right on target.

Why is that surprising? She's Diego. What's surprising is that she's feigning that what I wrote isn't the absolute total truth.

Although it's extremely uncomfortable, the two of us talk a little, and as I am leaving we make tentative plans for Sunday. The day before, I buy thirteen roses: four red, four pink, four yellow, and five white. The flowers are for naught, though; Anya calls and nixes the notion of any get-together, reminding me again that she has a boyfriend.

I guess that didn't go well. Hmmm . . . it appears a sober Anya has magically reclaimed her senses! Shit, at least we know she's sane! Not funny, Michael. Yes, it is!

During my next few encounters with Anya, all during the final week of the month, I take a slightly bolder approach, inundating her with outlandish claims and assertions. "Anya, you know, at least I don't have to wonder; I mean, I know I gave it a shot. Whereas you, you'll spend the rest of your life constantly reminded of me whenever you walk into a bookstore or turn on the television and will always wonder: 'What if?'"

Or: "Honestly, Anya, it's your loss. You'll never meet anyone like me as long as you live—never. There's no one. Do you have any idea who I am? There have been only a few people like me throughout all of history. You know that? Well, it's your loss."

And my personal favorite: "Anya, just so you know, I have the best mind, the best body, and the best soul of any man you have ever met or will ever meet. All right?"

Considering her giggles, I'm not so sure she takes that last one too seriously.

During the final week of May I receive my formal letter of acceptance from the prestigious George Washington University Law School, an extremely competitive school, one of the top twenty-five law schools in the country.

I immediately accept its offer of admittance and request a deferment to fall 2004, which is promptly approved. I want some time to devote to just drawing and writing, giving me some leeway to decide if law school is exactly what I want to do.

Lately I've become a much more thoughtful, deliberate decision maker, I think, quite pleased with myself.

THE GEORGE
WASHINGTON
UNIVERSITY
LAW SCHOOL
WASHINGTON DC

MICHAEL K. YOUNG

DEAN AND LOBINGIER PROFESSOR
OF COMPARATIVE LAW AND JURISPRUDENCE

May 1, 2003

Mr. Michael H. Winder
56 Partrick Road
Westport, CT 06880

Dear Mr. Winder:

It is my pleasure to inform you of your admission to The George Washington University Law School as a candidate for the Juris Doctor degree beginning next fall semester.

I am certain that you will enjoy the unique opportunity to study law in Washington, DC, the center of legal activity for the nation. In this environment the law school offers you a rigorous program and a diverse curriculum with a faculty distinguished in both scholarly and professional achievement. I am equally positive that you will appreciate the special atmosphere that exists here at the law school where students who are serious of purpose, nevertheless manage to find time for pleasurable pursuits. This campus has an abundance of activities which will enrich your life here, such as prominent speakers, sports events, and musical and theatrical productions.

You deserve congratulations for your outstanding record of accomplishments. You have much to contribute to our school and we therefore look forward to having you with us. Included with this letter is information concerning your acceptance of our offer, the submission of the required deposit, and opportunities for receiving financial assistance. If you wish to visit the school, please contact our Admissions Office. The telephone number is (202)994-7230. The people there will be very happy to see you and to answer any questions you may have.

Sincerely,

Michael K. Young

Michael K. Young

2000 H STREET, NW • WASHINGTON, DC 20052 • (202) 994-6288 • FAX (202) 994-5157 • myoung@law.gwu.edu

46

The Flamboyant Weirdo

June 2003

I t's June 1, 2003, and I am moving into the spare bedroom of the apartment that my sister Vanessa is sharing with her boyfriend, Mike. The street they live on, Arch Street, which is just a three-minute drive from downtown SoNo, is filled with houses virtually on top of one other, with each home divided into two or three apartments for renting. Theirs is the second home on the left: a nice, off-white, recently refurbished Colonial, with a front porch containing a few lounge chairs and a small barbecue.

Opening the apartment door, one is immediately confronted by a stairwell. The first flight of stairs leads to the second floor—the first real floor of the apartment. At the top of the stairs, one faces the door to Mike's bedroom, a high-tech haven for this electronics and computer aficionado. Off the stairs, to the left, is the living room, which is set up similarly to my living room at the Boulevard, with a couch, coffee table, and television.

In the middle of the living room's far wall is the door to the bathroom, right next to the entrance to the kitchen. If one continues up the staircase, one comes to the third (and last) level of the apartment. The upstairs bathroom is through the door at the top of the stairwell, and the two upstairs bedrooms are to the right, off a short hallway.

Although Vanessa usually sleeps downstairs with Mike, she has her own bedroom on the third floor, the one to the left. The right one is my bedroom, which doesn't contain many of my personal things. I haven't envisioned staying long, so I don't bring anything with me to the apartment besides clothes and toiletries. Virtually everything in the room is Vanessa's.

My bedroom has two windows: one straight ahead, in the middle of the far wall, and one in the middle of the wall to the right, above the foot of the bed. On the left side of the room are two dressers and a closet. In the far left corner of the room is the television, facing toward the bed.

As soon as I'm done unpacking, I eagerly take advantage of what is by far the room's best attraction, tucked in the far right corner of the room: a papasan chair. It's ridiculously comfortable. For reading, watching television, drawing, or sleeping, nothing beats a papasan chair.

Ensconced in the chair, I turn on the television, pop a Valium, and open a bottle of wine. With all the moving and the stimulants in my system, I need a brief reprieve before I head out to the bars in a few hours with Porter. I have only recently been speaking to Porter again, after our altercation in the club in Portchester months ago. At the end of last month I ran into him in a bar in a nearby town. Although the whole situation had basically been my fault, he just walked over as if nothing had happened, shook my hand, and gave me a hug. I think we both ended up apologizing, but it didn't matter. He makes some things real easy.

Damn, I love this thing, I think, as I drift off in the chair for a nap.

As my alarm clock blares, I languidly reach out of bed and turn it off, grabbing the two Adderall I've strategically placed on the table next to it. My body is used to this drill by now. Semiconscious, going on very little sleep, I pop the two pills in my mouth and swallow them. I allow myself to momentarily drift back to sleep while I still have the chance. It's 7:00 AM, three weeks after I first moved in.

A few minutes later, my eyes are wide open, and I leap out of bed. I secretly pop a few Paxil, careful not to let *them* see, before opening my window shades. After putting in my contacts and brushing my teeth, I take a quick shower.

"Damn, I look good!" I proclaim, examining my chiseled physique in the bathroom mirror. My New Year's resolutions sure have paid off. I've done quite well for myself. Five months of yoga, Pilates, cardio, weight lifting, and proper supplements have really made drastic improvements. I never could have imagined I could be in such good health. Furthermore, with the money I made from day-trading at the Academy, the residual West Point loan money, and three platinum credit cards, my new lifestyle is fully bankrolled.

"Well, you've got another busy day ahead of you. Let's make the most of it, Michael," I tell myself, as I finish styling my hair and give myself one last look-over in the mirror.

In light of the fact that I am chewing up a bare minimum of seven 30 mg pills of Adderall and snorting eight to ten Ritalin every day, which is a bit excessive on both counts (for "normal" people), I am getting extremely ripped.

Back in my bedroom, I'm ready to get down to business. I put *Lilo & Stitch* (my favorite movie) in the VCR and, still in my underwear, dance to the scene where Lilo teaches Stitch to act like Elvis. *The girls must love this morning treat.* I know they are watching me across the street, but I don't mind. I know it's for a good reason. I feel good. This is how I start my days.

Along with my move and change of scenery, there is great reason to be happy. I have realized, during the past week, that Anya has come to her senses and that *she* is now obsessed with *me*! Anya is obviously embarrassed about the fact that she likes me so much now, and since she had previously told me in no uncertain terms to take a hike, she wants to understand who Michael Winder truly is before approaching me. Thus, she has solicited a large consortium of her friends to help gather information about me.

During the past few weeks I have become aware of the fact that more than fifteen cars, filled with her friends and family, are watching me 24/7. It is easy for them to spy on me, since most of her friends live on the same street as Vanessa. From the moment I wake up in the morning, they're watching me through the windows, preparing to follow me as soon as I get in my car.

I throw on some cargo shorts, pack my gym bag, and close the shades. I need a brief moment of privacy as I pound some Ritalin into powder and do a few lines. I throw on my yellow Mr. Bubble tank top and go downstairs. As soon as I head outside, I have to keep myself from chuckling, because they are so obvious. I know they've been watching me since I first woke up.

Well, this oughta be fun. Let's see how many she has following me today, I think, as I pull out of the driveway. "That's definitely one, and there's another, and another, and another. Jesus, they're all over the place today," I announce with glee, as my wild eyes rapidly move between the mirrors of my car, examining the automobiles around me.

When I stop for breakfast, my body moving with the extreme swiftness and confidence that my medication imparts, I see them immediately. The girl behind the counter, who smiles at me as she takes my order, is clearly either one of Anya's friends or someone who has been solicited by them for inside knowledge, because this is the always the first stop in my daily routine.

And that mother, with her kid, who pretends that they just happen to be here at the same time as me—ridiculous! I've caught her looking at me at least three or four times already.

While I read the paper, I look outside and start chuckling. I can see some of their cars in the lots across the street, whereas others just drive back and forth along the busy thoroughfare that separates us. All I can do is smile. They think they're so clever!

When I'm done eating, I head to the gym for a three-hour marathon workout.

As I walk into the enormous fitness arena, strutting with

unbridled poise, I know that (almost) all eyes are on me. I've accepted the fact that they're just about everywhere. *Hell, why would today be any different? From morning till night, they are always here.*

Anya's friends watch me while I lift weights, and during Pilates and yoga I notice a few new women I have never seen before, obviously friends of Anya's mother who have been sent in to spy on me. When I'm finished, I head to a local restaurant for sushi and a wheatgrass shake. Shortly after I sit down, a group of girls sits down at a nearby table, obviously watching me. My suspicions are confirmed when I smile at the group and the two girls who notice return the gesture with genuine enthusiasm.

At least they're not as bad as that woman yesterday, who just came up to me out of nowhere and started talking. That was pretty absurd. But I guess they gotta do what they gotta do.

I look at my watch and hastily get up and throw out my trash. *Fuck. I'm almost late for my appointment,* I think, as I walk to my car.

Fifteen minutes later, as I'm getting acupuncture on the third floor of a medical building, they're watching through a closed curtain from cars parked in a lot across the street. When I'm done with my treatment, I head across town to the Westport Music Center.

During my piano lesson they watch from the store directly above, having slipped a small video camera through the connecting ventilating shaft. Several times I am forced to stop what I'm doing and bang my hands on the keys, shaking my head and looking at the ceiling with increasing frustration. I know my teacher is a little confused, but that's irrelevant.

After my lesson, I head to the beach. This is the worst, especially because it's where I typically spend the bulk of my day. They are everywhere, all around me, trying to blend in. It is actually kind of amusing: They give themselves away so easily. They are so loud that I can hear them all the time. I think a large part of me is actually enjoying the attention, confident that Anya will talk to me soon. I make sure not to let on that I can hear my watchers, or to otherwise let them know that I know they are there.

I spend the afternoon at the beach enhancing my dark tropical tan, continuing my Adderall and Ritalin consumption, as I read several magazines, write in my journal, and do some drawing.

After several hours, I've had enough; the amusement is gone. It's quite distracting and hard to concentrate on what I'm doing when they're always there. I loved the attention at first, but it's starting to get on my nerves. *Enough already. Why the fuck won't they leave me alone?*

Having reached my breaking point, I pack all my stuff and throw it in the car and drive to the library. Much to my chagrin, things don't improve. At the library, they are in the stacks, so close I can hear their breathing, and since I always use the desks next to the windows, they also keep watch on me from cars sitting in the parking lot across the street.

To regain focus, I crush up some Adderall and Ritalin, smiling as the orange and white colors mix together. I snort a few lines and anxiously look around from my clandestine, corner cubbyhole. After confirming that no one (besides Anya's friends) is watching me, I dive back into the powdery mix, confident that I'm quickly "sharpening up." Despite my efforts, my discomfort only increases.

Anya's friends have been following and watching me for three weeks now, yet still she has not said anything to me; moreover, although I know they have a good reason for their surveillance, the feeling of constantly having every movement of my life observed and analyzed is seriously starting to unnerve me. Now there are Anya's male friends as well as her female friends, and I even hear them talking.

::Why the hell does Anya like this dude?::

::Who the fuck knows, he's one hell of a freakin' weirdo.::

::Yeah, and what's up with all that goddam yoga and Pilates shit!::

::Forget that, how about the fucking manicures, pedicures, facials, and massages?::

::Yeah, it's all fucked up. The kid's a douche bag.::

::The fucking flamboyant weirdo!::

::You got that right! Damn, is he one flamboyant weird-ass motherfucker!::

You're all just jealous, you losers, I think.

During the past week it has become increasingly clear that all of Anya's male friends absolutely hate me, and for numerous reasons: they hate the fact that Anya likes me; that I am in such good shape; that I do yoga and Pilates; that I get manicures, pedicures, facials, and massages; that I take piano lessons; that I am able to spend so much time at the beach; that I get large checks in the mail for doing nothing; that I mainly wear little kids' shirts featuring Mighty Mouse, Pac-Man, Atari, Ghostbusters, Mr. Bubble, Lemonhead, and various other cartoon characters; that all it seems I listen to is Andrea Bocelli, Sarah Brightman, and Enya; that I do nothing besides eat, sleep, work out, write, and draw, which has assumed the largest role in my days since I realized I am Frida Kahlo; and, most important, that there seems to be no end to how much money I will spend. With a passion, they hate how I spend money so flagrantly.

In summary, they have nicknamed me "Flamboyant Weirdo"— and although they are unaware of my special abilities, they all realize that there's something very different about me. They just can't quite put their finger on what it is.

Typing away on my computer in the library, forced to listen incessantly to how much they all despise me, I become extremely agitated. One of Anya's male friends has thrown out the notion that I am surely an artsy queer, because I do so much weird "womanly" shit, and am probably the biggest pussy in the world. All I hear from the other male voices is overwhelming agreement, each taking his turn to offer insight into how much of a skirt I am.

Even though I don't want to give away the fact that I know I am being followed, after listening to this line of discussion for about a half hour, I truly flip out. With great haste, I leave the library, head down a set of stairs cut into the hill, and walk along a path by the river. Coming to a lone bench in a somewhat secluded area, I rip off my shirt and throw it to the ground. I beat my chest and scream: "Here I am, you motherfuckers! Here I am! You want me, come and get me! I'll take all of you fucking pansies! You hear me? All of you!"

47

The Force

July 2003

T he more I learn about myself, the more things fall into place," I whisper to myself, again working on my computer at the local library. *But then why am I getting more and more unsettled?* I wonder.

"Ahh . . . forget it. Just forget them, Michael! They're pathetic—pathetic and jealous," I say, smiling with renewed confidence and satisfaction. Tucked away in a clandestine corner of the library, I pop another Adderall, and after looking around once more to make sure no one is looking, I pour some of my already smashed-up Ritalin on the table and snort a few lines.

"All right, now I'm on point. Booyah! Let's get to work! All right, now what the hell was I working on? Hmm . . . ha! Who cares? Damn, was I right about that Adderall-Ritalin combination! I knew I had to be smarter than the doctors. They don't know shit. Just look at me: totally zoned in—perfecto! This is the key to unlocking the doors in each of us: 180 mg of Adderall, with nonstop lines of Ritalin. At last I'm on the right track!"

Yeah, but if only they would let up. I'm tired of listening to them! Why won't they ever let up? I've grown increasingly uneasy at the attention from Anya's friends and family, who refuse to stop watching and harassing me. For a moment I reflect on how odd it is that I can always hear them so clearly, even when I don't see them nearby.

"Yes, of course!" I realize suddenly. I can hear them not because they are being loud, but because I have incredible superhearing, yet another ability forged from my nervous system stimulation and spiritual awakening! My superhearing explains why I never actually see anyone; they must be maintaining a distance out of eyeshot, watching me with high-powered binoculars. I clearly have an awesome connection with a deep spiritual force.

Despite these revelations, a couple more pills, and several more lines, the voices of Anya's friends soon prove too much for me to handle. After another library incident, virtually identical to the one last month, I speed frantically back to the apartment, desperately craving privacy. Curling up in my papasan chair, violently shaking and hyperventilating, I am forced to confront yet another truth. *Fuck! How far will they go? This has to stop!*

On the verge of an emotional meltdown, I grab a pile of dirty clothes and some pillows and block out every square inch of both windows. This enrages them.

::Who the fuck does he think he is?::

::Yeah, I don't give a shit if he knows we're here watching him. It's not like we're doing this for our health. We're doing it for Anya. And if we want to watch him, then we're going to fucking watch him!::

::This kid's due for a beating.::

::Yeah, we should put him in the hospital. Then Anya won't like him so much.::

::You see him at the library earlier? Fucking moron thinks he's the Incredible Hulk or something.::

::I say we grab a couple of bats and wait for the right moment to beat him within an inch of his life.::

::I'm game. Asshole's got no fucking right blocking us out. I mean, what the fuck's he doing in there that he needs to hide from us?::

::Good point. Why are we even doing this shit, anyhow? Anyone have any fucking clue what Anya sees in this loser?::

::No one does, bro. Even the girls who used to like him think he's a fucking weirdo now.::

::You know, it really pisses me off that Anya says we can't kick his ass.::

::I'll tell you what, man. That shit's lifted. Earlier at the library Anya said that if he wants to act all tough, then he deserves what he gets. Plus, she thinks he needs a serious ass-whooping to humble him before she'd ever think of going out with him.::

::No shit, she said that? This faggot is going down.::

::I say we break his wrists and each and every one of his fingers so we don't have to watch queer-boy fucking draw or write anymore.::

::Sounds good to me, but while we're at it, why not also break his legs? I mean, we all know that this pecker has it coming.::

::And his face. We definitely have to break that asshole's face.::

::What if he says something?::

::Trust me, he won't say nothin'. He won't do jack shit to mess things up with Anya.::

::Yeah, but what does that really have to do with us? Why wouldn't he turn us in?::

::You don't get it, bro. Anya said she wants to take the first swing at him.::

::No shit! Guys, this is going to be too good.::

I've heard enough.

Severely unstable, in the preliminary stages of another panic attack, and unable to see an alternate means of bringing this to an end, I finally call the police. After a month and a half of living with strangers following me, watching me at every moment of the day, I have finally reached my decisive breaking point. *Fuck this, I'm done. I can't do this shit anymore.*

I take down the barrier from the window above the foot of my bed, giving me a view of the street. After just ten minutes, the cops arrive. I am aware that I am in the midst of another nice panic attack and in no condition to speak with them, but gathering myself as best I can, I go outside. It proves impossible for me to keep myself in check. Frantically pacing back and forth in front of the two police cars, and occasionally dropping to the ground to lie down and grab my heart, I can't put even one coherent sentence together. I attempt to communicate, but it comes out like mumbling. When one of them tries to grab my shoulders to keep me in place, my gut reaction proves poor. I swing around and punch the officer in the chest, which feels good for a brief moment before I am tackled to the ground by what are now six officers.

In a state of full-blown hysteria now, I scream holy havoc, swinging my arms in all directions, putting up as valiant a fight as possible. All that this earns me, however, is a baton to my back and ribs and a blast of mace in my face. Pushing my face into the concrete, the officers twist my arms behind my back and handcuff me.

The officers put me in the ambulance they have already called and ride with me to Norwalk Hospital, less than one minute away. On the way to the emergency room (yet again), I lose control of my emotions, crying worse than I have ever cried and screaming for help. Although I am aware of everything that is occurring, it is not until I wake up almost an hour later from a delightful Ativan-induced rest at the hospital that I have any clue who I am, where I am, or why I am in handcuffs.

Although they cannot prove anything, the doctors believe that, along with another panic attack, I have suffered some sort of emotional and nervous breakdown. Lucid now, I apologize to the officers who are still at the hospital to take my statement and possibly arrest me. I tell them why I initially called them, which I think explains why I acted as I did. The police, seemingly empathetic to my plight, whatever they believe that to be, let me off with just a citation for public disturbance.

The following day I am still quite anxious, though incredibly comforted by a new revelation. Having begun to hear Anya's voice continuously in my head, I have come to realize that we share a telepathic bond. She tells me to be patient, because she is just waiting for the perfect moment to speak with me in person. *Thank heavens! My conjecture that Anya and I are soul mates has been confirmed. I'm not crazy, after all!*

NORWALK HOSPITAL EMERGENCY MEDICAL SERVICES

RESPONDING STATION: ☒ NORWALK ☐ WESTPORT ☐ WILTON/WESTON ☐ NEW CANAAN

RUN NO. 2822

NAME: Winder, Michael

CITY/TOWN: Westport CT

DATE OF BIRTH: 04/04/1978 AGE: 26

DISPATCH/PU LOCATION: Arch Street CITY/TOWN: Norwalk ZIP CODE: 06850

STAFF 1: MGB MGS CREW #: 404404 Y N Y N DATE OF ONSET: 072703

CHIEF COMPLAINT(S): "People are following me" - per pt.

HISTORY: Pt. 26 y/o ♂ c̄ hx of psych problems. PD called to see pt. On EMS arrival pt. c̄o ~5 Pt officers. Pt. hyperventilating + agitated, lying on ground + grabbing hair. Pt. helped up to feet. Rega. to fight c̄ PD. Pt. arrested + maced by PD. (while fig.

CURRENT MEDS: Advil → per pt.

ALLERGIES: Per chart

OBSERVATIONS: 26 y/o ♂ lying on ground, yelling + grabbing hair. Pt. ⊕ hyperventilating ⊕ agitated. Pt. stating that people had been following him x 3-4 day. They wanted to fight him ⊕ head ache ⊖ recent trauma ⊖ pain → per pt. ⊕ Eye irritation p̄ being maced in fight.

TIME	BP	P	R	SpO₂	EtCO₂	GCS E	V	M	TRAUMA SCORE CS	R	BP
1 20:33	132/	P 90	20	% on O₂	mmHg	4	5	6	4	4	4
2	/			% on O₂	mmHg						
3	/			% on O₂	mmHg						
4	/			% on O₂	mmHg						

TREATMENT: Ambulated to ambulance c̄ assistance of PD. Pt. sat on bench c̄o c̄ 2 PD officers. Pt. in handcuffs throughout tx. → tx to observation unit @ NHED c̄ change.

CLINICAL IMPRESSION(S): 1. r/o psych

MR COPY DISTRIBUTED TO: ED chart BY MGB

PATIENT TRANSFERRED TO: Staff RN LOCATION: Observation

VALUABLES: ☐ None Describe: Cell phone, eye glasses

GIVEN TO: Nurse in observation unit

MEDICAL RECORD (PATIENT CHART)

Several hours later, as the darkness settles in, she gives me a tele-pathic ring, telling me that it is high time we get together. However, since I am the guy, she tells me that the onus is on me to make the date happen. Dutifully, I give Anya a call on her cell phone, leav-ing a message on her voicemail that I am going to a certain movie and that she can just meet me there.

"Hey, Anya, it's Mike, just calling because I'm going to see *Such and Such* and was wondering if you wanted to join me. All right, take care." Click.

"Hey, Anya, it's Mike again. Um, just wanted to let you know that *Such and Such* is playing right down here in SoNo in like thirty minutes. All right? Bye." Click.

"Hey, Anya, how's it going? Haven't heard from you yet and just wanted to let you know that I'm not sure I'm going if you aren't, so if you could give me a heads-up that would be great. Cool. Later." Click.

"Hey, Anya, still haven't heard from you, but I'm heading down to the movie anyway. If you decide to come, I'll be toward the back of the theater." Click.

"Hey, Anya, I'm down at the movie house. It seems they have stopped selling tickets, so what I'm going to do is leave the back door slightly ajar with a rock, so all's good if you still want to come." Click.

"Hey, Anya, just wanted to let you know that if you're hesitant about coming because you think it'll be awkward, don't be. You know, I'll have a seat saved for you, an aisle seat toward the back right, and all you have to do is just sit down and enjoy the movie. Nothing needs to be said. Cool? All right, take care." Click.

"Hey, Anya, last phone call, I promise. Um, I kind of didn't like how *Such and Such* was going, so I left and went to *This and That*, which is just a few theaters down. Oh, but I'll still be in pretty much the same spot. All right, hope to see you, bye." Click.

It occurs to me in passing that it's a good thing we have a tele-pathic bond; if we didn't, that set of phone calls might seem pretty darn weird. Hell, it might even surpass even my infamous mangled dinner invitation from several weeks earlier! No, worries, though. It's all good.

Much to my surprise, I watch the movie alone. I can only assume that her car isn't working or she is too nervous to call me back. So I make one more phone call because I am sure something must have happened.

Male voice: "Hello?"

Winder-Kahlo: "Hi, is Anya there?"

Male voice: "Who's this?"

Winder-Kahlo: "Mike. I think Anya's expecting my call."

Male voice: "Listen, man, this is Anya's boyfriend; she doesn't want to speak with you."

Winder-Kahlo: "First off, just so you know, Anya doesn't consider you her boyfriend, and second off, I'm pretty sure she would want to speak with me."

Male voice: "What? What are you talking about? I am her boyfriend, and just so *you* know, she's sitting right next to me and definitely doesn't want to speak with you."

Winder-Kahlo: "That's bullshit. But if that is the case, tell her if she doesn't stop following me, I'm calling the police. Understand?"

Male voice: "What? What are you talking about? Listen, I'm hanging up now, and I don't think you should call her again." Click.

Yes! Of course! Everything makes perfect sense! Anya accidentally left her cell phone with this cock-knocker, who, in desperation, overwhelmed by jealousy, erased all my phone messages and then finally picked up the phone only to tell me some unbelievable story about her not wanting to speak with me, so that I (his competition) might be eliminated from the picture. Ridiculous! Sorry, cock-knocker, you are just a bit too obvious.

I chalk this night up to a success for me; Anya will surely be furious with cock-knocker for not giving her the messages and for telling me that he's her boyfriend. I'll obviously just let her know telepathically everything that happened, and then cock-knocker will get his just comeuppance.

A few days later, Frida's spirit guides me in another direction. I am watching the news and see Osama bin Laden on the television screen. Something inside me lights up. *My God!*

For a while I have been assuming that Frida's spirit is inside me not just to guide me in personal matters but to affect the big picture as well. I know that I am supposed to use my connection and abilities to help humanity, but I've been uncertain how that would unfold. That is, until now!

I leap up off the couch. "I'm the one who's gonna find that bastard!" I shout triumphantly.

I grab my parents' big atlas, and, without looking, allow my hands and fingers to move on their own throughout the book. Ultimately, my hands stop on a page, my index finger slamming down in the middle of it. I've found his location.

In the days that follow I feel as though I ought to do more, that I am also meant to stop an evil plan he is preparing. Taking out my journals, I allow my hands to draw and write freely. My results are definitive and conclusive, compelling enough to warrant my bringing them to the attention of my family on numerous occasions and, eventually, the Federal Bureau of Investigation.

Without delay, I find the appropriate websites and send the FBI my privileged knowledge, praying that it will take heed of the imminent danger that I am disclosing.

The Terror Plot

> The overwhelming majority of the world is irate at the United States for making their own rules, acting like a supreme superpower that can do whatever it wants, and toppling regimes at will. Great Britain aside, the United Nations Security Council refused to support military intervention in Iraq. Even Canada and Mexico declined. Take careful notice of our neighboring countries' votes; this was meant to send a message: "Those that border you are not your allies!" The rest of the world realizes that in light of our focused efforts on homeland security after 9/11, the United States will only stay vulnerable to attacks and possible invasion for

another five years, max. For all intents and purposes, it is the rest
of the world against the United States and Britain. Canada, along
with France, has sided with many of the Muslim countries against
the United States. Accordingly, Canada is sheltering Osama bin
Laden; it's the last place we would ever look for the al Qaeda
leader. Bin Laden is living in the Monts Otish mountain range, in
the province of Quebec. He has shaved off his beard and all the
hair on his head, wears a mask and glasses, and walks with a cane.
     The United States is going to be attacked via water. Osama's
troops, stationed in camps in other mountainous regions near his
own, are going to be given false passports by the Canadian govern-
ment, and allowed to cross the Washington border into the United
States. They are going to arrive a week before, set the charges the
day of the attack, and afterward escape back into Canada. The
plan for initial attack, on December 31, 2003, is for al Qaeda to
blow up the Cle Elum Dam, in Washington State. This dam,
located only 124 miles from Olympia and 82 miles from Seattle,
has a drainage area of 260 square miles and no auxiliary spillway.
This one dam is going to flood both Washington state's capital and
her largest city, in one burst. They expect many to drown, especially
partygoers in the streets for New Year's Eve, too drunk to avoid the
flood waters. To make matters worse, they are going to drop gallons
of liquid LSD in the water before they blow it. Their hope: that
those who don't drown in the floods will ingest enough acid to
cause full panic and mayhem. If they get their wish, television will
broadcast a chaotic scene of madness: Americans brutally attacking
each other, getting in horrible accidents, mutilating themselves,
and committing suicide.

Since the attack never occurred, I can only assume that the FBI
managed to thwart Osama's evil plan—although it's a little disap-
pointing that I was never properly thanked.

Not having nearly enough on my plate as it is, I decide to round out
the increasing instability in my life this month by filing for bankruptcy.
Despite all the money I've received in the past several years from various sources, I am broker than broke, and roughly $60,000 in debt.
This is somewhat surprising to my family and my lawyers, because I
am just twenty-six and have no dependents. I'm not so fazed.

Am I doing the wrong thing? I wonder, alone in my room. After doing some lines and pills for added clarity, I stare at myself in the mirror. Things quickly sharpen up. "No, of course not, Winder. No worries, my good man! This is what's meant to happen. Remember, Frida is with you," I say, smiling, successfully reestablishing my momentarily waning confidence.

FORM B1	United States Bankruptcy Court District of Connecticut	Voluntary Petition
Name of Debtor (if individual, enter Last, First, Middle): **Winder, Michael**	Name of Joint Debtor (Spouse)(Last, First, Middle):	
All Other Names used by the Debtor in the last 6 years (include married, maiden, and trade names):	All Other Names used by the Joint Debtor in the last 6 years (include married, maiden, and trade names):	
Soc. Sec./Tax I.D. No. (if more than one, state all):	Soc. Sec./Tax I.D. No. (if more than one, state all):	
Street Address of Debtor (No. & Street, City, State & Zip Code):	Street Address of Joint Debtor (No. & Street, City, State & Zip Code):	
County of Residence or of the Principal Place of Business: **fairfield**	County of Residence or of the Principal Place of Business:	
Mailing Address of Debtor (if different from street address):	Mailing Address of Joint Debtor (if different from street address):	
Location of Principal Assets of Business Debtor (if different from street address above):		

Information Regarding the Debtor (Check the Applicable Boxes)

Venue (Check any applicable box)
☑ Debtor has been domiciled or has had a residence, principal place of business, or principal assets in this District for 180 days immediately preceding the date of this petition or for a longer part of such 180 days than in any other District.
☐ There is a bankruptcy case concerning debtor's affiliate, general partner, or partnership pending in this District.

Type of Debtor (Check all boxes that apply)
☑ Individual(s) ☐ Railroad
☐ Corporation ☐ Stockbroker
☐ Partnership ☐ Commodity Broker
☐ Other _____ ☐ Clearing Bank

Nature of Debts (Check one box)
☑ Consumer/Non-Business ☐ Business

Chapter 11 Small Business (Check all boxes that apply)
☐ Debtor is a small business as defined in 11 U.S.C. § 101
☐ Debtor is and elects to be considered a small business under 11 U.S.C. § 1121(e) (Optional)

Chapter or Section of Bankruptcy Code Under Which the Petition is Filed (Check one box)
☑ Chapter 7 ☐ Chapter 11 ☐ Chapter 13
☐ Chapter 9 ☐ Chapter 12
☐ Sec. 304 - Case ancillary to foreign proceeding

Filing Fee (Check one box)
☑ Full Filing Fee Attached
☐ Filing Fee to be paid in installments (Applicable to individuals only) Must attach signed application for the court's consideration certifying that the debtor is unable to pay fee except in installments. Rule 1006(b). See Official Form No. 3.

Statistical/Administrative Information (Estimates only)   THIS SPACE IS FOR COURT USE ONLY
☐ Debtor estimates that funds will be available for distribution to unsecured creditors.
☑ Debtor estimates that, after any exempt property is excluded and administrative expenses paid, there will be no funds available for distribution to unsecured creditors.

Estimated Number of Creditors
1-15	16-49	50-99	100-199	200-999	1000-over
☐	☑	☐	☐	☐	☐

Estimated Assets
$0 to $50,000	$50,001 to $100,000	$100,001 to $500,000	$500,001 to $1 million	$1,000,001 to $10 million	$10,000,001 to $50 million	$50,000,001 to $100 million	More than $100 million
☑	☐	☐	☐	☐	☐	☐	☐

Estimated Debts
$0 to $50,000	$50,001 to $100,000	$100,001 to $500,000	$500,001 to $1 million	$1,000,001 to $10 million	$10,000,001 to $50 million	$50,000,001 to $100 million	More than $100 million
☐	☑	☐	☐	☐	☐	☐	☐

48

Jesus

August 2003

I pretend I can't hear them.

It's a beautiful day: clear blue skies, warm (but not too humid) weather, children playing, and sailboats in the harbor. It's a picture-perfect afternoon for families who are looking to enjoy a gorgeous day at the beach. With its spectacular views, spacious sands, picturesque jetties, and incredible facilities, Westport's Compo Beach is absolutely beautiful. Everyone around me looks happy, smiling. I pretend that I am one of them.

Silently, I pray that Anya's friends will leave me alone, that they will stop following me. I don't know how much more of this I can take.

::You're not good enough for her.::

::Hey, you, you hear him? There's no way we're letting you spend the rest of her life in her head.::

::You're a dead man, shithead!::

::Yeah, you're one dead motherfucker!::

::Aw! You fucking flamboyant weirdo, you look so scared. Are you scared, fag-boy?::

::Yeah, he is. Look at him!::

::Is he trying to ignore us?::

::Oh, he better not try and ignore us, 'cause we're gonna fucking slit his throat!::

::No joke, bro. You're one dead son of a bitch!::

::Kill the queer!::

::Ha, ha, ha, ha . . . ::

::You still trying to ignore us, tough guy?::

::Yeah, he is.::

::Hey, we know you hear us!::

::We're watching you!::

::Yeah, don't ignore us, fag-boy!::

::What's he thinking, Anya?::

::Yeah, he trying to talk you at all?::

::No, not yet, at least, Anya says.::

::Anya? Is that you? Please make them stop, I beg her telepathically.::

::He just said my name. And then he asked you guys to stop, she tells her friends.::

::You kidding me?::

::That son of a bitch has got some nerve.::

::Man, we know you can hear us, so get this: we're gonna fucking cut you up, you little fucker.::

::Yeah, we know where you live—you ain't livin' through the night, queer.::

I slowly turn in a circle, scanning for Anya and her friends. They have been following me for more than two months now, yet she still doesn't approach me. I don't care about her anymore; I just want it all to stop.

From morning to night they are there, all around me, blending in.

To make matters worse, my recent realization that Anya and I have a telepathic bond has not been the blessing I had initially thought, because in addition to her thoughts, I can always hear what those around her are saying. There are voices everywhere, all the time, and almost all of them despise me.

There are so many of them—too many to count. They are relent-less. I cannot go on much longer.

> ::Aw, he's looking for Anya. Well, guess what, queer, she's done talking to you. We're in charge now, and we ain't going nowhere till you're dead!::
> ::Maybe he's looking for us.::
> ::Hey, you trying to find us, tough guy?::
> ::Hey, we're over here.::
> ::No, this way.::
> ::No, over here.::

"Stop. Stop. Stop. Stop. Stop!" I yell.

> ::Ha, ha, ha, ha, ha, ha . . . ::

I hear a thousand laughs, all directed at me, coming from every which way. More important, I finally feel the last ounce of control slip from my grasp. Screaming uncontrollably in all directions, I frantically begin pacing in circles, my palms continuously banging my temples. I grab my beach chair and begin smashing it repeat-edly against my car.

The voices are an unshakable, all-consuming presence in my mind.

I can sense the eyes of all the beachgoers fixed upon on me. They're not helping things. Anxiously scanning my surroundings, I see people staring at me as though I am that horrible accident on the freeway that they cannot look away from.

I am confident that I am putting the fear of God into the nearby children (and adults, for that matter!). I imagine that my unavoid-able presence must be something akin to Marilyn Manson (or per-haps Charles Manson?) invading a Norman Rockwell painting.

The parents look at me in disgust as they turn their children away from the crazy man; the little kids seem amazed (or are they afraid?). I hear crying (I think)—is it for me? Or, perhaps, *is* it me? A couple of tears trickle down the left side of my face. I quickly slap them away with my hand.

The entire beach has come to a silent, uncomfortable halt, watching me, waiting for the temporary cyst to be removed so that they can resubmerge themselves into Norman Rockwell. I acquiesce, but not out of concern for the public peace. It is survival, and nothing else, that sways me.

I jump in my car and start driving toward the apartment. Swerving in and out of both lanes, I contemplate sending my car into a tree, into a wall, or over a bridge. I'm driving with my head out the window, screaming *"Stop following me!"* at the top of my lungs, over and over.

Returning to my apartment, I take refuge in my bedroom, where the windows are still tightly covered. In my makeshift sanctuary (or is it a prison?) I can at least keep out the eyes of Those Who Are Watching; however, their voices permeate my very being.

With my mind in an uncontrollable, frenzied state, I am compelled to start organizing everything around me, down to the last Tic Tac and Adderall tablet, in various geometric, interconnecting patterns that ultimately cover the entire room. When I am finished, emotionally and mentally exhausted, I pass out in the papasan chair.

Two hours later, I wake up and look at the room around me.

"Did I do that?" I say.

There are so many colors, bright to dark, so many objects, big to small, interwoven throughout the floor of my room in the most amazing configurations. I feel such pride. It's beautiful. Yet part of me knows that something about it is very, very wrong—disturbing, perhaps.

First slowly, and then quickly, I put everything away. Not that I felt tremendously grounded before, but now something has decisively changed. I don't feel right anymore. I can't get my bearings, and despite the Adderall, I find it nearly impossible to concentrate on even the smallest things. I snort a couple of lines of Ritalin, hoping for clarity. To my surprise, clarity does not come. Suddenly, extremely dizzy, agitated, and confused, I lie down on my bed, but I am far from able to fall back asleep.

I'm overwhelmed by the loud, unrelenting voices in my head. I start crying, pleading with Anya to make them all stop yelling at me, but to no avail. I cock back my right fist and start punching my face as hard as I possibly can, over and over, hoping that I might knock them loose, or at least numb the pain for a little while. With the right side of my face sufficiently bruised, I move to my left, and after that I start butting the wall with my head, but this provides only momentary gratification.

After I have finished beating the shit out of myself, nothing has really changed, except that now it seems I've added a nice headache to my woes. Unable to move—or, actually, too scared to move—I continue to lie in bed for the next five hours, tears streaming down my face, until darkness comes. I spend the afternoon praying, asking both God and Frida Kahlo's spirit to help me, telling them that I don't want my abilities anymore, that I promise to act "normal," and that I don't want anything to do with Anya. I hope that someone is listening.

Someone is. Alas, it is none of my hopeful saviors. Having heard my thoughts, Anya is momentarily livid that I want nothing to do with her, but then she breaks down crying—and when her large entourage finds out what I have said, they decide that tonight is the night I am going to die.

I apologize to Anya, which actually works, for she is indeed obsessed—though not so much with me as with the notion of a telepathic bond. Unfortunately, the male members of her consortium still refuse to back off from their deadly decision. Anya therefore reasons that, for my own protection, tonight is going to have to be the night on which she finally speaks with me face-to-face.

Having finally passed out from complete mental and emotional exhaustion, I wake up several hours later. I'm lying on my bed, eyes wide open, staring at the ceiling. My hands rest just below my chest, tightly squeezing the open switchblade that lies flat against my body. I'm not sure if I'm holding it for protection or for a darker reason. I spend the majority of the evening in this position, virtually motionless, waiting.

Eventually I'm called on to prove my worth to Anya's mother, who refuses to let Anya speak with me unless I first take a few tests. These tests last through the night, conducted outside on my lawn for all to see. For example, I have to stand on my left foot with eyes closed and both hands covering my heart, until Anya's mother tells me to stop. All I have to do is pass just one test, but this never happens, because I always eventually mess up before I am finished, which sends Anya's mother into a rage.

::Who do you think you are? she screams in my head. In no way whatsoever am I going to let any daughter of mine speak with some loser who can't even complete such a simple task as standing on one foot with his eyes closed. What are you waiting for? Get back upstairs and wait for me to call you back down again.::

Up and down the stairs, up and down the stairs—faster and faster. At Anya's mother's direction, I scale the two flights of steps a dizzying number of times, my vision steadily growing more and more hazy, as I find myself grasping the banister with both hands as I climb. My hands white, my fingers tightly clenched, I hold on for dear life, for everything is so very distorted around me. Testing lasts straight through to the morning, over the course of which time I take eight tablets of melatonin (a natural herbal sleep aid) in the hope of falling asleep—but to no avail.

At around 9:00 AM, haggard and barely able to stand, I am finally given a reason for hope and the energy to keep going. Anya tells me to come outside. Apparently her mother has finally agreed to let us meet, with one final caveat: I have to prove my psychic abilities by finding her car, which is parked on one of the connecting side streets.

This test will be easy. Standing in the middle of Arch Street, barefoot and shirtless, I pull my eyelids back into my head as far as they will go and allow my right arm to swing free, my index finger slowly homing in on the exact location of Anya's car.

"Ah, there you are," I say triumphantly, as I start moving in the direction my spirit has shown me. As I look around, I realize it's just the beginning of yet another beautiful day. The birds are chirping, the sky is cloudless, and the sun is already beating down on my exposed chest. After the night I've had, I feel as if I'm making a final trek across the desert sands.

Dizzy and nauseous, I look toward the blurry horizon. I'm confident that Anya is there—in fact, I think I might even see her. As my vision slowly scrolls back down the street, my eyes take in the run-down, low-income, suburban housing, the houses cramped one on top of another. I wish they were a mirage. It all looks like shit: run-down, low-income, suburban shit.

As I continue walking down the street, something suddenly happens inside my head. It is sort of like a surge of lightning, a loud snap, followed by an immediate blackout. Any temporary energy burst is totally lost.

Severely exhausted and drained from not sleeping and, even more likely, from dealing with the combination of countless voices (and chemicals) in my brain, I suddenly feel asphyxiated. I barely manage to prop myself up against a neighbor's mailbox. Regaining my balance and consciousness, I start walking again, this time aimlessly because I am too disoriented to attempt to look to my inner spirit to guide me.

When a man comes outside, asking why I am stumbling across his lawn, I mumble an incoherent apology, aware that he is looking at me in a way that usually precedes a call to 911. *Jackass*, I think to myself, *he doesn't have a fucking clue who he's dealing with.* Suddenly I realize that Anya and her mother have driven off.

Half awake, half alive, and completely despondent, I slowly and circuitously walk back home. I pass another Joe Ordinary, dressed in the unkempt uniform of the indolent, potbellied, midlife man: bathrobe, boxer shorts, and slippers. I wish I had the energy to tell him to fuck off. His unabashed stare, surrounded by an ugly, unshaven face that doesn't even attempt to hide his disgust, is grating on my soul. Was he just sneering at me? Did I just see him shake his head? I can't be sure. But it doesn't matter; there's nothing I can do right now except, I hope, find my way home.

Jackass, I think to myself again, *he doesn't have a fucking clue who he's dealing with.* I wish I had the energy for original thoughts.

I serendipitously collide with my front porch just a few minutes later. The swirls of voices in my head and visions in front of my eyes are momentarily insignificant. I smile gratefully.

I dart up the stairs and head straight for the shower. Before getting there, however, I grab some Adderall, Ritalin, and Paxil. I'm hoping that a little drug cocktail might kick me into gear, or at least calm my growing instability. It does nothing of the sort.

The voices are so enormous in number that I can't even hear individual words, but the voices are all extremely angry. My hands clasp the sides of my head, tightly covering my ears, as I pace back and forth, my eyes closed, pleading with someone, anyone, to end my suffering. Although I am thankful for my telepathic bond with Anya, it has become indescribably tormenting to hear the voices from the moment I wake up in the morning until the moment before I fall asleep at night. I am unable to imagine that anything could be much worse.

I need them all to be gone. I need this all to be done.

I consider running a bath so that I might try drowning myself, but I figure that's totally unrealistic: I wouldn't be able to go through with it.

Stepping out of the shower, I think of the switchblade and wonder if I ought to slice myself. Much to my surprise, the vision of myself lying in a bloody mess brings me no fear, no anxiety. On the contrary, a large part of me feels comfort in the image; things would be resolved, and there would be no more pain.

I quickly dismiss this option, though, when I imagine Vanessa crying hysterically. There is no way I could ever let her find me in such a state. It is solely because of Vanessa that I decide not to go through with my final plan, either, which involves a couple of bottles of sleeping pills. I care about how my death would affect Vanessa a thousand times more than how much I care for my life. My younger sister is a bit wild, a bit insecure, and a bit immature, but she's selfless, loyal, genuine, and reliable to the max. My younger sister is my true best friend. Suicide is not an option.

Where this leaves me, I do not know.

On what feels like an inevitable course between here and *there*, for the moment I am unfortunately stuck here: in my bathroom; in Norwalk, Connecticut; in my head; in unrelenting anxiety; in ever-increasing madness; in life. *There* seems so much more appealing—so much more . . . peaceful.

Standing in the bathroom in my towel, I am staring at myself in the mirror, both hands gripping the sink as I desperately seek to regain composure and stable ground, when I suddenly hear a new, single, loud, clear voice ringing inside my head: *Arise, Jesus of Nazareth!*

At the point when I couldn't feel any lower or more hopeless, all my worries and problems are magically lifted. There will be no more pain.

I am Jesus of Nazareth!

Standing in the middle of My bedroom in only My boxers, windows now cleared and open, I am not afraid of anything. I close My eyes, allowing My arms to move freely, turning in all directions at My sides and around My head, as My torso, hips, and head twist in every direction. These fluid, time-consuming movements, meant to induce the coming physical transformation, are something similar to a musical interpretive dance, although I don't move My feet.

I'm a new man, in every possible way.

My dance is interrupted only by the occasional trip to the window, where, standing tall and unafraid, with chest out, head raised and slightly tilted back, eyes wide open and glaring down, and right arm fully extended outwards, I point My index finger toward those to whom I am speaking. In a deep, booming voice, loudly resonating throughout the house, I call out the names of Anya's male friends as they come to Me in My head and chant their terrible sins for all to hear.

Upon her return from work later in the day, Vanessa finds Me in My room. She looks harried from a long day of waitressing. Her long hair, draping her tall, slender frame, is as visibly frazzled as she is. She is, understandably, a little taken aback by My dancing, which I vehemently resist stopping. Eventually I relent, taking a transitory break from My transformation, although I do so only at the will of My "higher power," to speak my Father's wisdom.

After putting on my green cargo shorts, I walk over to Vanessa, rest My hands on her shoulders, and say, "Vanessa, daughter of Ruth and Alan, sister of Jason and Nicole. God bless you, my child. I am with you."

Barely able to move, let alone speak, Vanessa stares at Me as if I'm crazy. If only I could help her to understand that I'm not crazy. Nothing could possibly be further from the truth. I know this now. I know everything now. I continue to look straight into her eyes, My hands still resting on her shoulders, I am confident that, if not through My words, My eyes alone will help her to see more clearly and will comfort her. Slowly, she begins to make halfhearted attempts to speak with Me, to converse with Me on an earthly basis, but she simply can't understand.

After a few more unsuccessful tries at communicating with Me on her terms, Vanessa quickly removes herself from My presence and from her temporary paralysis to make a phone call. I can hear her whisper, "Mom, is Jason there? Put him on. Jason, Mike thinks he's Jesus. Please come quickly!"

Ten minutes later Vanessa, Jason, and My mother are all in My bedroom, trying to get through to Me.

Jason: "All right, so can I speak with Mike?"

Me: "Be calm, My child, Michael is Michael no more."

Jason: "Do you know where he is?"

Me: "He is fine, My son. All is well. You need not worry."

Mom: "Michael, come on, let's go, we have dinner waiting."

Me: "Ruth, wife of Alan, mother of Jason, Vanessa, and Nicole. Be not afraid. All is indeed well."

Jason: "Mike, do you know where you are? Do you know what day it is?"

Me: "Rest easy, My son. The time is near."

Mom: "C'mon, Michael. Snap out of it."

Jason: "Mike, can you stop moving? I just want to speak to you for a second."

Me: "Enough! The time for reckoning is upon us! For I am Jesus of Nazareth."

After an hour of negotiation, I finally get in the car with My brother, having ultimately agreed to go to dinner at My parents' house. I'm still wearing My green cargo shorts, but I refuse to put on a shirt or sandals.

As we drive down the street, My eyes are fixed on the same lawns I recently traversed, the same mailbox that barely kept me upright just hours ago, the same houses I stumbled by, with their same ordinary inhabitants walking about the neighborhood—but everything is so different, so far from ordinary. Everything is *extraordinary*. These are all My people, My children, living on My land. I am captivated by everything, all that I have let go unnoticed, unheeded—the wonders of society.

Amid My ethereal trance, My brother pulls a fast one, slipping up the street to the hospital. When Jason pulls into the emergency room parking lot and I realize where we are, I open the car door and attempt to jump out. I am unfazed by the fact that we are still moving, and I am disappointed that he, of all people, has chosen this option.

It's so obvious: My brother could never understand—My older, much more mature, and much more sensible brother. Of course

My brother doesn't believe; he is a worldly individual, a true non-believer.

When My brother slams on the brakes and reaches over and grabs me with both arms, he has crossed the line. No one, not even My brother, can touch Me, can stop Me from doing what I must do. I crack him in the face, leaving a nice fist print, jump out of the car, and take off running. Shaking off the blow, My brother hops out of the car and chases Me.

Shirtless and shoeless, I run down the asphalt sidewalk, impervious to the cuts ripping through My feet from the sharp rocks and broken glass. The faces staring at me from the cars I pass are as blurry as My thoughts. In fact, there are no thoughts, only an intense yearning to be free. I need to be somewhere else, so I can start helping My people.

In the distance I can make out Anya, calling to Me from the back of My mind, guiding Me toward her. I run, faster still, again crisscrossing lawns and driveways, confident that Anya's voice will bring Me to safety.

I can hear My brother, running just paces behind Me, calling the police from his cell phone, asking for assistance. After a nearly fifteen-minute run, and not before I've banged on at least one door screaming for Anya, the police finally stop Me, and demand that I explain why I am running from My brother down a residential street in just a pair of cargo shorts.

Realizing that these police officers will probably not be able to handle the fact that I am Jesus, I turn on my "Michael switch," pretending that I have no idea what Jason is talking about, that I have just been joking around with him about being Jesus, which unfortunately he has taken seriously. Just when I am certain that the police officers are about to let Me go, Jason tells them that I punched him in the face. This changes everything. Part of me feels sorry for My brother; he really just doesn't understand.

Suddenly I am under arrest. The police take Me to the hospital, where they give Me a citation for domestic violence and a court date. Furthermore, because Mom and Vanessa agree with Jason's version of events, I am ordered to stay overnight for psychiatric evaluation, during which time My bloodied feet, which I honestly never even felt, are also patched up.

The padded white walls I envisioned are nowhere to be seen. The doctors have placed Me in the emergency room's "holding cell" for the evening. There are eight beds in the room, but I am the only guest. This is how it is meant to be. This is My room. For the first time in a long time I am able to sleep in absolute peace. It's a very comforting thing to know that you are the son of God.

Although I know My true identity, when the doctors from the psych ward come down to see Me the following morning, I am confident that they, like my family and the police, won't be able to handle the truth. I therefore go the route of "Michael," tricking them into believing that I never thought I was Jesus.

As I leave the hospital, My mother and My sister look at me with uncertain concern. It is very evident that they do not know quite what to think. I hope I can help them. My brother, on the other hand, is absolutely livid. It is very apparent that he is not in agreement with My discharge.

"You might fool them, but you don't fool me. You understand?" My brother says to Me, staring straight into My eyes.

"That's fine. I'm sorry you feel that way," I respond. I can see that he is visibly taken aback by My calm demeanor, which I gather he had hoped to unsettle. As My family members look back and forth at each other, displaying an expansive spectrum of emotion, I move past them, walking out of the hospital—alone.

¼

NORWALK HOSPITAL CONSULTATION REQUEST | EMERGENCY

1900545795   NR 186053

PHYSICIAN OR HOUSE STAFF INITIATING CONSULTATION MUST CONTACT ___NDER MICHAEL
CONSULTANT BY PHONE BEFORE FORWARDING WRITTEN REQUEST.

CONSULTATION ONLY ☐   CONSULT & WRITE ORDERS ☐ X   04/04/1977 26Y

ACCEPT FOR TRANSFER ☐   08/03/03   21 11 00

CONSULTANT AND SERVICE

Psychiatry

DIAGNOSIS

REQUESTING PHYSICIAN & SERVICE

INFORMATION DESIRED

DR. _____   WAS NOTIFIED ON ____ (DATE) ___ BY ___ (SIGNATURE)

REPORT OF CONSULTATION IS AS FOLLOWS: (Please sign your Name and Date to each Consultation.)

This 26 y/o Swm, a West Point graduate was BBP p̄ an altercation c̄ pts brother which allegedly began c̄ an argument Sunday evening (last). Pt was "tricked" into coming to ED, fought c̄ brother outside hospital & fled. Pt stated he was going back home which is about 1 block from hospital. Bro called police who picked pt up & brought him in for psychiatric evaluation. Apparently pt was seen in ED 2 days ago for another confrontation, that one with police (resisting arrest). Pt explained 1st incident in very logical terms, his father however called ED & volunteered a different version of same incident. During interview, pt was calm, well spoken & cooperative. He was forthcoming c̄ info & called writer "Ma'am." Pt became slightly agitated when writer suggested he stay in hosp for further evaluation. Dr. _____ called to discuss pt as he is his OP clinician. Dr. _____ also consulted to determine whether pt was committable. * Past Whx - Pt grad from WPoint, served 2 of 5 yr commitment in army. Was discharged "honorably" but medically due to "nerve damage" pt explained as cervical radiculopathy & herniated L4-5 disc. Pt stated that he then studied for & took the LSAT - was accepted @ GW but

DATE 8/04/03

SIGNATURE OF CONSULTANT

Psychiatry

CONSULTANT'S SERVICE (MEDICAL AND SURGICAL, ETC.)

FORM 17-181 REV. 12/68   ORIGINAL - CHART COPY   DUPLICATE - CONSULTANT'S COPY

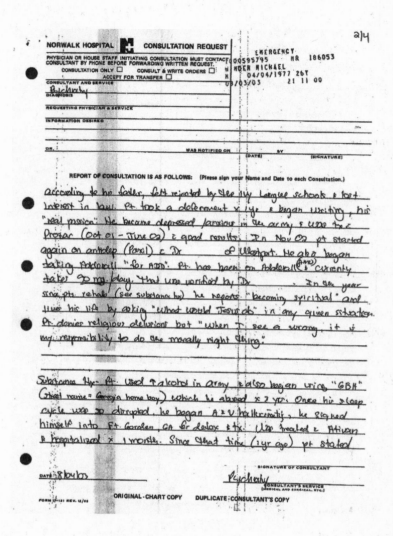

NORWALK HOSPITAL   CONSULTATION REQUEST

PHYSICIAN OR HOUSE STAFF INITIATING CONSULTATION MUST CONTACT CONSULTANT BY PHONE BEFORE FORWARDING WRITTEN REQUEST.

EMERGENCY
00595795   HR 186053
NDER MICHAEL
04/04/1977 26Y
09/03/03   21 11 00

CONSULTATION ONLY ☐   CONSULT & WRITE ORDERS ☐   ACCEPT FOR TRANSFER ☐

CONSULTANT AND SERVICE
Psychiatry
DIAGNOSIS

REQUESTING PHYSICIAN & SERVICE

INFORMATION DESIRED

DR.   WAS NOTIFIED ON   BY
                                   (DATE)   (SIGNATURE)

REPORT OF CONSULTATION IS AS FOLLOWS: (Please sign your Name and Date to each Consultation.)

according to his father, felt rejected by the Ivy League schools & lost interest in law. Pt took a deferment x 1 yr & began writing, his "real passion". He became depressed /anxious in the army & was tx'ed Prozac (Oct 01 - June 02) & good results. In Nov 02 pt started again on antidep (Paxil) & Dr ___ of Westport. He also began taking Adderall "for ADD". Pt has been on Adderall (Amp) currently takes 90 mg/day. That was verified by Dr ___. In the year since pt rehab (see substance hx) he reports "becoming spiritual" and lives his life by asking "what would Jesus do" in any given situation. Pt denies religious delusions but "when I see a wrong, it is my responsibility to do the morally right thing"

Substance Hx - Pt. used ↑ alcohol in army & also began using "GBH" (street name = Georgia home boy) which he abused x 2 yrs. Once his sleep cycle was so disrupted, he began A & V hallucinating, he signed himself into Ft. Coralen, GA for detox & tx. Was treated c Ativan & hospitalized x 1 month. Since that time (1 yr ago) pt stated

DATE 8 loy/03

SIGNATURE OF CONSULTANT
Psychiatry
CONSULTANT'S SERVICE
(MEDICAL AND SURGICAL, ETC.)

FORM 17-121 REV. 12/98   ORIGINAL - CHART COPY   DUPLICATE - CONSULTANT'S COPY

3/4

NORWALK HOSPITAL ▪ CONSULTATION REQUEST   Winkler, Michael #18,053

PHYSICIAN OR HOUSE STAFF INITIATING CONSULTATION MUST CONTACT
CONSULTANT BY PHONE BEFORE FORWARDING WRITTEN REQUEST.
CONSULTATION ONLY ☐   CONSULT & WRITE ORDERS ☐
ACCEPT FOR TRANSFER ☐

CONSULTANT AND SERVICE
Psychiatry
DIAGNOSIS

REQUESTING PHYSICIAN & SERVICE

INFORMATION DESIRED

DR.   WAS NOTIFIED ON   BY
                                        (DATE)   (SIGNATURE)

REPORT OF CONSULTATION IS AS FOLLOWS: (Please sign your Name and Date to each Consultation.)

that he "made a pact with God" to do His work if God could
help him stay clean & sober. He has maintained sobriety to date.
Family- M & F A & W in Westport. Pt has a sis, 1 bro - he is #3
in sibship. Lives = younger sister. Has no friends, prefers to be alone.
MSE - Pt. A & O x3 - Appears sweaty, states he is "starving" & asking
for food (1030h) and water. Mood = sad, slightly guarded.
Affect - mood congruent, occasionally odd i.e. when he spoke
of "Enya" his "lady friend." He got a very strange look on his
face & had a strange smile. Pt articulate, good eye contact,
well spoken. Speech- Rate & rhythm WNL no push except when
under suggestion he stay in hosp for a couple days. He then becomes
defensive. T/P No sign of formal thought disorder except for what
appeared to be thought blocking - he explained as "lack of focus due
to not taking Adderall today." T/c Denies A/V/H, preoccupations,
OCD, phobias, thoughts of self-harm or harming anyone else.
Is religiously focused, not delusional at this time. Explains paranoia
P/t neighbors as "a real threat." The same neighborhood men he
was worried about apparently assaulted a young man yesterday which
resulted in hosp of young man.

SIGNATURE OF CONSULTANT

DATE 8/04/03   [signature]
                                      CONSULTANT'S SERVICE
                                      (MEDICAL AND SURGICAL, ETC.)

ORIGINAL - CHART COPY   DUPLICATE - CONSULTANT'S COPY

FORM 17-121 REV. 12/84

414

NORWALK HOSPITAL — CONSULTATION REQUEST

Winter, Michael # 186063

PHYSICIAN OR HOUSE STAFF INITIATING CONSULTATION MUST CONTACT
CONSULTANT BY PHONE BEFORE FORWARDING WRITTEN REQUEST.

CONSULTATION ONLY ☐ CONSULT & WRITE ORDERS ☐
ACCEPT FOR TRANSFER ☐

CONSULTANT AND SERVICE
Psychiatry
DIAGNOSIS

REQUESTING PHYSICIAN & SERVICE

INFORMATION DESIRED

DR. _____ WAS NOTIFIED ON ____ (DATE) ____ BY ____ (SIGNATURE)

REPORT OF CONSULTATION IS AS FOLLOWS: (Please sign your Name and Date to each Consultation.)

Organization- logical, goal oriented. Pt appears to be above average intelligence. When questioned about 2 ED visits in 4 days, pt was defensive & attempted to explain away alterations. Judgement - Understands consequences of his behavior, but does not alter behavior in spite of knowledge (incident c brulla). Insight - pt denies illness beyond mild depression / anxiety.

Impression- Axis I: Substance induced anxiety disorder (Adderall)
Dysthymia, R/o Bipolar Dis
Axis II Deferred Axis III Nonspecific Axis IV: housing - mod Axis V GAF 4

Plan- After speaking c Dr _____ decision was made to discharge pt from ED c promise to see Dr _____ today @ 4:30. Pt intended to take No Adderall today & Dr plan to discontinue same. Will begin antipsychotic as an OP. Pt does not seem to be a danger to himself or anyone else at this time. He is able to care for himself & owns no firearm. Agreed to OP treatment & also agreed to keep Dr _____ appt today. Family notified of pt discharge (as he was leaving) who disagreed plan to discharge (brother). Instructed him to call Dr _____ & continue discussion of concerns. Pt has no hx of self-harm / suicide attempt.

SIGNATURE OF CONSULTANT

DATE 8/04/03

Psychiatry

CONSULTANT'S SERVICE
(MEDICAL AND SURGICAL, ETC.)

FORM 12-141 REV. 12/86

ORIGINAL - CHART COPY   DUPLICATE - CONSULTANT'S COPY

NORWALK HOSPITAL

MEDICAL RECORDS

Discharge Summary

WINDER, MICHAEL - 186053

Result Type: Discharge Summary
Collected/Performed: Friday, August 08, 2003 00:00
Result Status: Unauth
Result Title: Discharge Summary

Discharge Summary

`scharge Summary
..MISSION DATE: 08/04/03 to the psychiatric holding area. He was admitted to the unit of CP-3 on 08/07/03.

DISCHARGE DATE: 08/08/03.

HISTORY OF PRESENT ILLNESS: This is a 26-year-old man who came to the emergency department for his third visit in several days, from Dr. Israely's office. The patient said the police were called. This was his third visit, the first occurring on 08/01/03, which involved his being restrained by the police, and he returned on 08/03/03 at the request of his brother, after he had assaulted his brother in the process.

The patient was guarded and tangential. His brother reported episodes of paranoia in the past week and also grandiosity where he felt that ᵉe was Jesus. He was frightened by neighbors, which originally lead   m to call the police. The patient has seen Dr. Israely since November 2002. The patient has been taking Adderall from Dr. Israely and also has been taking Paxil on his own, which he has obtained over the internet.

EDUCATION: Includes graduation from West Point; this was followed by two years in the Army. He was honorably discharged for medical reasons, which was related to disc disease. He also had treatment for depression and alcohol dependence.

Printed by: MAHER, ALICIA
Printed on: 08/25/2003 15:41

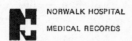

NORWALK HOSPITAL

MEDICAL RECORDS

Discharge Summary | **WINDER, MICHAEL - 186053**

The patient is on a disability pension from the Army. He is currently unemployed. He sees himself as a writer and is working on one book at the present time and has several other ideas. He managed to take the LSATs and was accepted to George Washington University Law School. He deferred going there for one year and currently says he does not want to pursue that.

PAST MEDICAL HISTORY: Includes disc disease and scoliosis.

His substance abuse in the Army included drinking to a level of a fifth of Vodka per day. He also took a drug called GPC throughout his four years and in the Army, which he said was undetected by urine tests and was a psychoactive drug. He denies any recent use of drugs or marijuana at the present time.

The patient has no current relationship. He had a girlfriend who he lost with his substance abuse.

The patient had called one of his sister's co workers and during his period of psychosis left an inappropriate message on her phone that when taken out of context could have frightened her.

MENTAL STATUS: The patient was oriented to person, place and time. There was no evidence of any cognitive dysfunction. On admission, on 8/5/03 when I saw him, his thoughts were fragmented. He was delusional with decreased insight and judgment. He denied voices then but after he cleared, he admitted that he was hearing background conversations. He denied suicidal thoughts or suicidal intent. There was a history of being suicidal when he was depressed in the Army two years ago.

The patient had been assaulted prior to admission.

The patient was treated with Zyprexa 10 mg h.s. His Adderall was discontinued. The patient did well. He had one dose of Haldol on 08/04/03, and two days later, he had a dystonic reaction. He was continued on the Zyprexa, however, and the dystonia has not recurred, and it responded to intramuscular Benadryl.

The patient is willing to be discharged. If his family and Dr. ____ are onboard with this, he will be discharged home with followup as an outpatient by Dr. ____. He will live with his family, at least initially; his parents in Westport, and he will return to his home in East Norwalk when appropriate. The patient

Walking back to the apartment, a five-minute stroll, still shirtless and shoeless, I carry myself as the new man I have become, standing tall, shoulders back, chest out, head high, and eyes wide open, scanning. I feel a bit of déjà vu, though, as I walk down My street: I'm still scarcely clothed, walking through My neighborhood on yet another beautiful early summer morning. Nevertheless, things are quite different now. In the past twenty-four hours I have become all that is truly Me. My presence is to be felt. Let there be no doubt about it: the Lord has arrived.

I am going to have to be strong, however, for along with this awesome responsibility come great new gifts, new characteristics of My changing persona, which initially seem like a great burden. My brain is slowly opening itself to everyone, to all God's children, so that everyone might find comfort in My message.

This is quite a lot to bear; I slowly come to terms with the fact that Anya is just the first of many to realize a telepathic connection with Me. The voices in My head are growing exponentially by the minute. The most frustrating aspect, by far, is that it seems to go one step further than telepathy. My mind is now totally open, with all My thoughts available for all to dissect.

Back at the apartment, I continue My transformation dance until it is time to see My psychiatrist. Meeting with him this afternoon was the one condition of My release. I am unconcerned.

Sitting in Dr. Elionder's office, a posh workplace befitting the exorbitantly expensive surrounding real estate and rows of Mercedes, BMWs, and upscale SUVs parked out front, I find myself unable to control all My thoughts and feelings as I am forced to answer question after question under the close scrutiny of his critical eyes.

Flustered, I stand up to catch a breath. I realize that I can finally prove to someone—someone respected, even—that I'm not crazy, that I have indeed been followed for the past few months. In the parking lot just outside his window I clearly hear the voices of Anya's friends and My family. Pulling back his shades, I stare out his window in all directions, searching for the people who must be attached to the voices I hear, but there is no one.

"They must have just sped off," I offer lamely, but Dr. Elionder apparently doesn't agree. He gives Me an extremely unreasonable ultimatum: I must begin taking Seroquel, an antipsychotic, or else he will call the police. He is clearly not the open-minded academic that I had originally taken him to be. He is incapable of seeing the truth.

I call his bluff and sit quietly, refusing his ridiculous offer of medication. For one thing, I am obviously far from psychotic. Besides, I can tell from his middle-aged, pseudo-intellectual uniform of black shoes, khakis, blue button-down shirt, gray wool vest, glasses, and calm demeanor that he is all talk.

Unfortunately, My doctor acts in sharp discordance with My preconceived notions. A few minutes later, the cops arrive and I am again taken against My will to the mental ward at Norwalk Hospital.

I still don't see padded white walls, but I have many reminders of where I am: daily medication lines, meetings with social workers, crisscrossing nurses and psychiatrists, and strict security (highlighted by the locked doors that provide the only exit off the floor). I am thankful to be given a room to Myself, allowing Me the privilege to come unglued in complete privacy.

Rocking back and forth on My bed in a fetal position, I cry for hours on end, grateful that My seclusion provides Me this one much-needed escape. When My mother and sister come to visit the following day, the tears don't stop streaming, especially when I see how they look at Me. These images are immediately ingrained in my mind: such sadness and uncertainty, concealed by ever-so-thin masks of forced smiles and cracked voices that make false promises of hope and full recovery.

To say that things are horrible is perhaps one of the most egregious understatements of the century. The doctors refuse to let Me have the drugs I actually need, limiting Me to the Seroquel they demand I take each morning.

Quitting Adderall, Ritalin, and Paxil cold turkey, after taking so much for so long, is a big "no fun" experience: uncontrollable shaking and tremors, nausea, headaches, delirium, increased hallucinations, and throwing up. Withdrawal from Adderall is right up there with quitting GHB, benzos, and painkillers; in some ways it's better, but in other ways it's much more terrible. Suffice it to say that these were not some of my finest, happiest hours.

To make matters worse, as I slowly come to the realization that I am (probably) not Jesus, the voices only increase in number. After a week of this madness, I turn on as much of the "Michael switch" as I can. I need to leave.

I'm not sure what I say to the head psychiatrist, but whatever it is, it apparently works. With my family's agreement, I am discharged from the hospital later that afternoon, thus ending what I am confident will always be the worst two weeks of my life. Upon being released from the ward, I move back in with my parents.

As soon as I get home, I make a beeline for my old bedroom. After sealing up the several large adjoining windows in the room, I lie down to stare at *Le Champ de Mars*, the painting that has been a steadfast advisor over the past several months. Rarely does she let me down. This night is no different. The angelic, motherly figure reaches out to me, speaking to me in her own way. As she moves, her thoughts and words flush through my mind: *Be calm, Michael. We are watching over you. Don't despair. It will all soon be fine. Now go to sleep.* I dutifully comply.

The next day, I am behind the wheel of my Altima, nervously wiping the sweat that's pouring down my face as my eyes frantically search the rearview mirror. I am being followed.

Just minutes from my house, as I'm driving down the quiet suburban back roads, I am stricken with fear. As far as I'm concerned, my family might as well be a million miles away. I can't imagine feeling farther from safety. Although the Seroquel is doing nothing to control my psychotic symptoms, it does seem to noticeably slow my thought processes and, accordingly, my reaction time.

Swerving across the yellow line, with my foot pressed tightly on the accelerator pedal, I struggle to keep my car on the road. I am driving like a madman, desperately trying to escape those who would kill me.

Cresting a hill, I happen upon a car that appears to me to be parked in the middle of the road. I slam on the brakes, my tires screaming, as the Altima seems to fly in all directions. I pray that I will not hit this family that has just pulled out of its driveway, but to no avail. Having lost all control of my car (and myself), I smash into the left side of the vehicle, coming to a screeching halt about thirty yards down the street.

My car is totaled; the other has about $4,000 in damage. It is a miracle that no one is hurt. When the police arrive I receive several tickets: for driving without registration (the car is being repossessed because of the bankruptcy), driving without insurance (recently canceled), and driving recklessly and in the wrong lane. In addition, my license is immediately and indefinitely suspended.

A week later, borrowing Vanessa's car, I forget to watch the road and hit a stopped motorcycle at a red light, barely braking at the last second to avoid what could have been a major collision. Despite more damage, again no one is hurt. After this second incident, I decide that it would be prudent for me to stop driving.

I spend every day of the rest of the month of August running through the dense woods surrounding our home, switchblade in hand, trying to catch Those Who Are Watching and to confront the heavy hitters that Anya has hired to kill me. As a result, my family is graced with the presence of the police more than a few times, responding to numerous calls from our neighbors reporting a man running across their property, wielding a knife. Because the voices, instability, and paranoia are only getting worse, regardless of how much the doctors increase my daily dosage of Seroquel, I am reinstitutionalized, this time at the Veterans Administration (VA) Hospital in West Haven, Connecticut.

I am growing surprisingly well accustomed to places, thoughts, behaviors, and medications from which I once felt totally shielded.

To whom it may
concern, over the
past 4 wks I've
been followed by
a woman Anya (works
w/visitor at Ambersacks)
and her family & friends.
At first I was attracted
to her & she rejected
me but then she slowly
grew an attraction
for me, though unsure
of how to approach.
After initial rejection.
She to solve her dilemma
she decided to follow
me w/ all her friends
and family, they watched
— at work, movies, bath
& bedroom etc....

They watched as I
was brought into the
emergency room on 3
separate occasions, my
most recent & most
damaging incident being
up "schizophrenic" out-
burst that brought me
to the psych ward for
3 days of cast lots. I
am anxious
for my safety personal
well-being & family
members (as well as
my own) privacy. I am
writing this letter as a
last resort in attempts
to savage something
something
of my life, etc....

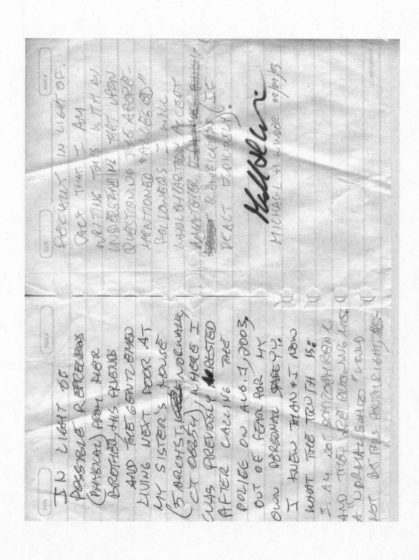

```
WEST HAVEN                          12/27/2005 10:13    Page:  1
------------------------------------------------------------------
PATIENT NAME                 | AGE | SEX |  SSN    | CLAIM NUMBER
WINDER,MICHAEL               |  26 |  M  |         | 049763935
------------------------------------------------------------------
  ADM DATE  | DISC DATE  | TYPE OF RELEASE | INP | ABS | WARD NO
AUG 27, 2003| SEP 05, 2003| REGULAR        |  9  |  0  | 1-8WPSY
------------------------------------------------------------------
DICTATION DATE: SEP 29, 2003        TRANSCRIPTION DATE: SEP 29, 2003
TRANSCRIPTIONIST: jlb
```

DIAGNOSIS:
AXIS I: Schizophrenia (?first psychotic break);
        r/o substance induced psychotic disorder;
        r/o bipolar d/o
AXIS II: deferred
AXIS III: Scoliosis, Eye Surgery, Nasal Surgery, Disc impingement
AXIS IV: Familial discord
AXIS V: GAF: 80

OPERATIONS/PROCEDURES:
None

CHIEF COMPLAINT:
"I thought I was Jesus and that I had ESP."

HISTORY OF PRESENT ILLNESS:
       This 25 y/o white male with an extensive substance abuse history
presented to the PER on 8/22/03. He was brought to the PER by his
parents who, as per ER reports, stated that patient believed
he was "Jesus", was behaving in "a bizarre manner", and "was not
himself". Three weeks prior to his presentation at the PER, he was
living with his younger sister and her boyfriend. He reports that at
this time he was taking Adderal and Paxil (drug history to be
delineated fully below). He was taking the Adderal prescribed by his
psychiatrist, Dr.   , whom he was seeing for "his ADHD". He
obtained Paxil via an internet drug store. He reported that 3w ago, he
was taking approximately 90-120mg Adderal q2h, and PaxilCR 50mg qd. At
this time he reports that the "Adderal and Paxil combination completely
cleared his mind such that he was able to hear other peoples
thoughts." "I had ESP". "I would be walking down the beach, and I
would hear what other people were thinking about me, and what they were
thinking in general." At this time, he reports having "a breakdown".
His brother attempted to help him, and he "punched" his brother "in the
face". Charges were brought against him for "disturbing the peace", and
for "menacing a family member". He was brought to the ER at Norwalk
hospitalwhere he stayed for one night, and was subsequently discharged.
He then saw his psychiatrist, who he told he had "special powers" (pt
had powers). He felt that his family members were "mocking and
chastizing him". He was brought back to Norwalk Hospital where he
stayed for 4-5d. He was discharged with the diagnosis of Schizophrenia
on Zyprexa, and "didn't like it". "It wasn't working. I still had the
belief that I was Jesus, and that I could read peoples' minds."
Zyprexa was changed to Seroquel by Dr.   , and he "didn't like it
either". "It made me feel sleepy". Patient reports that he doesn't

PATIENT: WINDER,MICHAEL   VA FORM 10-1000 DISCHARGE SUMMARY

WEST HAVEN   12/27/2005 10:13   Page: 2
```
------------------------------------------------------------------
PATIENT NAME                    AGE | SEX |  SSN   | CLAIM NUMBER
WINDER,MICHAEL                   26 |  M  |        | 049763935
------------------------------------------------------------------
   ADM DATE  |  DISC DATE  | TYPE OF RELEASE | INP | ABS | WARD NO
AUG 27, 2003 | SEP 05, 2003 | REGULAR        |  9  |  0  | 1-8WPSY
------------------------------------------------------------------
```
understand why they would say he had Schizophrenia. "I believe that it
is more likely that I have bipolar disorder, because I have these mood
swings all the time, and sometimes I get really depressed." He reports
that symptoms continued, and his psychiatrist recommended
hospitalization.

In the few months preceeding this episode, Mr. Winder became
somewhat reclusive, "writing a novel, and drawing". He reports that he
was trying to achieve a higher plane. He deferred acceptance to
Yeshiva University School of Law, and George Washington University
School of Law in order to pursue his writing. He reports that at this
time, he was "living in his own head", and that he would write because:
"You can speak to people, and they don't hear what you are saying. But
if you write words down, the words can't help but make it into their
head." He reports that his parents were surprised at his decision not
to enter law school.

Mr. Winder has an extensive drug history. He is selective with
whom he shares this history. He reports being treated by a
psychiatrist, Dr. _____, whom he never related his drug history to.
He states: "I didn't feel it was important, since I was there only for
the Aderall".

Mr. Winder reports that in high school, he frequently abused
alcohol, but nothing else. His first year in college, he used "weed
and mushrooms". When he was a sophmore, he began abusing GHB, and Acid.
He reports that at the same time, he was using pain killers, and muscle
relaxants given to him at College for scoliosis and severe back pain.
By Junior year, he was using GHB daily (obtained via internet), and was
using Acid three times perweek. At this time, he was also using
Ecstasy, and reports using up to 20 pills per weekend. After graduation
from college (12/22/00), he had 3m free before beginning training. He
reports using "Coke, Weed, and Steroids". He reports using the
steroids to "bulk up" for training since he wasn't working out. He
began training in El Paso on 3/15/01. He reports that he would "walk
to Mexico to buy D-Ball, and Cocaine". He also was using Hydroxycut at
the time. At this time, he "stopped using acid". He began training,
and states that he would drink up to 1L of Vodka daily in addition to
GHB. He also reports obtaining "Climbuterol, and Sussincd obtained in
Juarez, Mexico". In Mid-May 2001, he states that his "body gave up"
He reports taking "sick call a lot". During his last test of PT
training, he reports that his "legs failed". He was diagnosed with
Mononucleosis and Monohepatitis at the time. In mid-July 2001, he
graduated from training. He was on Convalescent leave Mid July. He
was partying at home for a while. He went to the ER "a few times", and
was told that he had an enlarged spleen and liver. At this time, he
began taking 10mg valium each evening.

October 4, 2001, he was admitted to a "mental ward for depression,
and having a breakdown. I woke up every morning in tears and drinking.
December 2001 he was put in Detox, and "failed for sleeping through

PATIENT: WINDER,MICHAEL   VA FORM 10-1000 DISCHARGE SUMMARY

49

Commitments

September 2003

D uring my week-and-a-half commitment at the VA hospital, I spend most of my free time writing poetry, almost all of it about Anya, who, I have come to suspect, might also have been Mary Magdalene, long before she became Diego Rivera.

Despite the fact that my symptoms are not at all in check, I am released on Zyprexa, another antipsychotic; Depacote, a mood stabilizer; and Celexa, another antidepressant. My tentative diagnosis is schizoaffective disorder, which has characteristics of both schizophrenia and bipolar disorder.

Upon returning home, I immediately browse the Internet for more information on these previously foreign illnesses. This is what I find:

> Schizophrenia is a severe brain disease that interferes with normal brain and mental function—it can trigger hallucinations, delusions, paranoia, and significant lack of motivation. Without treatment, schizophrenia affects the ability to think clearly, manage emotions, and interact appropriately with other people. Bipolar depression, also called bipolar disorder or "manic-depressive" disease, is a mental illness that causes people to have severe high

and low moods. People with this illness switch from feeling overly happy and joyful (or irritable), to feeling very sad. Schizoaffective disorder is a mental disorder that combines the symptoms of mood disorder and schizophrenia.

Source: www.webmd.com

Well, I can see why the doctors were fooled. But that's certainly not me, I think, confidently.

I've been home for a week now. I close my eyes, hoping to shield myself from what I know will come next. The devil's demons have started taking solid form, walking on the walls and ceiling in my bedroom at night. They appear intermittently, for flashes of two to three seconds, their grins a haunting reminder of how truly unhappy I am. At times, when the devil thinks I am weakest, he sends blood cascading in streams down the walls around me. The angelic figure from the painting laughs at me, taunting me, as tears roll down my face.

I get out of bed, my languid body slowly stumbling across the room, as my limbs shake relentlessly. Frightened of having to look at Chagall's painting anymore, and hopeful that a change of scenery will allow me some sleep (and sanity), I decide that I'll try to sleep the rest of the night in the den—that is, until I grow overwhelmed by the tree spirits outside the window who twist and turn into writhing dragons, homicidal maniacs, and satanic creatures, all staring at me, slowly edging their way toward the room's wall of windows.

"The devil knows that the time of rebirth is at hand and has sent his minions to destroy me. I will not yield!" I proclaim, in desperation.

Despite my affirmations to the contrary, I find myself reaching another breaking point. I pull the covers tightly over my head, praying for relief.

"Please. Please. Please, God. Please. I just can't take it anymore. Please. This is just too much," I whisper, as tears roll down my cheeks.

I spend the rest of the night in a similar position, curled in an uncomfortable ball underneath my blankets on the couch, while the voices and demons incessantly harass me and my tears blanket the darkness.

Since returning from the hospital, I have become a full-blown insomniac, sleeping only when I finally pass out from severe exhaustion. All day, every day, and all night, every night, I am tormented, living in a state of ongoing agony I never dreamed possible. The voices incessantly threaten me, berate me, criticize me. They twist my thoughts and tell me how they want me to die.

Things have been better, I think sarcastically, as the sun's rays poke through my blankets. Lying on the couch, gripping my covers tightly with clenched fists, I stare wild-eyed at the ceiling.

Despite all the medication and the complete lack of sleep, the first rays of dawn give me great cause for comfort. My old friends from West Point have all arrived (Anya has urgently requested their presence), hoping to learn more about me. When my West Point friends realize that some of Anya's friends are trying to kill me, they stay in the woods with rifles to protect me.

"Thanks, guys. I knew you'd never let me down," I say, wiping the tears away, with renewed hope.

I go to the kitchen and prepare some breakfast plates, then head outside to lay out food for them. When it isn't eaten, I realize that they clearly don't want to expose their position to the enemy, which prompts me to throw the food away. In addition, I leave out a peace offering for Anya and her friends, placing my last bottle of Vicodin in the garage for them.

Things are finally going my way, I think, joyously.

However, several hours later I realize that my situation has taken a decidedly negative turn for the worse.

"Fuck. Fuck! Fuck! Fuckin' Parker has to go screw everything up, doing his whole Parker thing," I stammer, as I pace my small bedroom in frantic circles.

Apparently Anya has fallen in love with Parker. It didn't help my cause that he showed up in his officer's uniform, sporting his Ranger tab and rows of medals from the Iraq War. Parker, my old friend, has suddenly changed sides and convinced the rest of the guys to do the same.

"Why? You were my only hope! Why?" I ask my former friends, who refrain from answering at first, but later they come back with a challenge: I'm supposed to buy a gun and shoot myself in the foot. They say that I am constantly "shooting myself in the foot" by my strange actions, and that if I were really Jesus, which none of them actually believes, I ought to be able to take the pain.

"Well, we'll soon see who's right," I say, smiling a crooked grin of smug self-satisfaction. *Yes, that gun is numero uno on my agenda. Now I just need to borrow a car and someone's credit card. That shouldn't be too hard. No, not for the son of God!* I think, smiling. *I wonder if it'll hurt, or if I won't even feel anything?* I ask myself.

::Ha ha ha . . . we knew you'd back out, you scared pussy! You're no son of God! You're nothing—nothing but a dead, crying pussy!::

The shouting comes at me from all directions.

"Fuck you! Fuck all of you! I am Jesus, and I'll prove it! I'm not fuckin' scared. Fuck the foot—I'll even aim higher, if you want. I'm not scared!" I yell, with unflinching conviction. *How high I'll aim is the only question.*

In light of the fact that numerous voices are telling me that they can always see me, regardless of how much I tape up the windows, I search for a hidden camera—which thanks to my keen awareness, I am ultimately able to find.

"How in the hell did they pull this off? Ridiculous! These are indeed professionals I'm up against! Good work, Winder!"

Somehow they have attached a microscopic spy camera to my glasses, which have recently become a fixture on my face because I no longer feel comfortable wearing my contacts. After I consider destroying the glasses, I suddenly realize that I know how to disable a microscopic spy camera. I soak my glasses in a carefully prepared mixture of water, lemon juice, salt, cumin, and paprika, and voilà! Their hidden eye is destroyed.

"Ha, ha, ha, ha, ha, ha!" I proclaim, with great enthusiasm.

> ::That motherfuckin' piece of shit!::
> ::Who the fuck told him?::
> ::Forget that. How the fuck did that asshole know how to disable it?::
> ::That fucking asshole is dead!::

They are all extremely angry, and for good reason!

"Yes, I have won the battle!" I shout. *However, it is all far from over, Winder. The war rages on, my good man,* I remind myself.

> ::You're goddam fucking right it does! 'Cause you're not dead yet!::

A few minutes later, the joy that came from this victory is nowhere to be found. *Jesus Christ, no matter what I do, they keep coming. They're everywhere. They're surrounding me, with more and more troops by the day . . . by the minute . . . by the second.* "Fuck. What am I going to do?" I wonder, growing increasing unsettled—to put it mildly.

The police? "Fuck, yeah, that's what I'll do! Now we'll see what's up, you fuckers!" I scream out the window at the trees that I'm sure are concealing their positions.

Accordingly, I call the police, demanding that they do something about the individuals watching me from outside my window. When they come and do nothing, I call them again later, unequivocally insisting that action be taken. Each time the cops show up at my house, they speak with my father and then quickly depart.

"What the fuck? Dad, what the hell's going on here? Aren't they gonna freakin' do something? Don't y'all believe me?" I ask my father, bewildered by their departure.

"Yes, of course they, and we—that is, your mother and I—do, Michael. It's just that . . .," my father says, clearly struggling to say what's actually on his mind.

Why *don't you say what you actually mean, jackass! You think I'm a nut-job!* "Ah, fuck it!" I shout, as I walk away from him, throwing my hands up in the air in frustration. "I'm not crazy. Despite what you all might think, I'm not fucking crazy!" I shout over my shoulder.

I'm not, am I? Hmmm . . . if I am crazy, the antipsychotics sure aren't doing their job. They're having little or no effect on me; so if I am crazy, that would make me overwhelmingly pro-psychotic! Ha!

I'm momentarily amused by my own cleverness, But then my spirit quickly sours. *Fuck! Regardless of what I am, I can't live here, like this, anymore. I need help through this.*

Of this I am certain: I won't survive alone. I am left with no option but to commit myself, once again, to the VA hospital in West Haven, Connecticut. I ask my parents to drive me immediately, this very night. I can't stay one more evening in their house.

The gun will have to wait. Maybe that's a good thing, I think, as we roll down the highway, my eyes glaring at the shapes that are taunting me in the distance.

/es/
REGISTERED NURSE
Signed: 08/27/2003 18:52

      TITLE: MENTAL HEALTH ATTENDING PROGRESS NOTE
DATE OF NOTE: AUG 28, 2003@15:27:17   ENTRY DATE: AUG 28, 2003@15:27:17
     AUTHOR: EXP COSIGNER:
    URGENCY: STATUS: COMPLETED
 INSTITUTION: CONNECTICUT HCS
   DIVISION: WEST HAVEN

Mr Winder is a 70%SC single veteran from Westport, Ct who is admitted for diagnosis and treatment of psychotic disorder and substance abuse. He had a psychotic break several weeks ago, was hospitalized and continued to be symptomatic, thus was referred here by private psychiatrist. Symptoms emerged while he was taking selfobtained large doses of Paxil and Adderal, he denies other drug use, though has lied about this in the past, and in past year has obtained drugs from Europe, alcohol, cocaine, stimulants bought illegally and from health food store. He has history of long time alcohol/drug abuse, and self mutiliation (burning self) and of depression. He says that for past few months he has been "living in his head", isolated, and doing a lot of writing and drawing, which makes him feel better, for he believes that writing is the only way of getting ideas into other peoples heads.

Symptoms recently have included - belief he can read other peoples minds/ has ESP, IOR, belief he is Jesus. He is pleasant and superficially cooperative, though guarded. Thought process is tangential at times, and content is expansive with focus on philosophical issues - themes of life is meaningless for most in society. Speech not pressured. He describes auditory hallucinations, that maybe his own critical thoughts. He denies current si, though has thoughts of hitting his head to punish self, and contracts for safety on the unit.

Diagnostic question is whether current psychotic break is secondary to substances, a manic episode or a first schizophrenic break. He is started on Seroquel, and initially the task will be to gather further history and information.

/es/
Attending Psychiatrist
Signed: 08/28/2003 15:40

CLIN DOC: Multi-Document   Page: 8
WINDER,MICHAEL   Division: 308
Printed on: Oct 23, 2003 11:35:36 am   System: WEST_HAVEN

Admitting Diagnosis:

AXIS I: Schizophrenia; r/o substance induced
       psychotic disorder;
AXIS II: deferred
AXIS III: Scoliosis, Eye Surgery, Nasal Surgery, Disc impingement
AXIS IV: Familial discord
AXIS V: GAF: 40

Treatment Plan:
1. Psychosis: Mr. Winder is demonstrating a marked increase in psychotic
           symptoms since last admission. In addition to an increase in
           the intensity of auditory hallucinations that were present
           during last admission, he is presently experiencing prominent
           visual hallucinations.
           a. Diminish psychosis
           b. Initiate antiepileptic

2. Polysubstance abuse: As was related during last admission, Mr. Winder has a
           long history of substance abuse. He presently reports
           to taking no substances other than those prescribed in
           addition to Melatonin for "aid in sleep".

3. Elevated Ammonia: Mr. Winder had 2 isolated elevated levels of ammonia

CLIN DOC: Multi-Document   Page: 38
WINDER,MICHAEL SSN#   Division: 308
Printed on: Oct 23, 2003 11:35:36 am   System: WEST_HAVEN

40, and 72.

50

Indecent Proposal

October 2003

M r. Winder, rise and shine," a voice chimes, with unwelcome enthusiasm.

"Huh?" I whisper, as I turn over, my mind an uncertain haze.

"Yes, good morning, Mr. Winder. It's 7:00 A.M., time for you to get up," a nurse proclaims, as she switches on the lights in my room.

"Yes, ma'am," I groggily reply.

"Please get dressed, brush your teeth, and perform all your other hygiene needs so that you can be in line at the nurse's station by 7:30. Okay?"

"Yes, ma'am," I reply.

"Thank you."

I've been back in the hospital for about two weeks now. This morning, similar to most, I am hopeful for all of five to ten seconds, while I pray that the voices won't return today, but they always do. *C'mon. Not today. Please. How about a second to myself? To just think. That would be nice.*

::Is he awake yet?::

::I think I just saw him move.::
::Yup, he's out of bed.::
::Dead man walkin'!::
::Ha, ha, ha, ha, ha … ::
::Time ta die, faggot!::

I am still hearing them—lots and lots of voices. They criticize everything I do and manipulate my thoughts, often masquerading as my own. At times they even keep me from such simple tasks as brushing my teeth or getting dressed, while they describe the thousands of extremely vivid ways in which I ought to die.

As I stand in line with the rest of the patients, all of us in standard-issue light-blue pajamas, I'm vaguely aware of what time it is, though unaware of how much time has passed. Of roughly thirty patients, I am definitely the youngest, and by at least ten years. Some of the others, with all their mutterings and bizarre actions, scare me somewhat. Three of these yahoos even had the nerve to say that I was an extremely disquieting element. Nonetheless, I am glad to have my own room now.

I like these socks, I think, looking at the gray, treaded hospital socks they've given me. *I wonder what's for breakfast. I like grits. That would be nice. Yeah, I like mixing them with the scrambled eggs and a lot of ketchup, creating a bug mushy mess. Yeah, I'd like that.*

Eventually, after an undetermined amount of time passes, I'm the one at the front of the line, standing in front of the counter of the nurses' medicine station.

"Name?"

"Winder, Michael. Uh, Michael Winder," I stammer.

"Last four?"

Silence.

"Mr. Winder, I see here that your medications and dosages have been adjusted again. Has your doctor apprised you of these changes?

"Uh, I think so, ma'am," I reply, genuinely. I can't remember my last meeting with my psychiatrist. "I think I'm seeing her today, or maybe tomorrow."

"Well, regardless, Mr. Winder, I'm providing you with printouts that contain information on all the medications that you're currently taking, for you to read once you get back to your room. All right?"

"Yes, ma'am," I say, as I grab the handouts she provides me.

"All right, now I just need to see you take these, and we're all set. Oh, and here's your glass of water."

"Yes, ma'am."

"Here you go."

"Um, ma'am?"

"Yes?"

"Are you sure this is all for me, because it just seems like a lot, and last time . . ."

"Yes, Mr. Winder. The information is all in the packets I just gave you, and any medication questions you have you can bring up with your doctor later, all right?"

"Yes, ma'am," I say, as I swallow the handful of pills, under her careful watch.

"Thank you, Mr. Winder, and have a good day. Next!" she shouts.

It's official, I'm a prisoner, I think.

Back in my room, I look indifferently at the sheets I've been given. I'm reasonably aware of my growing apathy.

Determined to put my symptoms in check, the doctors have indeed increased my medication upon my return to the mental ward. My new drug cocktail includes: Zyprexa, Risperdal (another antipsychotic), Depacote, Celexa, Cogentin (from the anticholinergic family, commonly used to treat the involuntary movements associated with Parkinson's disease), and clonazepam (from the benzodiazepine family, often used as an anticonvulsant).

"Huh. Well, I guess this all makes sense," I say, pausing for a moment, "Ha! Kind of a lot," I add, trying to force a mild chuckle, but there's nothing there. "Kind of a lot," I repeat, solemnly, staring out the window, as the voices weigh down on me.

Looking back at the sheet, I realize something: "Hmm . . . these last two drugs might have been added at my request, to help me with all the problems I've been feeling from the antipsychotics. Yeah, that might be it. Maybe they'll help me walk or talk better."

Yeah, that would be nice, I think, pinching my eyes with my fingers to suppress the mawkish tears that are on the verge of forming. *Things have gotten so awful. Even if the doctors are right, and I am crazy, I think I'd almost prefer the voices to all this medication.*

I'm not exaggerating. As much as I dread the voices, that's almost how much I dread the antipsychotics. They slow my brain down so thoroughly that my thoughts can't come together correctly and I can't talk properly. I am unavoidably tired and slowed down physically, which causes me to walk very sluggishly and strangely. I am extremely edgy and unable to sit still; my whole body, especially my hands, shakes relentlessly. To make matters worse, I've started gaining an enormous amount of weight. I'm confident someone would be hard-pressed to recognize me based on my appearance three months ago.

The drugs are just so hard on my body. Especially the antipsychotics— they mess my world up something fierce. It's just so hard. But I can't let them see . . .

::Can't let them see what, girly-boy? You crying, again, little boy? Oh, poor boy—life's so hard right now. Well, don't worry, loser, it's all ending—really soon!::

They're shouting at me from outside the window; laughter penetrates from all directions.

"I'm not listening, I'm not listening, I'm not listening," I repeat for an undetermined amount of time, with my hands tightly covering my ears, as I rock back and forth on my bed. Eventually I remove my hands, hoping that I might have earned a brief reprieve from the madness. I'm wrong. I still hear the voices, but I do my best to ignore them. "Fuck you! I've got more important worries right now," I shout.

::Yeah, we're sure you do! Like, which way are you going to die?::
::Ha, ha, ha, ha, ha . . . ::
::I say he hangs himself!::
::I say a razor!::
::I say . . . ::

"Please, please stop," I beseech.

::Ha, ha, ha, ha, ha!::

The laughter cascades across the walls, all around me.
"Fuck all of you!" I shout, in a brief moment of bravery. *You can't get me in here,* I think.

::Can't we?::
::What a jackass!::
::Does he even think we need to? Ha! He'll do it for us—won't you, ya fuckin' loser?::
::Yeah, you're a dead man, boy!::

Fuck, just please stop. You know, I don't even care anymore. Even if you aren't real, I don't really care, I reply.

I honestly believe that the full horror of serious mental illness (such as schizoaffective disorder or schizophrenia) cannot be truly appreciated unless one experiences it. To be honest, I had never really believed that delusional individuals actually believed their delusions. A few years ago, when I saw *A Beautiful Mind* about the life of Nobel Laureate John Nash, I simply couldn't comprehend how someone, especially someone so incredibly intelligent, could believe such fantastic delusions and have constant interaction with auditory and visual hallucinations. Furthermore, I didn't quite know what to make of his medicated appearance in the movie: his arms contorted and shaking as he struggled just to put one foot in front of the other.

Similarly, when I watched the television show *The Osbournes*, I was amazed by the deteriorated and shaky mental and physical state of famed rocker Ozzy Osbourne. The show drew unexpectedly high ratings. Many viewers were no doubt fascinated by Ozzy's condition, which was most likely assumed by many to be related to recreational drug use. However, I read a magazine article that claimed he'd been taking antipsychotic medication for years, and was actually displaying the side effects of those prescribed drugs.

Until now, neither John Nash nor Ozzy had made any sense to me. Lying here in the VA hospital, however, I finally understand all too well that the effect of these illnesses and these medications on one's body and mind are very real and extremely serious.

::Ohh . . . poor boy.::
::Ha, ha, ha, ha, ha . . . yeah, poor little boy.::

"Fuck you! The doctor says you're not even real."

::Ha, ha, ha, ha, ha . . . we're not real? We're not real? Well, then what does that make you, crazy boy?::

Fu-u-uck! I want to shout, uncertain of what's truly occurring. I don't even know what's true anymore, which is perhaps the most frightening part of all. "Which is worse?" I wonder aloud, as the voices and laughter envelop me.

After several hours, despite all the medication, the voices are undeterred, and they continue with their own agenda. Everyone is outside my window, screaming at me; the voices come from inside my head and out. Lynn is here; so is her father, who, I have come to learn, is secretly a capo in the largest, most powerful American crime family.

Whose crime family, though? Yes, of course! Anya's! Hmm . . . yes, that must be it. Anya's parents are not her real parents. They are actually members of the Family. Anya is the last living descendant of Al Capone! Besides my increased cocktail of medications, the realization of Anya's true identity is the only significant change I've had upon returning to the mental ward.

Amid these revelations, I attempt to ignore the huge battle being fought outside my window. It is a bloody, medieval-style fight involving all of Anya's friends, my former West Point friends, Sarah's friends from Kentucky, and even the associates of the pimp of the girl I slept with in Niagara Falls, who apparently is a huge crime boss in Canada. The sides are uncertain, and ultimately, with a nod to *Murder on the Orient Express*, they cease their internecine fighting and decide that everyone will have a chance to stab me.

Please go away . . . please . . . just leave me alone . . . please, I implore, but they respond simply with laughter. Curled up in the corner of my bed, trembling, I grip the sheets tightly, my knuckles turning white. I stare through the white wall in front of me, aware of the ever-vigilant video camera in the upper right-hand corner of the room. *Always watching. Always,* I think, as the tears stream down my face. *I wonder if they're with Them.*

After breakfast and morning rounds, I return to my room to sit on my bed and draw. During this hospitalization I've spent every waking second of my free time working on one charcoal drawing, an abstract piece I call *Heaven and Hell.*

Without a doubt, this is my favorite piece to date. I stare at the drawing with great satisfaction. Perhaps there *is* beauty somewhere inside me.

::Are you fucking kidding me, faggot?::

::The only beautiful thing you'll ever be part of is your own death.::

::Why don't you just hang yourself and save us the trouble, you queer?::

::Ha, ha, ha, ha, ha, ha . . . ::

Similar negative thoughts reverberate through my mind as the
voices continue unabated, determined to destroy me. Later in the
afternoon, I am provided with some unexpected relief when Josh
comes to visit.

"Hey, what's up, Mike?"

"Nothing much," I say, somewhat embarrassed.

"Hey, you hungry? I brought some pizza," he says.

"Yeah, definitely," I reply.

As we eat in the communal recreation area, I am once again surprised by how relaxed Josh appears, despite the setting and my fellow patients surrounding us. I anxiously wait for him to say
something about my situation, something about my using drugs,
which he's always been firmly against; he has made a point of
telling me (without preaching) that I ought to stop using every
time we've seen each other since I left the army. However, similar
to the last time he came (and the time before that), he never brings
any of that up.

We eat the pizza, watch some television, and then play Ping-
Pong. Just as he did on his previous visits, he again treats me completely normally, as though nothing serious has happened. He is
my only dose of sanity.

As he leaves, I'm sad to see him go, but that's not why I want to
cry. For a moment, the voices have no meaning. I feel strong.

It is only during times of such severe lows that one learns who
one's true friends are. My family's unconditional, nonjudgmental
support is not surprising; they're my family. However, Josh really
impresses me. He's the real deal. Despite everything, he's here.
With my world crashing down, Josh has visited me several times—
not just once, to check off the box. I believe people are lucky if they
have one friend like Josh in life. Porter's a lot of fun, but I'd take
one Josh to a thousand Porters any day of the week. (Porter: sorry,
bro. You know I love ya, but I have to keep it real.)

::Awwww! Little boy gonna . . . ::

"Fuck off, assholes! Fuck off!" I shout, as the maddening voices resurge.

This torture continues day in, day out, until Anya finally gives me a break from my agony. I am in the mental ward one afternoon, minding my own business, when Anya suddenly decides to give me a telepathic ring.

::Hey, Mike, what's going on?::

"Not much. You know, it sucks in here. Is there any chance you guys will go away soon and stop yelling at me?"

::That's your problem, not mine. I'm leaving with Parker tomorrow to get married in Vegas. I just wanted to let you know.::

"What? You're kidding! That's ridiculous. You can't leave me here with them. You can't."

::I'll tell you what, I'll give you one last chance. If you call me right now and propose, then I'll consider not having you killed and will marry you instead. Understand?::

"Yeah, on my way."

Standing at the ward's pay phone, I call Anya's cell phone.

"Hello?" (This time, it's actually her.)

"Oh, hey, Anya, it's me. Um, so here I go: Anya, will you marry me?"

Receiving no answer, I disappointedly hang up the phone and walk back to my room. As I lie back down on my bed, she gives me another telepathic ring.

::Hey, jackass. You're kidding, right? That pathetic excuse of a proposal was the best you could do?::

"Sort of."

::Well, that's not what I wanted at all. You did it all wrong.::

A wave of comfort rushes across my face as I realize that instead of wanting a conventional contractual marriage, Anya instead believes in a spiritual union between two people, as I do. Ecstatic that we are indeed so similar, I immediately run back to the pay phone and call her again.

"Uh, hello?"

"Anya, it's me again. Listen, I totally understand. I want you to know I feel exactly the same way. I think conventional marriage is bullshit. Honestly, I never wanted a real marriage anyhow. Anya, will you do me the pleasure of being my spiritual partner?"

Click.

Hmmm . . . we must've been disconnected. I mean, I know I said everything right—at least, the second time, I think, smiling, as I walk back to my room and lie down on my bed, satisfied. Since she actually listened to everything I had to say both times, and I never received a response, I can only believe that Anya's still carefully considering this attractive proposal.

After an almost one-month stay in the hospital, I am finally released. As with other mental wards, although I have committed myself voluntarily, the doctors decide when I am able to leave. I've had to lie to all the staff about not seeing visual hallucinations and not hearing voices anymore, because they are adamant about keeping me this time until all aberrations are gone. My diagnosis has not changed: schizoaffective disorder, or perhaps full-blown schizophrenia; it is still too early to tell.

Maybe, maybe, the voices might not be real, but I still don't see any end in sight, I think from the backseat of my parents' car, as my eyes gaze impassively out the window, with a lackluster awareness of our approaching home.

51

"Fuck You, Weirdo!"

November 2003

It is my first time out on the town in more than three months. I am meeting Vanessa for a few drinks at Amberjacks, and upon sitting down I notice Anya in a seat at the bar. Certain that she sees me walk in, I start drinking as fast as possible, unsure about what I should do.

Along with the incessant voices, numerous questions run through my mind: *Are the voices real or not? Did she ever actually follow me? Did I imagine proposing to her from the hospital?*

Having decided that there is nothing wrong with a little drinking, especially during my recovery, I do my best to ignore Anya's presence, focusing on nothing besides guzzling alcohol. She eventually leaves, and I am relieved. I sit with my sister, drinking in silence, lost deep in thought. The answers to my questions are still an irritating mystery. "Fuck!" I unwittingly say aloud.

"What?" my sister asks.

"Nothing," I say. "It's nothing at all," I continue halfheartedly, as the knowledge starts to set in that I am indeed possibly insane.

Regardless of the answer, I just wanna know. One way or another, I just need to find out what's what. A strange feeling of comfort slowly begins to take hold of me, with the thought that there might be answers in my near future.

About a week later I make my second appearance out on the SoNo scene, this time heading to The Loft, a bar next door to Amberjacks. Just my luck: my second time out means my second Anya sighting. After drinking for a couple of hours I feel courageous enough to recognize her existence, saying hello as I pass her on my way out.

She turns, smiles, and returns the greeting as though nothing has happened, leaving me in an annoyed state of confusion. *Fuck! Goddam motherfucking—what the fuck is going on?*

The voices around me laugh.

::Ha, ha, ha, ha, ha::

"Fuck!" I shout.

"What's wrong?" Vanessa asks me.

"Nothing, don't worry about it."

That's a lie. I'd so hoped that Anya's response might help me to solve this puzzle. She was *not* supposed to be cordial to me. She was supposed to say something like "Fuck you, weirdo!" or "Mike, I'm sorry I was following you, but I'm finally ready to talk." But she wasn't supposed to act like nothing had happened.

Now what do I do? I ask myself, as the voices laugh all around me.

Another week later I have my third Anya encounter. I've unknowingly gone to Amberjacks on a night when she is working, and our paths cross as I am looking for a seat. At this point, with the help of the outpatient psychiatrist I am seeing and the increased dosages of medication I am taking, I am leaning toward an acceptance that all the voices, hallucinations, and everything involving Anya, except for me calling her (again and again and again), were not real.

I want to cry when, instead of running away from me, ignoring me, or berating me, Anya just gives me a big hug. *You gotta be kidding me. Honestly, if the same thing happened to Vanessa, with some psycho harassing her, I would have forced her to speak with the police and file a restraining order against the wack job,* I think, as I slink down into a nearby seat, straining to keep the tears from forming in my eyes.

Jesus, what the fuck have I done? Seriously, how many girls envision a marriage proposal from a heavily medicated guy they don't really know, from the pay phone of a mental ward? I reflect, smiling, providing myself some humor and a momentary escape from the incredible sadness.

Overwhelmed by Anya's compassion and understanding, I resort to the only thing I can think of, the only thing I have ever really felt confident doing, and offer her drugs (some Klonopin).

"Uh, no," Anya quickly replies, as she hastily slips into the kitchen.

My presence is clearly a disruptive element, so I decide to do the only kind thing I can think of for her: I drain my glass of wine and leave the bar with a purpose. As I slink off to my car, I am left alone with my unhappiness.

Well, one thing's for certain: if she wasn't frightened before, she definitely is now.

"Fuck! Good work as always, Winder!" I say, trying to force a smile.

For a moment there are no voices except my own, and there are no tears except for the ones I quickly wipe from my face.

52

A New Day Rising
December 2003

L ying on my bed in my parents' house, I could not possibly be more disgusted with myself and, for that matter, with living. My symptoms are finally somewhat in check, at least to the point where I realize without a doubt what is real and what isn't, and I've become severely depressed. Alone, I find myself caught in yet another sad conversation with myself. I grow weary of the same, tired themes.

What have I done to myself? I wonder, despondently.

"You've destroyed yourself. You're nothing," I answer, feeling quite confident in this response.

I know, I know. But why?

"No reason, you just wanted to destroy yourself. You're a loser. You realize now that the entire last year of your life was all in your imagination, primarily consisting of delusional, psychotic episodes," I say with a firm but disheartened voice.

Yes, of course I do. No one, absolutely no one, pictures themselves hearing voices, watching blood flow down their walls, or thinking they are Frida Kahlo or Jesus. This is a hard thing to come to grips with.

"And what about your family? What have you put your family through?"

Yeah, no shit. It wasn't enough to be sent to a mental ward and rehab in the army; once I was discharged, I chose to devote virtually my entire life to drinking and using drugs. What a fucking loser.

"Exactly. A fucking loser."

I have been totally apathetic—not only to any possible personal consequences but also to the impact these consequences might have on my family. That's done now. I'm a fucking loser, without question. But is the damage permanent? *Probably. At least that's what all the statistics and the doctors are saying.*

Even if my diagnosis is changed to schizophreniform (which means I basically just suffered one isolated schizoid episode—a purely drug-induced psychosis—that does not require psychiatrically prescribed medication, and will never return—as long as I never do drugs again!), according to the statistics there is still roughly an 85 percent chance that within a year off medication I'll relapse, and that my diagnosis of schizophreniform will be changed back to either schizoaffective disorder or schizophrenia.

"What the fuck did I do?"

You fucked up—real bad, my friend.

Either diagnosis will require lifelong medication. In summary: if I discontinue my meds, I officially have just a 15 percent chance of avoiding a relapse during the first year alone. Since I've had relatives who experienced some similar crap, my chances are below 10 percent, because it seems I have a genetic predisposition. Things don't look good for me.

"Great."

I can't handle this shit.

I simply can't handle the fact that I am probably schizophrenic (or schizoaffective) and will have to take antipsychotic medication for the rest of my life. I just can't. Honestly, I'm a fucking mess. I'm not going to sit here and say I'd rather hear voices, but antipsychotics are the worst medication I can possibly imagine. The moments I want to be awake these days are extremely few and far between. Everything is so incredibly slow, distorted, and shaky. I can't walk right, talk right, or sit still without intense shaking. I can't focus on anything. I sleep a minimum of fourteen hours a night, and on waking up, I just move to the den to sleep some more in front of the television. I'm nothing anymore.

Yeah, too true. And what makes everything even worse is that I've gone from being completely physically jacked and cut, to a sickening mess of a blob who's put on twenty-five pounds of fat in just three and a half months.

I recently started yoga and cardio again, but it isn't doing much for my waistline; the antipsychotics strongly resist a loss of weight. I am moving so slowly it is nearly impossible to sweat much. I'm a fat fucking loser.

Yeah, and lifting weights, well, that's absolutely out of the question; I am far too insecure about my weight, the shaking, and my insanely slow body movements. It's just so fucking embarrassing.

I'm such an embarrassment. As I see it, I've done irreparable damage, and my life, as I've known it, is over. *There is nothing anymore, nothing to look forward to.*

I pull out the bag of weed I picked up earlier in the day, grab my bowl, and start puffing, with my bottle of vodka close by my side. *Who really cares anymore? I can't kill the pain with drinking alone, and marijuana might make things just a little more bearable, I think,* wistfully.

I am dead wrong. About fifteen minutes later, while I am drunk and high, a cacophony of voices begins attacking my brain, overwhelming me, demanding that I take a knife and stab myself to finally put an end to all the pain. Chagall's painting, which hasn't moved in almost a month, suddenly begins swirling around, the angelic woman tilting her head slightly and smiling at me.

::Michael, we're still here.
Fucking end it, you loser!::

No, you're not back, I beg.

::Ha, ha, ha, ha, ha, ha, ha!::
::We never left, faggot!::

Stop. Please. What have I done?

::It's what you're about to do that matters.::
::Time for you to do the deed.::
::Kill yourself, you bastard!::
::Stop being such a pussy and stab your weak-ass heart out!::
::Slit your fucking wrists, queer!::

But my parents . . .

::You think they'll give a fuck? Think about all you've put them
through. End this—now!::
::Go get a fucking knife from your fucking kitchen and stab the
fuck out of your pathetic fucking body!::
::End this shit, you fucking waste!::

Pulling the covers over my head, crying uncontrollably, I begin
to pray for the last time.

"Please God, please! Please make them go away! Why won't
they go away? I know they're all in my head, but they're so real, so
intense, and so compelling. Please stop them. Please!" I lament,
underneath the blankets.

However, my prayers are not answered—far from it. The voices
only intensify. Feeling very close to doing something terrible, I
jump up, grab my bottle of Klonopin, and swallow seven pills,
quickly putting myself to sleep.

You know, there are those mornings when one wakes up and
thinks, *Today marks the beginning of an important new chapter in my
life.* December 16, 2003, is exactly such a day for me. On this
morning, a *miracle* happens.

When I returned from the hospital in October, my father had

put up shades across all my bedroom windows in order to alleviate my fear of Those Who Are Watching. This morning, for the first time since then, I decide to pull back the shades to let the sun in. A somewhat foreign feeling consumes me. The light fills not only the room but me as well.

A couple of tears roll down my cheek, but they are quite different from those of the previous night. I don't wipe them away, but rather welcome their presence, and I let them stream to the floor.

I'm actually happy, I think, with disbelief. *I'm happy to be alive.*

Although many voices are still present, the worst of them are gone, along with the paranoia. Moreover, knowing that they are not real, I am able to push the remaining voices into the background and allow myself to hear my own thoughts clearly. A sudden realization dawns on me.

I might be able to beat this thing, after all! I pause, amid my thoughts, smiling as if for the first time in my life. *At least I have my family close by, supporting me.*

Family is real—concrete. Drugs, I now realize, are just an illusion—a dangerously seductive, beautiful illusion that seems to offer so much and yet takes away so much more. Drugs will always be available, but I know that only my family will ever be able to provide me with the true support and help I will need during my recovery. Accordingly, there will always be a choice, and making the right one is something I can never take for granted. Although I've suffered a serious blow, I'm not going to let it be my destruction.

"I don't care what anyone tells me; I'm not schizoaffective, or schizophrenic, or bipolar, or anything other than a relentlessly self-destructive drug addict and alcoholic. I'm gonna get my life back," I say, firmly.

Looking out the window, I'm confident I see the sun on my horizon. However, the happiness reverts to sorrow as my thoughts turn back to my family. I just can't help feeling sad when I think of all the pain I've put myself and, more important, my family through.

"I can't help it. I'm such a piece of shit. My poor sister—and my mom—what have I put my poor, sweet mother through?" I wonder, with genuine remorse. *My mother, so diminutive in stature— reserved, kind, and soft-spoken; she's a constant reminder of how appearances can be so deceiving. She has real strength; she's what I ought to be.*

"And what of me? What the fuck have I done to myself?"

I reflect on all the terrible damage that I've done to my brain, which I'll most likely have to deal with for the rest of my life. I'm so very, terribly stupid.

I pause for a moment, lost without thought, as I stare out my window. "I can't undo the past, but at least I will have a life, a new life, and it's beginning today."

Today is another day.

AFTERWORD

Despite what transpired in December, I not only continued using marijuana and alcohol, I also started a regular daily regimen of cocaine. Choices, choices—some are bad, and others are worse. Eventually I came to my senses, but I suppose that's another story.

I want to make it clear that I do not hold the U.S. Military Academy or the army accountable for what happened to me. Although the demanding military lifestyle might have been a contributing factor, it would be a completely immature cop-out for me to blame others for the poor decisions I've made. A large part of being a cadet, in preparation for becoming an officer, is learning to get tasks done properly and under a great deal of stress. One is expected to make sound decisions, often with extremely limited time to think. When push came to shove, I clearly did not rise to the occasion. I would also love to be able to blame a bad set of friends, my psychiatrist, God, or just bad luck, but no one believes any of that—least of all myself. I did this. All of it.

I play things out in my head over and over, trying hard to understand when and where things really got out of control, when I should have stopped. The existentialist philosopher Søren Kierkegaard wrote, "Life can only be understood backwards; but it must be lived forwards." That's undoubtedly true; however, each time I think about it, the cause-and-effect trail slides back further and further as I struggle to pinpoint the moment when I began risking my life, my sanity, and my future. I'm sure I could have avoided this entire mess, but the answers aren't obvious, not even in retrospect—at least not yet.

All this being said, I don't have many regrets. My philosophy is something akin to "what happened, happened—now make the most of it and move on." I obviously can't do anything to go backward and take it back, but I can use what I've learned to my advantage as I move forward. Accordingly, I honestly see it all as a blessing. Although it might be hard for some to believe, I'm truly glad for everything, especially those desperate nights in the mental ward, because it's those moments that are the most deeply ingrained in memory and that prevent me from ever wanting to use drugs and alcohol again. Moreover, along with my recovery, there has been a definite change for the better in my perspective on life. Simply put: I feel like I'm a better person. I suppose I probably could've taken a more direct path, but who's to say?

The only regret I do have is the pain and suffering I inflicted on my family and close friends. Along the way I've stolen, lied, cheated, and hurt everyone I ever cared about. These memories are also clearly embedded, and they only further reinforce my conviction to maintain my sobriety.

At this point, there are only three things that I know for certain: life is quite beautiful, even though I did have to travel through hell to get some perspective; I love my friends and family, and am grateful for their ongoing support, despite the pain I've caused them; and, most important, I want to live a clean and sober life.

People from all walks of life have fancied themselves too wealthy, successful, conscientious, focused, intelligent, athletic, or strong-willed to fall prey to addiction's sharp talons, yet they have found themselves consumed by this sinister disease. I pointed this out at the very beginning of this book; however, I was wrong about one thing. Even the drug of choice stays the same across all demographic lines: *more*. Left untreated, addiction will not stop until you are in jail, institutionalized, or dead. I was lucky; many learn too late, if at all. I suppose there are very few people who take note of the countless individuals who have been destroyed by addiction or who recognize that maybe they are not so special, that maybe they too could be vulnerable, or that maybe, just maybe, they should heed the warnings of the poor lost souls who've gone before them.

Except for you, of course, because you are different.

Before the storm, me, 1985.

Michael Winder was born in Westport, Connecticut, in 1977. A graduate of the U.S. Military Academy at West Point and former U.S. Army officer, he currently resides in his hometown, where he is working on his second book.